JEAN BAUDRILLARD

RHETORIC IN THE MODERN ERA

Arthur E. Walzer and Edward Schiappa, Editors

The goal of the series Rhetoric in the Modern Era is to prompt and sponsor book-length treatments of important rhetorical theorists and of philosophers and literary theorists who make substantial contributions to our understanding of language and rhetoric. In some cases, a book in this series is the first book-length treatment of the figure; in others, a book in the series is the first to examine a philosopher or theorist from the perspective of rhetorical theory.

The intended audience for books in the series is nonspecialists—graduate students coming to the study of a theorist for the first time and professors broadly interested in the rhetorical tradition. The series books are comprehensive introductions—comprehensive in the sense that they provide brief biographies, descriptions of the intellectual milieu, and discussions of the major scholarship on the figure as context for a detailed examination of the figure's contribution to rhetorical theory or history.

We envision these as the first books on their subject, not the last. While books in the series may exceed these modest aims, their focus is on achieving them. A complete list of the books in the series can be found at the end of this volume.

Jean Baudrillard

The Rhetoric of Symbolic Exchange

BRIAN GOGAN

Southern Illinois University Press
Carbondale

Southern Illinois University Press
www.siupress.com

20 19 18 17 4 3 2 1

Library of Congress Cataloging-in-Publication Data

Names: Gogan, Brian, 1982 February 26– author.
Title: Jean Baudrillard : the rhetoric of symbolic exchange / Brian Gogan.
Description: Carbondale : Southern Illinois University Press, 2017. | Includes bibliographical references and index.
Identifiers: LCCN 2017006136 | ISBN 9780809336258 (softcover) | ISBN 9780809336265 (e-book)
Subjects: LCSH: Baudrillard, Jean, 1929–2007. | Rhetoric—Philosophy. | BISAC: LANGUAGE ARTS & DISCIPLINES / Rhetoric. | LANGUAGE ARTS & DISCIPLINES / Communication Studies.
Classification: LCC B2430.B33974 G55 2017 | DDC 801/.95092—dc23 LC record available at https://lccn.loc.gov/2017006136

Contents

Short Titles

A	*America*
AA	*Arte and Artefact*
BL	*Baudrillard Live: Selected Interviews*
CA	*The Conspiracy of Art: Manifestos, Interviews, Essays*
CC	*Carnival and Cannibal, or the Play of Global Antagonism*
CM	*Cool Memories*
CM2	*Cool Memories II, 1987–1990*
CM3	*Fragments: Cool Memories III, 1990–1995*
CM4	*Cool Memories IV, 1995–2000*
CM5	*Cool Memories V, 2000–2004*
CPS	*For a Critique of the Political Economy of the Sign*
CS	*The Consumer Society: Myths and Structures*
DL	*The Divine Left: A Chronicle of the Years 1977–1984*
EC	*The Ecstasy of Communication*
ExD	*Exiles from Dialogue*
F	*Fragments: Conversations with François L'Yvonnet*
FF	*Forget Foucault*
FS	*Fatal Strategies*
GW	*The Gulf War Did Not Take Place*
HD	*Jean Baudrillard: From Hyperreality to Disappearance; Uncollected Interviews*
IE	*The Illusion of the End*
IEx	*Impossible Exchange*
LP	*The Intelligence of Evil, or The Lucidity Pact*
MP	*The Mirror of Production*
P	*Paroxysm: Interviews with Philippe Petit*
PC	*The Perfect Crime*
PH	*Photographies, 1985–1998*
PW	*Passwords*
RA	*Radical Alterity*
RC	*Revenge of the Crystal: Selected Writings on the Modern Object and Its Destiny, 1968–1983*
S	*Seduction*

SA	*The Singular Objects of Architecture*
SC	*Screened Out*
SED	*Symbolic Exchange and Death*
SO	*The System of Objects*
SS	*Simulacra and Simulation*
SSM	*In the Shadow of the Silent Majorities, or The End of the Social*
ST	*The Spirit of Terrorism and Other Essays*
TE	*The Transparency of Evil: Essays on Extreme Phenomena*
UB	*The Uncollected Baudrillard*
UD	*Utopia Deferred: Writings from* Utopie *(1967–1978)*
VI	*The Vital Illusion*
WD	*Why Hasn't Everything Already Disappeared?*

A Note on Baudrillard's Original French

With few exceptions, Jean Baudrillard produced his original work in French. He wrote in French, heavily relying on the subtleties of the French language to make some of his most important theoretical points. Only occasionally did Baudrillard pepper his work with borrowings from other languages. Save for a handful of English-language lectures, he delivered papers in French, and he participated in interviews that were almost exclusively conducted in French. The vast majority of this work—including Baudrillard's essays, books, interviews, and lectures—has been translated into English, and these translations provide English-language audiences access to Baudrillard's oeuvre.

This book presents the English-language translations of Baudrillard's work in the chapters and, wherever possible, his original French in endnotes. In the places where word-for-word French-to-English correspondences are not possible, the endnotes present only the essential French behind the translation. In the instances where Baudrillard delivered his original work in English (e.g., *The Vital Illusion*) or in the instances where an interview with Baudrillard was immediately translated into and published first in English, no endnotes are provided. The author has, to the best of his own ability, verified the accuracy of these translations. Bibliographic information for the original French works that were consulted is included in the list of works cited as part of the entries for their English-language translations.

Acknowledgments

Jean Baudrillard embraced the challenge of writing, rhetoric, and the world. Once, in an interview with Guy Bellavance, Baudrillard opined that "livelier things come into existence" through a "mode of challenge" ("The Revenge" 57).[1] During this same interview, Baudrillard suggested that "interesting relations between people" only exist in the mode of challenge (57).[2] In offering these remarks, Baudrillard might well have been speaking about this book—a challenging thing that has been made livelier by a good number of people who, by way of their relationships to me, have encouraged, counseled, and, also, challenged me as I completed this project.

Learning is a challenging endeavor, and I want to acknowledge the energy and the effort of some formidable scholars and tremendous teachers who worked with me early on in my studies. I had the privilege to be guided by dozens of sage pedagogues, among them Geraldo U. de Sousa, Trudelle Thomas, and Tyronne Williams at Xavier University and Virginia Chappell and Krista Ratcliffe at Marquette University. The educational experiences that they produced inside and outside their classrooms are models—if only more educators would work to copy them. Trudelle, Kris, and Virginia deserve special mention, here, for introducing me to the study of rhetoric and writing and for continuing to orient me as I map new territory in my own career.

A debt of gratitude is owed to the people at Virginia Tech for the lively exchange of ideas from which this project emerged. Faculty and colleagues —namely, those affiliated with the Ph.D. in Rhetoric and Writing program—offered their regular perceptions of many, many versions of this project. Their willingness to share these perceptions forced me to confront the problem of meaning-making in, around, and through Baudrillard. Bernice Hausman, Paul Heilker, Kelly Pender, and Katrina Powell were extraordinarily helpful in this regard, as they read and responded to very early drafts of this study. In particular, Bernice and Kelly allowed me to better meet the challenge of Baudrillard's work by offering very honest and very insightful feedback on this project.

At Western Michigan University, my colleagues in the Department of English have been as they appear to be—that is, fantastic—and my colleagues in the rhetoric and writing studies program have been especially so.

As department chair, Jonathan Bush arranged for research release time, and, without this time, the drafting of this book would been delayed. Charlotte Thralls and Thomas Kent have been invaluable mentors to me over the past five years. I simply cannot thank them enough for their reassurance and support in all areas of my work. I am fortunate to count Staci Perryman-Clark and Maria Gigante as superb friends, first, and wonderful colleagues, second. When the stakes seem to be the highest, both Staci and Maria have stood behind me and this project.

The Rhetoric in the Modern Era series editors, Arthur Walzer and Edward Schiappa, have lent their wisdom to this manuscript at every stage of its development. Years ago Art reviewed an initial plan for this book and, since that time, has been ever willing to advise me on the book's direction. Ed conducted an extremely thorough and insightful review of the initial manuscript, and his suggestions improved this book's quality immensely. Art and Ed should be further commended for their patience with the development of this project. Likewise, Bruce McComiskey's reviews of this book were both timely and formative, and I extend my gratitude to him. Helpful, too, have been Karl Kageff and his production team at Southern Illinois University Press. I am particularly appreciative of the assistance they offered in the late stages of this project.

While little has been written about Baudrillard's relationship with those people closest to him, I want to write a little about those people closest to me. To complete this book—a book about the relationship between disappearance and appearance—I quite literally had to disappear from my family, retreat to my office, bury myself under books, and compose for hours, days, and weeks at a time. This kind of disappearance would not have been possible without the appearance and tireless support of Karen Coleman, Chris Coleman, and Barb and Jim Gogan. At the most crucial times in this project, these individuals made huge appearances as grandparents to my children and as parents to me. Over the course of writing this book, my daughters Linnea and Natalie made their big appearances, too. They are both lively and lovely, and, together with their mom, they serve as the daily inspiration behind my work.

Of all the people who have seen this book come into existence, Amanda Coleman deserves the single greatest acknowledgment for her love and encouragement. From the very beginnings of this project right through to the last edits, she listened, read, spoke, and wrote alongside me in a way that only a best friend would or could. She challenged me to make the project better, and that challenge was met only with her support. I am forever grateful.

INTRODUCTION

CHAPTER 1

Cross-Disciplinary Perceptions of Baudrillard and Rhetoric

Today it is concepts, much more than individuals, that are under house arrest, under the fierce control of each discipline. Interdisciplinarity merely plays the role of Interpol.

Bien plus que les individus, les concepts sont aujourd'hui en résidence surveillée, sous le contrôle féroce de chaque discipline. L'interdisciplinarité joue simplement le rôle d'Interpol.
—Jean Baudrillard, *Cool Memories II, 1987–1990*

Interdisciplinary structures in all their forms are symptoms of this: every discipline is aligned on the degenerate concepts of another.

La multidisciplinarité sous toutes ses formes en est le symptôme: chaque discipline s'aligne sur les concepts dégénères de l'autre.
—Jean Baudrillard, *Fatal Strategies*

I pity—a figure of speech, since no one is to be pitied, neither oneself nor anyone else—an intelligence that's always getting caught up in its own outdated facts, its own values. There's the internalizing of a discipline or a reality or a group; a siding with something. Then there's no cross-disciplinary outlook, but sheer immersion. There are lots of people who can live only fully immersed in something, a variant of perfectionism. Without it, life would be too much to cope with.

Je plains—c'est une façon de parler, car personne n'est à plaindre, ni soi ni un autre—une intelligence qui se prend toujours à ses propres données révolues, à ses propres valeurs. Il y a intériorisation d'une discipline, d'une réalité, d'un groupe, on prend fait et cause pour quelque chose. Alors, il n'y a plus de regard transversal, c'est l'immersion. Nombreux sont les gens qui ne peuvent vivre qu'en immersion—une variante du protectionnisme—, la vie sans cela serait trop difficile à vivre.
—Jean Baudrillard, *Fragments: Conversations with François L'Yvonnet*

In 1997 an editor named Michael Fordham interviewed Jean Baudrillard. At the time Fordham worked for the British magazine *Dazed and Confused*, a publication that targeted an audience of youth and young adults by featuring a mix of popular culture and underground culture content. Fordham's interview with Baudrillard, which consisted of ten questions, was relatively brief, and it opened with a question that acknowledged the peculiar fact that a magazine targeting youth would want to interview Baudrillard: "Are you surprised," asks Fordham, "at the interest of a youth culture magazine in your work?" (*HD* 113). In response Baudrillard indicates that he is surprised, but pleasantly so. Baudrillard further explains that he can understand why a younger audience might take an interest in his work, noting that "there can be an affinity between an enquiry which is, on the one hand, piercing and incisive, but which is not specialised, not professional," since the "young generation doesn't have too much of an historical or traditional reference and I don't either" (113). Here, then, in response to an interview question about audience appeal, interest, and understanding, Baudrillard remarks on his lack of reference to history, tradition, specialization, or profession.

Baudrillard's remarks receive elaboration later in the interview, as Fordham presses him about his identification with academic disciplines and professions. Recognizing that Baudrillard's "work has tended to be viewed by academia—very often sociologists, philosophers, and so on—as deliberately undermining the establishment," Fordham prods: "Is this a kind of philistinism?" (*HD* 116). Baudrillard answers that he "was a little rejected by all the various disciplines" and that he's "basically been on the outskirts of academe, of university, of discipline" (117). Describing the subtleties of his relationship with academic disciplines, Baudrillard discusses the slight feelings of loneliness and of "pollution" that he associates with his peripheral position (116–17). And, Fordham, in posing his final interview question, queries Baudrillard even more directly: "Today, what is your profession: are you a philosopher, are you a sociologist, are you a poet, are you a prophet?" (121). Baudrillard replies honestly, admitting that he "can't really say" and that "[t]here really isn't a definition" (121). He quickly eliminates the disciplines of philosophy and sociology from his consideration, noting that members of each discipline "don't recognize [him] as one of them" (121). Toward the titles of "worker," "writer," and "thinker," Baudrillard is more open. However, he questions the meaning of each of these titles in terms of their professional significance (121). Eventually, Baudrillard decides that he has "no response," and he ends the interview by turning the question back onto Fordham (121). "That's *your* problem!" exclaims Baudrillard (121; emphasis original). By the end of the interview, then, neither Fordham nor his readers are able to pinpoint Baudrillard's profession. The interview, thus, defies attempts at definitively categorizing Baudrillard's work and words as belonging to a particular set of academic traditions, histories, and practices.

To a great extent, Fordham's interview concentrates on Baudrillard's complicated relationship with academic disciplines, as well as his tepidness toward the traditions, histories, and practices associated with most disciplines. Given the interview's young target audience and its relative brevity, the interview's focus on academic specialization and professional identity is somewhat perplexing. Nonetheless, the interview is revealing, for it captures Baudrillard's thoughts on disciplinary identification: Baudrillard's disciplinary identification is not his problem; instead, it is the problem of his interpreters. As such, Fordham's interview serves as a point of departure for the present study—a study that identifies Baudrillard with rhetorical studies and argues for Baudrillard's professional identity as a rhetorical theorist. Rhetoric, as Steven Mailloux defines the term, connotes "our use of language in context" (73). And, Mailloux further observes that rhetorical practice, theory, and study heavily depend on location: "Rhetoric," writes Mailloux, "is often about who's in and who's out, what's included and what's excluded, who is placed inside and who outside a cultural community, a political movement, a professional organization" (124). As Mailloux suggests, rhetoric shifts, and the aim of this book is to nudge scholars in such a way that they more fully perceive Jean Baudrillard as an individual who, to borrow Mailloux's phrasing, is "in" rhetoric—both as provocative practitioner of rhetoric as well as a novel theorist of rhetoric.

Jean Baudrillard: The Rhetoric of Symbolic Exchange locates Baudrillard inside rhetorical studies by demonstrating how the histories, traditions, and practices of rhetoric prove central to his use of language. By examining Baudrillard from the perspective of rhetoric, this study follows its predecessors in the Rhetoric in the Modern Era series (cf. Agnew; Gross and Dearin; McKenna; Ritivoi; Walzer). Indeed, as the first book-length treatment of Baudrillard and rhetoric, this study aims to encourage a shift in the way in which Baudrillard is perceived—namely, this study argues that Baudrillard should be perceived as a rhetorical theorist. To return to the epigraphs that opened this chapter, perceiving Baudrillard as a rhetorical theorist should not be understood as an attempt to place him and his work under the "arrest" of rhetorical studies, nor should it be viewed as forcing him to "align with" or "side with" rhetorical studies. Rather, the current study stresses the commonalities shared by Baudrillard and rhetorical studies. Baudrillard, himself, would appear to support this perceptual shift, in large part because of his reticence about identifying with various academic and intellectual labels as well as his openness to a cross-disciplinary perspective.

To be sure, Baudrillard views disciplinarity with disdain and views claims of interdisciplinarity with suspicion. Disciplines, according to Baudrillard, arrest concepts and immerse scholars in a set of idealized values and practices (*F* 57–58). Individual disciplines maintain their definition by leaning hard on the decrepit concepts of other disciplines (*FS* 82). As such, interdisciplinarity mediates disciplines and, ultimately, works to preserve disciplinary boundaries (*CM2* 19). In fact, Baudrillard declares that his work is "reducible to no particular discipline" (*PW* 4). He further locates his work "outside the disciplines" in which he trained: German philosophy and sociology (*HD* 47; cf. *F* 55). He identifies with neither of these (*HD* 121). Moreover, Baudrillard eschews a wide range of labels that attempt to classify his work as belonging to particular intellectual epochs. Most prominently, he rejects the label *postmodern* (cf. *BL* 22–23, 158; *HD* 187). Speaking with John Strand, Baudrillard explains the difficulty of this label, which is "hard to fight against" (*HD* 45). Referring to the label as a "false image," Baudrillard attests to the stubbornness of this apparition, stating, "If other people accuse me of being postmodern, I say 'I'm not postmodern,' but everyone tells me I am and I can't do anything about it" (46; cf. Best and Kellner 111). The problem with labels such as *postmodern* or the disciplinary monikers *sociologist* or *philosopher*—at least as Baudrillard expresses it here—is that these labels conjure up erroneous perceptions of intellectual histories and academic traditions and produce false images of the individual on whom they are foisted. In other words, the problem with these labels is one that stems from language use and its effects: the problem is a problem of, with, and for rhetoric.

Rhetoric effects perception, perception is rhetorical, and the relationship between perception and rhetoric is one that has been subject to contemporary rhetorical study. Barry Brummett, for one, contends that perceptions are "constructed" (*The World* 26). In *The World and How We Describe It*, Brummett draws on the work of Susanne K. Langer, Richard L. Gregory, and C. K. Ogden and I. A. Richards, among others, in an attempt to explain how language use constructs perception (24–44). Indeed, much of Baudrillard's own work, which not coincidentally figures prominently in Brummett's study, examines the same relationship—that is, the relationship between language use and perception. Arguably, then, Baudrillard's aversion to intellectual and academic categorization can be understood as demonstrating his rhetorical savvy. Baudrillard remains keenly aware of how intellectual and disciplinary labels work rhetorically, and he does his best to avoid the rhetorical effects brought about by such labels.

Baudrillard's resistance to disciplinary and academic labels should not, however, be taken as a disavowal of rhetoric. Quite to the contrary, Baudrillard identifies his work as rhetorical, admitting in a 2007 interview with Truls Lie that he was "very aware" of the "rhetoric in [his] writing" (*HD* 186). Importantly, though, the rhetorical dimensions of Baudrillard's work far exceed his writing, encompassing his speech and his photography as well as his persona and his delivery. Indeed, as even Baudrillard acknowledges, his work is rhetorical, and the rhetorical dimensions of his work are underscored by its cross-disciplinarity. In an interview with Dianne Hunter, Baudrillard asserts that his "work has a transversality, a cross-disciplinarity" (*HD* 47). He explains that his work required him to move across disciplines and that "it forced a cross-disciplinarity on [him]" (*PW* 4).[1] For Baudrillard, cross-disciplinarity is preferable to either disciplinarity or interdisciplinarity because a cross-disciplinary outlook encourages the exchange of ideas and facilitates the challenge of thought. Such exchange, it should be noted, is central to Baudrillard's rhetorical theory. Douglas Kellner, a scholar who has studied Baudrillard extensively, corroborates Baudrillard's assessment of his own work. Kellner sees Baudrillard's work as influencing "a diverse numbers of disciplines" to such a degree that the work "promotes cross-disciplinary thought" (*Jean* 53; "Jean Baudrillard (1929–2007)" 25). The cross-disciplinary outlook endorsed by Baudrillard further opens his work up to rhetorical study. As Mailloux observes in his discussion of rhetoric's disciplinary status, "disciplinary-identified praxis constitutes perhaps the most powerful conditions of academic work, both constraining and enabling intellectual accomplishment, closing down and opening up possibilities for thinking," and, facing the prospect of "isolated disciplinary work," rhetoric is ripe for cross-disciplinary application (125, 129). Chronicling rhetoric's place among and between disciplines, Mailloux, in fact, urges rhetorical studies scholars to continue their "efforts at cross-disciplinary cooperation" (129). Thus, both Baudrillard and rhetorical studies maintain an openness to cross-disciplinarity, and it is within this cross-disciplinary space that the present study emerges.

In particular, this study of Baudrillard and rhetoric positions itself in the space alongside two cross-disciplinary lines of inquiry: the study of rhetoric and the study of Baudrillard. The first line of inquiry—known as rhetorical studies—has, in the United States, emerged primarily from the subfields of literary studies, composition studies, and speech communication studies in departments of English and communication (cf. journals such as *Rhetoric Society Quarterly*, *Quarterly Journal of Speech*, *Philosophy and Rhetoric*, *Rhetoric and Public Affairs*, and *Rhetoric Review* and conferences such as the biennial Rhetoric Society of America conference). The second line of inquiry—known as Baudrillard studies—has emerged from international conversations (cf. the *International Journal of Baudrillard Studies* and conferences such as "Engaging Baudrillard") about the relevance of Baudrillard's work to a wide range of disciplines. Indeed, the founding editor of the *International Journal of Baudrillard Studies*, Gerry Coulter, rightly observes that Baudrillard's work "passes through many disciplines" ("Reversibility"). Included among these are "cultural studies, visual culture, design studies, human geography, photography, film studies, sociology, art history and theory, social and cultural history, philosophy, architecture, cultural politics, media and communication studies, and cyberculture" (Clarke, Doel, Merrin, and Smith, "Introduction" 5). This study assumes that these two cross-disciplinary lines of inquiry might themselves be crossed in a way that leads to a number of provocative insights germane to scholars who identify with rhetorical studies and Baudrillard studies.

The present study also assumes that the relationship between perception and rhetoric is a relationship that is not only central to the traditions and histories of rhetoric but that is also central to Baudrillard's work. To repeat, language use brings about perception; perception is rhetorical. Accordingly, *Jean Baudrillard: The Rhetoric of Symbolic Exchange* is decidedly less interested in foisting the label of rhetorical theorist on Baudrillard than it is in exploring the ways in which Baudrillard might be perceived as a rhetorical theorist. Put differently, the present study attempts to move from the question "What might we call Baudrillard?" (a question about definition, labeling, and naming) to the question "How might we perceive Baudrillard?" (a question about the relationship among thought, discourse, experience, and judgment). Such a shift is a subtle one, as definitional questions necessarily involve perceptual questions, but the shift toward perceptual questions is a shift intended to stress the rhetorical nature of perception. Perception, itself, is rhetorical; it maintains deep roots in the histories and traditions of rhetoric and occupies a prominent position in discussions about the relationship between rhetoric and reality. Furthermore, perception is of central importance to an understanding of Baudrillard and his work, given that widely varying perceptions of each persist. In fact, Baudrillard defies "established academic ways of proceeding and thinking" to such a degree that Baudrillard studies scholars Chris Rojek and Bryan S. Turner describe him as an individual who "emerges as a chameleon figure" (i).

Organization of the Study

The perception of Baudrillard as a "chameleon figure"—that is, an individual who can travel across and yet blend into many different scenes—is where this study begins. Arguably, such a perception emerges from Baudrillard's cross-disciplinary rhetorical practice, and the next chapter in this study presents a brief biographical sketch of Jean Baudrillard along with seven vignettes involving him. Together, the sketch and the vignettes are intended, first, to introduce readers to Baudrillard and, second, to stress the eminently rhetorical nature of his writing, speaking, and composing in different scenes. Touching down in 1968, 1976, 1986, 1991, 1996, 1999, and 2002, this chapter demonstrates Baudrillard's decades-long prowess as a practitioner of rhetoric through biographical illustration. The scene from, or sketch of, 1968 illustrates the way in which Baudrillard took action through writing and demonstrating in solidarity with the March 22 Movement. The sketch of 1976 chronicles Baudrillard's interactions with Michel Foucault, illustrating his relish in rhetorically challenging his audiences—particularly his readers. As this sketch suggests, these rhetorical challenges often produced personal and professional consequences for Baudrillard. The 1986 sketch traces the relationship between Baudrillard, the Bonaventure Hotel, and Fredric Jameson's widely read treatment of that hotel, exhibiting the way in which Baudrillard regularly played upon the fluid relationship between texts and contexts and often used this relationship to his rhetorical advantage. The 1991 sketch describes the way in which Baudrillard, in his three writings on the Gulf War, mobilized place and commonplace for an uncommon effect. The 1996 sketch explores Baudrillard's iconic address to the attendees of the Chance Event at Whiskey Pete's in Primm, Nevada. This sketch presents Baudrillard as an individual who understood delivery as indispensable to effective rhetorical performance. The 1999 sketch focuses on Baudrillard's photography—compositions heralded for their opportune timing, or *kairos*. Finally, the 2002 sketch outlines Baudrillard's controversial and unconventional use of the requiem genre following the events of September 11, 2001. Focusing on an address Baudrillard delivered at the "Rencontres Philosophiques Outre-Atlantique" debate in Manhattan, this sketch stresses the deliberateness with which he approached genre.

Part One

Moving away from Baudrillard's rhetorical practice and toward his rhetorical theory, part one of this study explains Baudrillard's theory in such a way that it reveals the theory's compatibility with the histories and traditions of rhetoric, as well as the theory's novel understanding of rhetoric as art—or, more precisely, of rhetoric as two mutually dependent arts. As part one shows, Baudrillard's theory locates itself in an ongoing discussion concerning rhetorical effect and audience perception. Key to Baudrillard's theoretical intervention in this discussion is his focus on rhetorical invention and, more specifically, the turning, or troping, of appearance into disappearance and disappearance into appearance. As part one explains, the tropings of thought, discourse, and perception serve as the means to symbolic exchange.

Chapter 3 situates Baudrillard's rhetorical theory in rhetorical history by connecting his work to Plato's *Sophist* dialogue. Arguing that Baudrillard's rhetorical theory is indebted to Plato's work, in general, and the *Sophist* dialogue, in particular, this chapter surveys treatments of the *Sophist* in rhetorical studies. The very few treatments of the dialogue suggest that the field of rhetorical studies is largely reluctant to engage with it on account of its unflattering characterization of rhetors, its overly philosophical take on ontology, its decidedly less literary approach to the interlocutors, and its inability to adequately define the Sophist. Following this survey, this chapter outlines three arguments supporting the dialogue's relevance for rhetorical studies and for Baudrillard studies. First, the *Sophist* dialogue addresses questions of reference and reality, questions that pervade both cross-disciplinary fields. Second, the dialogue circumscribes a semantic field that cuts across histories of rhetoric from classical to contemporary times and draws two rhetorically significant terms—*phantasia* (φαντασία) and *simulacra*, along with their cognates—into an almost synonymous relationship. Third, the dialogue suggests a new approach to studying the sophistic characteristics of rhetors, including Baudrillard, and that approach depends on the appearance of the rhetor as evaluated against the appearance of the Sophist outlined in the *Sophist* dialogue.

With the rhetorical compatibility of Baudrillard's theory having been articulated in chapter 3, chapter 4 outlines the first half of Baudrillard's rhetorical theory, which he terms the *art of appearance*. For Baudrillard, the art of appearance uses thought and discourse to produce perceptions, and, as such, this first half of Baudrillard's rhetorical theory resembles what Plato describes as the art of the Sophist in the *Sophist* dialogue and, more generally, what rhetorical studies scholars traditionally understand as the art of rhetoric. This chapter's central aim, then, is to describe Baudrillard's art of appearance in a way that distinguishes it from other proximal arts by way of its effects. Accordingly, this chapter builds its argument around Baudrillard's discussion of simulation and simulacra—a discussion that, besides being widely read and referenced across fields, is itself a discussion of the art of appearance. As this chapter argues, simulation and simulacrum are, respectively, process and product that emerge from the art of appearance in its most dominant and extreme form. Throughout his work Baudrillard positions simulation as a process that opposes representation (as it dismisses reference to truth) and functions circularly (as it ignores the linear trajectory of time). Likewise, Baudrillard positions simulacra as models, which self-proliferate (in a way that wrests agency away from humans) and function tropologically (in a way that turns perceptions into reality). Baudrillard, however, does not endorse the unchecked dominance of the art of appearance; rather, he views this dominance as symptomatic of the contemporary world.

For Baudrillard, the only viable challenge to the unchecked dominance of the art of appearance in the contemporary world is what he calls the *art of disappearance*. Chapter 5 outlines the art of disappearance—an art that constitutes the second half of Baudrillard's rhetorical theory. As this chapter argues, the art of disappearance is his most unique theoretical contribution to rhetorical studies. Emerging from the classical notion that perceptions lead to effects, the art of disappearance, as Baudrillard describes it, is a process by which thought and discourse can be mobilized to destroy perceptions. The art of disappearance is, in other words, not a productive process. This chapter argues that Baudrillard's art of disappearance is, indeed, a rhetorical art that deserves closer rhetorical study. To support this argument, this chapter follows three of Baudrillard's claims about the art of disappearance—one, that the art of disappearance is aptly figured through the trope of metamorphosis; two, that the art of disappearance involves alterity and ambivalence; and, three, that the art of disappearance can be discussed either as a fatal strategy or as a seductive game. Ultimately, this chapter explains Baudrillard's notion that the art of disappearance draws on alterity and ambivalence to transform perception; in doing so, this chapter details the most radical component of Baudrillard's rhetorical theory.

The final chapter of part one, chapter 6, builds on the two preceding chapters, with their respective discussions of the two component arts in Baudrillard's rhetorical theory, to discuss the goal of Baudrillard's rhetorical theory—or, what he calls *symbolic exchange*. Symbolic exchange is a rhetorical relationship brought about by a reversal of the effects of thought, discourse, and perception. Baudrillard describes symbolic exchange as "the complete symbolic operation" (*HD* 126)—that is, an operation that locks the art of appearance in an agonistic relationship with the art of disappearance. Key to the exchange operation is movement—a constant turning, or troping, of appearance into disappearance, disappearance into appearance—and this chapter locates rhetorical invention as the pivot on which symbolic exchange is sustained. In the ever-moving symbolic exchange relationship, thought and discourse are invented either to construct or to destruct perceptions. Reading Baudrillard alongside Hannah Arendt, Karl Popper, and Lloyd Bitzer, this chapter expounds on the rhetorical nature of symbolic exchange, stressing the importance of invention, perception, supposition, refutation, and even situation to the symbolic exchange relationship. This discussion of symbolic exchange provides the first sustained engagement with Baudrillard's own uses of the term *rhetoric* (*rhétorique*) in rhetorical studies scholarship. Concentrating on a number of revealing instances where Baudrillard uses the term *rhetoric* in his writing, this chapter solidifies his theory as a rhetorical theory—albeit an untraditional one. Baudrillard's rhetorical theory, as this chapter argues, positions exchange, not change, as rhetoric's goal and works to test hypotheses against the perceptions of the rhetor's experiences in the world.

To illustrate the parts of Baudrillard's rhetorical theory explained in part one of *Jean Baudrillard: The Rhetoric of Symbolic Exchange*, each chapter therein concludes with an "Illustration" section that applies Baudrillard's theory to Rebecca Skloot's 2010 book *The Immortal Life of Henrietta Lacks*. An award-winning best seller that has been widely adopted as a curricular common reading at over 150 colleges across the United States, Skloot's book demonstrates how a text might enact symbolic exchange and thereby sustain the goal of Baudrillard's rhetorical theory. As a piece of nonfiction documenting the decades-long saga of one woman, her cells, and her family, the book further captures a series of events that lends itself to an analysis grounded in Baudrillard's rhetorical theory. In fact, his work on the art of appearance, the art of disappearance, and the goal of symbolic exchange offers a novel explanation of the rhetoric at work in the events chronicled by the book—events that are, to be sure, ethically fraught. Baudrillard's rhetorical theory allows rhetorical studies scholars to better understand rhetoric on two levels: one phenomenological, involving a general analysis of the symbolic exchange sustained by the thoughts, discourses, and perceptions that mark the events involving Henrietta Lacks, her cells, and her family; the other textual, involving a particular analysis of Skloot's text and its ability to initiate and sustain symbolic exchange. While these four "Illustration" sections are meant to advance an understanding of the main parts of Baudrillard's rhetorical theory—the art of appearance, the art of disappearance, and the goal of symbolic exchange—they might fruitfully be read together as a piece of rhetorical criticism that mobilizes a Baudrillardian perspective to better understand *The Immortal Life of Henrietta Lacks.*

Part Two

Part two of this book includes four chapters, each of which evaluates a perception of Baudrillard—as, respectively, an aphorist, an illusionist, an ignoramus, and an ironist—in two ways. First, because each of these perceptions resonates with one defining characteristic of the Sophist as outlined by Plato in the *Sophist* dialogue, each chapter assesses Baudrillard's fit with a particular component of the Sophist's art. By measuring Baudrillard's work and words against these defining characteristics, the four chapters demonstrate a relatively uncommon approach to the study of sophistical rhetoric, at least as it pertains to Baudrillard. Thus, the first kind of evaluation that occurs in part two exemplifies an uncommon historiographical approach. Second, each chapter of part two evaluates a perception of Baudrillard against his own words and work. Together, these chapters collectively intercede in the thought and discourse that have produced certain appearances of Baudrillard. In this second kind of evaluation, questions of historical accuracy and fidelity abound; yet, these questions are only answered through extended inquiry into a specific facet of Baudrillard's rhetorical practice or theory. Thus, the second kind of evaluation uses perceptual appearances of Baudrillard as provocations to elaborate further on his rhetorical practice and theory.

Chapter 7 opens part two by considering Baudrillard's appearance as an aphorist. At stake in this appearance of Baudrillard is an understanding of the way he performs symbolic exchange through a written genre. This chapter elucidates a performative dimension both to the Sophist's imitative art and to Baudrillard's aphoristic writing. After examining how much these arts might be said to be comparable, and Baudrillard might be said to be a Sophist, the chapter investigates Baudrillard's writing and his theory. In the first place, it argues that less critical emphasis should be placed on Baudrillard's rhetorical use of style in his writing and more critical emphasis be placed on his rhetorical use of genre. To support this argument, the chapter analyzes Baudrillard's performance of and commentary on the genre of the aphorism. In the second place, the chapter reveals the deliberateness with which Baudrillard approaches writing and, more particularly, writing theory. To demonstrate his deliberateness, the chapter draws on his extensive commentary on writing and theory as both relate to symbolic exchange and to the rhetor's place in the world. In its entirety, chapter 7 offers a sustained treatment of the performative nature of Baudrillard's rhetorical theory.

Chapter 8 assesses Baudrillard's appearance as an illusionist by examining the discussions of illusion, illusion-making, and illusion makers that occur in Plato's *Sophist*, Aristotle's *Rhetoric*, and Baudrillard's own work. This chapter necessarily revisits the classical term *phantasia*, which works around Parmenides's thesis and preserves the potential for illusion-making. As the chapter explains, Plato and Aristotle understand *phantasia* differently, and, in this regard, Baudrillard's work on illusion and illusionists aligns much more closely with Aristotle's notion of *phantasia* than with Plato's. Pursuing the provocative connection between Aristotle's work on illusion and Baudrillard's work on illusion, this chapter contends that both theorists attribute illusion-making to rhetors as well as audiences. To support this argument, the chapter advances a novel interpretation, first, of what Aristotle refers to as an apparent enthymeme and, second, of Baudrillard's controversial text *America*. The chapter also examines the position of both thinkers—Aristotle in his *Rhetoric* and Baudrillard across his oeuvre—toward facts, holding that the two thinkers occupy a similar stance toward them: facts are produced by the communication between rhetors and audiences—that is, the invention, arrangement, delivery, perception, belief, and judgment that accompany an apparent enthymeme. Ultimately, Baudrillard endorses an exchange between fact and illusion wherein illusion is turned into fact and fact into illusion.

Chapter 9 gauges Baudrillard's appearance as an ignoramus by entering into the disagreement between Baudrillard and Susan Sontag. Despite the striking number of similarities in these critics' work, Baudrillard and Sontag openly criticized—if not outright insulted—each other in the 1990s and early 2000s. As this chapter argues, Sontag's critique of Baudrillard not only invokes one characteristic of Plato's Sophist, but her critique also provokes a consideration of each thinker's position with respect to meaning-making. In particular, this chapter views the disagreement between Baudrillard and Sontag as rooted in each thinker's different approach to repudiating interpretation and signification. While Sontag wants to recover a sensory experience that precedes the production of meaning, Baudrillard wants to turn meaning against itself. Accordingly, this chapter details how Baudrillard's rhetorical theory emerges from Ferdinand de Saussure's work on anagrams—work that predated Saussure's work on signification and that embraces a radical kind of rhetorical invention. By taking up Saussure's work on anagrams and signification as well as attempting to turn one body of work against the other, Baudrillard suggests that ignorance, idiocy, and stupidity might be preferable to intelligence. Chapter 9 closes by considering this suggestion and by applying Baudrillard's rhetorical theory to his remarks on stupidity and intelligence.

The final chapter of part two, chapter 10, entertains Baudrillard's appearance as an ironist. This appearance leads to a reading of Baudrillard alongside both Plato and Kenneth Burke. Irony proves central to the definition of the Sophist that Plato offers in the *Sophist* dialogue. But, whereas the irony that defines the Sophist depends on human knowledge and is a feature of human being, the irony endorsed by Baudrillard has no connection to knowledge and is an essential feature of all being. Baudrillard argues that irony works independently of human perception, harboring the alterity and ambivalence that initiate and sustain symbolic exchange. Irony, for Baudrillard, is integral to tropological movement, and the association of irony with tropes connects Baudrillard's work to Burke's. This chapter elaborates on the connection by demonstrating how Baudrillard and Burke both mobilize a similar set of terms and concepts—including *identification*, *motivation*, *symbolic*, *poetic*, *rhetoric*, and *ambiguity*—to articulate quite different rhetorical theories. Thus chapter ten contrasts the theories of Baudrillard and Burke to clarify Baudrillard's lesser-known rhetorical theory and, more generally, to stress the importance of irony to rhetorical theory.

Conclusion

The concluding section of this book encompasses an eleventh chapter, which responds to concerns about the status of invention and interpretation in rhetorical studies, and an appendix, which offers a critical review of the sources and scholarship on Baudrillard and rhetoric. More specifically, chapter 11 outlines the way that the present study of Baudrillard and its emphasis on the relationship between rhetoric and perception alleviates worry, first, over the interpretive redescription of influential thinkers as rhetoricians and, second, over the function of rhetoric with respect to reality. This chapter positions Baudrillard's rhetorical theory as the kind that accounts for the appearance and disappearance that necessarily accompany the study of rhetoric. The appendix is intended to promote cross-disciplinary study of Baudrillard—initially by orienting rhetorical studies scholars to important sources and reference works on Baudrillard and, reciprocally, by introducing Baudrillard studies scholars to the three most significant treatments of him by rhetorical studies scholars.

CHAPTER 2

Biographical Sketch: Jean Baudrillard, Rhetor

Scholars who specialize in the study of Jean Baudrillard frequently remark on his ability to travel across, yet blend into, many different intellectual scenes and milieus—that is, in spite of his reluctance to identify with these same scenes and milieus. Quite aptly, then, Chris Rojek and Bryan S. Turner characterize Baudrillard as a "chameleon figure" (Rojek and Turner i), for the hue of his work is perceived quite differently depending on the disciplinary or cross-disciplinary line of inquiry against which it is examined. On the one hand, the ability of Baudrillard and his work to move across disciplinary divides and different intellectual milieus invites a consideration of both Baudrillard and his work against the scene of rhetoric. Rhetorical studies scholars would, in other words, be interested in seeing how Baudrillard and his work appear against the background of rhetoric and, moreover, what these appearances reveal about his use of language. On the other hand, the ability of Baudrillard and his work to move across different scenes in an imperceptible way speaks to the adaptability of his thriving rhetorical practice. The eminently rhetorical nature of his writing, speaking, and composing functions as his camouflage, in that his work exhibits a quality that is perceived to absorb the color of its surroundings. If rhetoric, as Mailloux defines it, is language use *in* context, then the ability of Baudrillard's language to be used *across* contexts suggests an uncommon rhetorical flexibility.

This chapter addresses the appearance of Baudrillard against the scene of rhetoric and also the rhetorical adaptability of his work by, first, presenting a brief biographical sketch of Baudrillard and, then, offering seven vignettes of particular scenes from his life. This chapter perceives Baudrillard as a rhetor—that is, as an individual who uses language for effect in context—and it profiles his life in a way that highlights his skill as a practitioner of rhetoric. The brief biography that begins this chapter introduces Baudrillard to readers and chronicles the experiences and education that contributed to his rhetorical practice. The seven vignettes that follow the biography detail scenes from his life—in 1968, 1976, 1986, 1991, 1996, 1999, and 2002, respectively—that exemplify his use of language for effect. These vignettes might be understood as rhetorical touchstones in Baudrillard's life, and, together, they demonstrate his decades-long dexterity as a practitioner of rhetoric through biographical illustration.

The Abnormal Career

Baudrillard's life and work were far from what might be considered typical or normal for intellectuals of his generation. Indeed, by Baudrillard's own account, his career "always missed" the typical sequence of events or "the normal stages of a career" (*BL* 19). Baudrillard was born on July 27, 1929, in Reims, France. His parents, who were children of peasants, had "left the countryside and settled in a town" to take up careers of civil servants (19). Baudrillard, in fact, was the first member of his family to "do some studying," and his education functioned as what he described as a "point of rupture" with his family (19). He describes the environment in which he was raised as "not a cultural environment," and he goes so far as to contend that he "was not brought up in an intellectual milieu" (19).

Baudrillard's early schooling involved hard work that yielded a mix of successes and failures. Mike Gane profiles Baudrillard as "a brilliant pupil," who nevertheless maintained a "highly unusual" academic career (*Jean* 1). Baudrillard, who underwent an initial formation in "languages and literatures" (Gane, "Foreword" ix), describes having to compensate for his upbringing in his secondary studies "by working extremely hard at the Lycée" (*BL* 19). Baudrillard's studies in the lycée included years at his local secondary school, as well as an additional year of "intensive study" at the Lycée Henri IV in Paris (European Graduate). Baudrillard reports reading Friedrich Nietzsche early in his studies (in the sixth form) and also being tested on Nietzsche for both the written and oral German *agrégation* examinations (*F* 1; *BL* 19). Although Baudrillard took the *agrégation* examinations, he "didn't succeed" and was denied entrance into the École Normale Supérieure (*BL* 19). On this point, Baudrillard jests that Nietzsche did him "a favour by preventing [him] from passing the exam," recounting that his "examiners didn't agree at all" with his interpretations of Nietzsche (*F* 1).[1]

Eventually, Baudrillard began careers in the discipline of German and the discipline of sociology. Once his secondary studies concluded, he arrived at the Sorbonne, where he was trained in German (European Graduate).

Baudrillard contends that he was, "by training," a "Germanist" with background in "German philosophy, the history of philosophy and the history of ideas" (*HD* 47). This training prepared him for work as a teacher and as a translator. During the 1950s Baudrillard began teaching German in various lycées and would continue to do so for ten years (Gane, *Jean* 1; Gane, "Foreword" i). Around this time he also began translating works from German into French. As Gary Genosko explains, the "bulk of his work in translation was in the area of theatre" and specifically focused on the work of the playwright Peter Weiss (*Baudrillard* xi). Nonetheless, Baudrillard managed to produce "a significant number of translations of quite diverse texts" that, besides those by Weiss, included texts by Bertolt Brecht, Wilhelm E. Mühlmann, Friedrich Engels, and Karl Marx (xi). This "prolific" translation work—for which Baudrillard became "widely known"—would continue through the early part of the 1960s, even after he "made the transition to sociology under the guidance of Henri Lefebvre and Roland Barthes" (Gane, "Foreword" ix; Gane, *Jean* 1).

Baudrillard's transition from the study of German to the study of sociology would indeed launch his career in the university. He spent twenty years teaching in Paris at the Université de Nanterre (the Université de Paris X), first joining the school's teaching ranks in 1966 as an assistant lecturer of sociology (*assistant de Sociologie*) and later rising to the position of junior lecturer (*Maître-assistant*) in the Faculté des Lettres et Sciences Humaines at Nanterre (Genosko, *Baudrillard* xi). Baudrillard also held a number of visiting positions in the United States, including a 1975 appointment alongside Jean-François Lyotard, Michel de Certeau, Louis Marin, and Edgar Morin at the University of California, San Diego (Lotringer, "Introduction: Domination" 11). This particular position was arranged by Fredric Jameson and grew into an offer for Baudrillard to join the faculty at the University of San Diego (*P* 80). He turned down the offer and would hold his position at Nanterre for twelve more years. In 1987 Baudrillard, who had one year earlier earned his doctoral degree at the Sorbonne, decided to retire from academia to focus on his writing (Gane, *Jean* 1).

From 1987 until his death in 2007, Baudrillard wrote prolifically. By the most conservative counts, he produced over forty book-length pieces, long essays, and interview dialogues. The one-time translator would see most of these forty-some works translated into English and a smaller number translated into at least ten other languages. He published scores of short essays and consented to dozens of interviews. He was also a practicing photographer who not only exhibited his photographs but who also published two books of them in the late 1980s (cf. Bonnal; *PH*). Baudrillard further influenced a number of journals, including *Utopie*, *Traverses*, and the *International Journal of Baudrillard Studies*. He served in an editorial capacity for all three journals, beginning in 1967, 1975, and 2003, respectively (Genosko, *Baudrillard* xii). Finally, Baudrillard maintained a regular lecturing presence at two institutions apart from his work at Nanterre. From 1969 to 1973 he lectured at the École Practique des Hautes Études, in what was then called the Centre d'Études des Communications de Masse, and, "from the earliest period [of the school] to his death," he taught at the European Graduate School in Saas-Fee, Switzerland (Genosko, *Baudrillard* xiii; European Graduate). His lectures at the former institution focused, at least from 1969 to 1971, on design (Genosko, *Baudrillard* xiii), while his lectures at the latter institution encompassed topics such as "The Principles of Seduction" and "Cultural Identity and Politics" (European Graduate). Baudrillard's contributions to the European Graduate School and the *International Journal for Baudrillard Studies* ended when he succumbed to a yearlong battle with cancer on March 6, 2007.

Uprising at Nanterre, March 22, 1968

Baudrillard was a rhetor who, early in his career, used language in an attempt to effect change. In particular, he was involved with the protest movement in the spring of 1968 that would eventually lead to demonstrations, strikes, and riots throughout France. On March 22, 1968, a group of 142 students at the Université de Nanterre responded to growing animosity between school administrators and students by storming and occupying a room in an administrative building at the university. This initial occupation soon ballooned into a large-scale movement, and, on May 2, 1968, the Université de Nanterre was temporarily closed as a result. Daniel Cohn-Bendit, a student most often described as a leader of what would become known as the March 22 Movement, was studying sociology at Nanterre. Baudrillard, at the time, was teaching sociology at Nanterre and was clearly familiar with the movement. When questioned, in an interview with Jean-Louis Voileau, as to his "relationship to the 'enrages' at Nanterre," Baudrillard invokes the second person plural *we* (*nous*) to describe the relationship: "We were at the center of the 'events,'" he recalls, noting that "we participated in AG [general assemblies]" and that "we went to the barricades" ("On *Utopie*" 16; cf. Riley 118).[2]

These comments indicate that Baudrillard seems to have, at the very least, identified with the movement and perhaps even taken action himself.

Alexander Tristan Riley, for one, contends that Baudrillard's relationship to the uprising was one of "active involvement in the political radicalism that was then endemic at Nanterre" (118). Riley's contention, here, is supported by the fact that, over one year prior to the events at Nanterre, Baudrillard was among eight signatories who sent a February 17, 1967, letter to *Le Monde* (cf. Brillant 72 n. 1; Duteuil 129). This letter voices support for a group of activist students at the University of Strasbourg in advance of their trial for using university resources to promote Situationist thought (Brillant 71–72). Baudrillard's letter attempts to persuade the public "that the problems of the University will not be ruled by only 'cracking down' on the students who are most conscious of the elements of the environment" (Duteuil 129).[3] This letter aside, Richard G. Smith is more circumspect about Baudrillard's active involvement in the March 22 Movement. Letting Baudrillard's words to Voileau speak for themselves, Smith stresses the significance of the uprising and pursuant events to Baudrillard, stating "that the failure of May 1968 was an important watershed for Baudrillard" and noting that the uprising forced him to "question the role of the intellectual" ("May 1968" 121). Through his own rhetorical action leading up to May 1968—action that ranged from writing a letter to going to the barricades; action described as "*prendre la parole*," "*taking the floor to speak as part of taking power*," or acting "against those who controlled power" (*HD* 51; emphasis original; cf. *MP* 11–12)—Baudrillard understood the potential of language use to bring about change. As such, this action stands as a first rhetorical touchstone in Baudrillard's life.

Forgetting Foucault, December 1976

Baudrillard was a rhetor who took risks with his audience, and perhaps the best example of his unique ability to confront his audience is found in the history behind the publication of his essay *Forget Foucault*. Upon its French-language publication in 1977, this particular essay "made Baudrillard instantly infamous," for the essay "was widely perceived as an attack on the great philosopher" Michel Foucault (Lotringer, Kraus, and El Kholti 8). The essay, for example, points out that which "Foucault does not see"—namely, "that power is never there and that its institution, like the institution of spatial perspective versus 'real' space in the Renaissance, is only a simulation of perspective"—and further asserts that "the whole analysis of power needs to be reconsidered" (*FF* 50–51).[4] The essay was, in fact, "problematic" to such a degree that its English-language translation was not published until 2007 (Lotringer 7). Sylvère Lotringer, general editor of the Semiotext(e) series

Foreign Agents, explains the delay in publishing the translation as a result of the rareness of Baudrillard's particular rhetorical act: Baudrillard's essay confronted Foucault "publicly," and this public confrontation was further complicated by Foucault's stature and his eventual death in 1984 (7). Baudrillard issued his challenge to Foucault as a way to pay respect to Foucault and assert his independence from him (Lotringer, Kraus, and El Kholti 8; cf. Hegarty 155). Yet, this kind of rhetorical challenge was one that Baudrillard "enjoyed"—so much so, that reminiscing about it two weeks before his death in 2007 brought a sparkle to his eyes (Lotringer, Kraus, and El Kholti 8).

As Lotringer explains, Baudrillard's audience and his intentions with *Forget Foucault* were clear ("Introduction: Exterminating" 7). Baudrillard sent this piece to the journal *Critique* during a time when Foucault served on the journal's editorial board (7). And, although the essay was submitted as a review of Foucault's *History of Sexuality, 1: The Will to Knowledge*, it did not merely limit its comments to Foucault's most recent publication; instead, the essay took issue with Foucault's "entire oeuvre" (7). The plan, reportedly, was for *Critique* to publish it alongside a response from Foucault (Butler 78). The plan, however, was abandoned when Foucault withdrew his involvement at the insistence of his friends (78). As Rex Butler surmises, the experience resulted in Baudrillard being "ostracized from the French intellectual community" and perhaps also his departure from "orthodox academic" writing (78). Here, then, in the publication history of *Forget Foucault,* the brashness of Baudrillard's rhetorical practice becomes evident. He seizes on an opportunity to address Foucault directly, ostensibly for the purposes of eliciting a response. Baudrillard's essay was published instead by Éditions Galilée—not by the journal *Critique*—and Foucault never responded to Baudrillard's challenge (Lotringer, "Introduction: Exterminating" 25). Despite the essay's failure to generate its desired effect, its history can be interpreted as a second rhetorical touchstone in the life of Baudrillard.

Checking Out the Bonaventure Hotel, 1986

Baudrillard was a rhetor who understood the relationship between texts and contexts as a fluid relationship, and the fact that he used this fluid relationship to his rhetorical advantage is illustrated by his treatment of the Bonaventure Hotel. Baudrillard's writing on the Bonaventure Hotel is, of course, less well known among American scholars than that of Fredric Jameson, who featured the hotel in his 1984 essay "Postmodernism, or the Cultural Logic of Late Capitalism." Published in the *New Left Review*, Jameson's essay navigates the postmodern architecture of the Bonaventure Hotel, arguing that the visitor's experience of the architectural space functions as a "symbol and analogue" of the human subject's experience of the globalized economy and communication network (80). Ultimately, Jameson contends that humans "do not yet possess the perceptual equipment to match this new hyperspace" (80). Baudrillard's treatment of the Bonaventure Hotel, published as a two-paragraph-long entry in his 1986 *America*, responds to the postmodern context that was crystalized, encapsulated, or perhaps popularized with the publication of Jameson's essay. Whereas Jameson's treatment commences at the hotel entrances (81) and eventually ascends to the rotating cocktail lounges perched atop the hotel (83), Baudrillard's treatment begins at the cocktail lounge (*A* 59) and descends in an attempt to find the hotel's exit (60). Jameson, on the one hand, understands the hotel as a transformative and transcendent space—one that gives humans a new view (83) and one that requires new perceptual capacities (84). Baudrillard, on the other hand, understands the hotel as an "internal refraction" that lacks mystery (*A* 59).[5]

However, if text and context are understood to relate to one another fluidly, then both of these treatments of the Bonaventure Hotel can be understood as emerging from Baudrillard's 1977 essay "The Beaubourg Effect." This earlier essay theoretically challenges the Centre Georges Pompidou in Paris to the point of envisioning its collapse (cf. Armitage, "Beaubourg"). As Mike Gane's "From the Beaubourg to the Bonaventure Hotel" explains, Jameson used Baudrillard's essay on the Centre Pompidou "as a resource" for his seminal essay and viewed the 1977 essay as "an exercise in postmodernism" (*Baudrillard's* 143, 151). After documenting some striking oppositions between Baudrillard's 1977 essay and Jameson's 1984 essay that suggest Jameson used "The Beaubourg Effect" as more of a stylistic model, Gane directly compares the two treatments of the Bonaventure Hotel: Jameson's 1984 essay and Baudrillard's 1986 treatment (150–51). Gane chronicles six similarities and a number of significant differences between the two treatments, heralding Baudrillard's treatment as "remarkable" for its "structure of imagery" as well as for its ability to address the salient critical points that emerged from scholarly discussion of Jameson's essay (153). According to Gane, Baudrillard's short treatment of the Bonaventure Hotel "is more effective, forceful, unified, and evocative, even in its humor, its wit," than Jameson's longer treatment of the same storied Los Angeles hotel (156). Baudrillard's rhetorical success, here, might very well be attributed to his larger sense of the multiple contexts—from the architectural to the historical, the cultural to the popular—and the multiple texts—from his essay on the Centre Pompidou to Jameson's essay on the Bonaventure Hotel—that encompassed and informed his treatment of it. His navigation of the complex network of texts and contexts serves as a third rhetorical touchstone in Baudrillard's life.

Replacing the Gulf War, 1991

Baudrillard was a rhetor who made significant use of the commonplace, or the ordinary, and often for an uncommon effect. In the early months of 1991, Baudrillard published three pieces in the daily newspaper *Libération*. All three of these pieces commented on the Gulf War, and they would eventually be collected (and, in the case of the latter two pieces, expanded) into Baudrillard's controversial book *The Gulf War Did Not Take Place*. The first essay, originally published on January 4, 1991, speculated through its title that "The Gulf War Will Not Take Place." Baudrillard wrote this first essay as the United Nations Security Council's deadline for Iraq to withdraw from Kuwait neared. The essay suggests that the build-up toward war will actually prevent the Gulf War. Baudrillard, himself, refers to his suggestion in this essay as "a stupid gamble" (*GW* 28).[6] The second essay, part of which was initially published on February 6, 1991, was more circumspect about the occurrence of war—that is, even as air campaigns had commenced and military arsenals had been launched. Using its title to inquire "The Gulf War: Is It Really Taking Place?" this essay serves as a rejoinder to the first, arguing that the information about and reportage on the war was cleaning, "laundering," or bleaching the war into a nonwar (*GW* 43, 51).[7] The third essay, part of which was published on March 29, 1991, mobilized its title to declare defiantly that "The Gulf War Did Not Take Place." Written as the war concluded, this last essay retrospectively considers the conflict to be "a war won in advance" (*GW* 61).[8]

Whether understood together or approached separately, these three essays provoked what William Merrin describes as a strong critical reaction (82). The reaction—typified by Christopher Norris's *Uncritical Theory: Postmodernism, Intellectuals and the Gulf War*—was, according to Merrin, so strong that it perpetuated hostility toward Baudrillard and his work decades after the essays were published (82). Part of the adverse critical reaction to these essays resulted from the titles that Baudrillard chose. As both Merrin and Richard G. Smith observe, Baudrillard's choice for the first essay's title alluded to a 1935 Jean Giraudoux play titled *La guerre de Troie n'aura pas lieu* (*The Trojan War Will Not Take Place*) (Merrin 87; Smith, "Gulf" 93). The allusion—what Merrin calls "a key reference essential for any understanding of these essays" (87)—was initially lost on critics. Similarly, Gary Genosko recognizes the significance of the original French essay titles, which move from future tense to present tense to *passé composé* (*Baudrillard* 104). According to Genosko, these titles signal "the question of the 'place' at which the war has not transpired" (104). Merrin concurs, noting the significance of the war's nonplace in these essays (92). The place (*lieu*) or nonplace of the Gulf War was, indeed, significant to Baudrillard. In the third essay and with reference to Bertolt Brecht and Carl von Clausewitz, Baudrillard writes that "[a]t the desired place (the Gulf), nothing took place, non-war" and also that "[a]t the desired place (TV, information), nothing took place, no images, nothing but filler" (*GW* 82).[9] He further observes that "[n]ot much took place in all our heads either," concluding that "[t]he fact that there was nothing at this or that desired place was harmoniously compensated for by the fact that there was nothing elsewhere either" (82).[10] The argument that Baudrillard advances in these lines and throughout these three essays is, ultimately, an argument about commonplace: What was once commonplace to and about war—for instance, images of battlefields (40),[11] antagonistic confrontation between enemies (62),[12] relatively equal forces engaged in a duel (69)[13]—is no longer. Rather, Baudrillard argues that a simulacrum founded in "dupery," "hyperreality," and "trickery" has replaced war commonplaces (67).[14] Since Baudrillard advanced this argument in 1991, commentators, such as J. Marshall Beier (114) and Merrin (83), have defended his essays. Both Beier and Merrin recognize that these three essays identify characteristics of the Gulf War that have become the new commonplaces of contemporary warfare. Merrin perhaps puts it best when he declares, "The simulacrum, therefore, has become a commonplace" (44). To be sure, Baudrillard's ability to identify, controversially yet clairvoyantly, new wartime commonplaces stands as a fourth rhetorical touchstone in his life.

Rolling with Chance, November 9, 1996

Baudrillard was a rhetor who recognized the importance of delivery to the effectiveness of speaking, and his delivery was arguably most distinctive at an event in Primm, Nevada, on November 9, 1996. The Chance Event was organized by Chris Kraus, a faculty member at the Art Center College of Design in Pasadena, California, and a former employee with one of Baudrillard's American publishers, Semiotext(e) (Swed, "Accidents"). The conference brought together individuals who studied poetry and philosophy, as well as those who studied finance and meteorology, to discuss the chaotic nature of the world (Swed, "Hundreds"). Baudrillard was an invited speaker, and as the *Los Angeles Times* reports, his fifty-minute talk was "not easily understood," for it was delivered with a heavy accent.

To be sure, though, the most notable part of the delivery was not Baudrillard's accent. Instead, scheduling difficulties wreaked havoc on arrangements for the talk, making it so that Baudrillard delivered the talk in the showroom of Whiskey Pete's casino on a dance floor that had been prepared for dancing. Marc Swed describes a setup where "the audience sat or reclined on the floor, at the philosopher's feet" ("Hundreds"). What is more, Baudrillard shared the stage with a pickup band named the Chance Band. As the band "noodled" along playing "'Twin Peaks'–like music," Baudrillard delivered an English-language "lecture on the Demise of the Real," and his message was received as "gloomy," "arcane," and "fatalistic" (Swed, "Hundreds"; Kraus; Swed, "Hundreds"). The event would continue "into the wee hours of the morning" with the band playing and Baudrillard, who sat in a corner of the room and leafed through his writing, occasionally stepping to the microphone to speak (Swed, "Hundreds"). The tone of the performance was described later as monotonous to the point of putting audience members to sleep ("Hundreds"). Nonetheless, the night was punctuated by Baudrillard's choice of attire—a metallic lounge jacket with a sequined lapel that some describe as silver and others as gold (Swed, "Hundreds"; Kraus). The color of the jacket is, though, less important than its effect on the audience: Baudrillard's decision to switch his denim coat for the lounge jacket helped this address achieve iconic status among individuals interested in Baudrillard. Despite the scheduling snafu, the heavy accent, the gloominess of the address, the monotonous tone, and the audience members who fell asleep, Baudrillard has been described as "the star" of the entire conference (Swed "Hundreds"). Kraus recalls that Baudrillard "was a reluctant guru" and the "response was ecstatic." Thus, Baudrillard's delivery at the Chance Event functions as a fifth rhetorical touchstone in his life.

Capturing *Kairos* with Photography, January 8, 1999

Baudrillard was a rhetor who understood the importance of timing to a composition, and his mastery of timing is perhaps best showcased in his photography. Baudrillard began practicing photography in conjunction with his travels as, he says, "a kind of diversion or hobby" (*AA* 32). As Alan Cholodenko documents, Baudrillard received a camera in 1983 from his partner, Marité Bonnal, so that he could capture images of the United States (155). By the late 1980s, Baudrillard began taking photographs more earnestly and, by the early 1990s, pursued photography even more seriously (*PH* 207). His prowess in photography was on full display at the Neue Galerie in Graz, Austria, in the early winter of 1999. Between January 8 and February 14 of that year, the Neue Galerie ran an exhibition titled *Within the Horizon of the Object* (*Im Horizont des Objekts*) that featured ninety of Baudrillard's photographs taken between 1985 and 1998 (*PH* 216–17). These photographs, by and large, possess striking color and present images of objects and architecture, often in contrast with a landscape element. Although human figures are occasionally present in these images, their faces and gazes are obscured, suggesting that they were unaware of their photographer. While the 1999 exhibition was not the first exhibition of Baudrillard's photography, it was, according to the Neue Galerie, the first exhibition of Baudrillard's photographs "in a large solo show and in an extensive catalogue" (*PH* 19), and, according to Cholodenko, the exhibition was likely "the most significant" of Baudrillard's photography (155). The main exhibition space consisted of a large rectangular room. Some of Baudrillard's photographs hung—framed and mounted—on the walls of the space, while even more were matted and displayed on one of three tables that ran diagonally across the large hall. A semicircular alcove occupied one end of the exhibition hall, and it was in this alcove that Baudrillard delivered the exhibition's opening lecture.

His lecture aside, Baudrillard's photography highlights his grasp of timing. Peter Weibel, who wrote the epilogue for the exhibition, describes the effect of Baudrillard's photography best when he writes, "Baudrillard is a photographer of the *kairos*, not of the *chronos*, of the here and now not of time" (*PH* 211). Weibel's remark captures what Baudrillard's photography captures—that is, a reaction to "the instance, the elusive moment, the coincidence of image" (211)—and it does so by invoking the rhetorically seminal concept of *kairos*. Weibel's description suggests that Baudrillard's photography seizes the opportune moment and that each of his photographic compositions capitalizes on the delicate timing involving the photographer, the camera, and the world. While the "image is an acting out of technology," the timing of Baudrillard's photographic compositions clearly shows that "the object succeeds in putting its stamp on the subject and its perception" (214). The exhibition in Graz—Baudrillard's most significant photographic exhibition and also the exhibition where his photography was lauded for the way it captured *kairos*—can, subsequently, be read as a sixth rhetorical touchstone in Baudrillard's life.

Bidding a Generic Farewell to the Twin Towers, February 23, 2002

Baudrillard was a rhetor who deployed genre in unconventional ways to maximize the impact of his rhetorical action. Among the genres repeatedly used by Baudrillard is the genre of the requiem—that is, a written, musical, or ecclesiastical composition that works to bring about peaceful repose for the recently deceased (cf. Gogan, "Rhetoric" 170). Because the effect of a requiem is spiritual or symbolic in nature, the requiem genre departs from instrumental or pragmatic understandings of rhetoric (170). Baudrillard deployed the requiem genre first, in 1971, when he crafted a "Requiem for the Media." This particular requiem was originally published in the journal *Utopie* and later collected in the 1972 *For a Critique of the Political Economy of the Sign* (*UD* 326). In this early composition, Baudrillard used the requiem genre to put the media and its emphasis on communication to sleep, favoring symbolic exchange. Baudrillard deployed the requiem genre a second time in the months following September 11, 2001. This second requiem, "Requiem for the Twin Towers," was crafted for the World Trade Center and was first delivered as part of a February 23, 2002, panel organized by New York University and France Culture. The audio of this address is archived by France Culture, and the requiem has been published in Baudrillard's *The Spirit of Terrorism*, which was his contribution to Verso's 9/11 series.

"Requiem for the Twin Towers" demonstrates the way in which Baudrillard twisted genre to bring about an unconventional effect, for this piece overflows with lines that do not convey the conventional impression of peaceful repose. The line that is perhaps most unconventional and also the most egregious reads, "The Twin Towers were worth destroying" (*ST* 46).[15] This line and some others like it confirm that Baudrillard uses the requiem genre in an unconventional manner to maximize the effect of his composition. Rather than conveying peaceful repose, "Requiem for the Twin Towers" seems to promote violence and destruction. In fact, this requiem was so unconventional that it drew the ire of most reviewers and irreparably tarnished Baudrillard's reputation for many (cf. Gogan, "Rhetoric" 169, 171). Nonetheless, according to William Merrin, "Requiem for the Twin Towers" played a part in "restoring" Baudrillard's "intellectual profile and cutting-edge cachet in the English-speaking world" (*Baudrillard* 105). Considering Merrin's statement alongside Baudrillard's use of the requiem genre suggests that this use worked to bring about an effect less focused on the peaceful repose of the Twin Towers than on the reclamation of his intellectual cachet. In this respect—and perhaps this respect only—his use of the requiem genre seems shrewdly effective and serves as a seventh rhetorical touchstone in Baudrillard's life.

From Rhetor to Rhetorical Theorist

The seven rhetorical touchstones outlined above suggest that Baudrillard was a bold, if not novel, practitioner of rhetoric. He was, indeed, a rhetor who was deliberate in his choices regarding action, audience, context, commonplace, delivery, timing, and genre. He wrote about *and* went to the barricades in the spring of 1968. He challenged an expert audience in Foucault and the *Critique* editorial board in 1976, only to find himself on the outside of certain intellectual circles in France. He drew on his fluid understanding of context and text in his 1977 work on the Centre Pompidou and his 1986 work on the Bonaventure Hotel. He exploited a tension between place, commonplace, and the uncommon argument in his 1991 writings on the Gulf War. His sequined delivery of remarks at the 1996 Chance Event carried his address through difficulties with the event's speaking schedule and the venue. Likewise, his opportune timing shone through his 1999 photography exhibition in Graz, Austria. And, his unconventional use of genre was at no time more pointed than during his talk on the Twin Towers in 2002. Above all, however, Baudrillard was an inventive rhetor, and his expansive notion of invention—its brash, challenging, and provocative potential—is one that proves central to his rhetorical theory. Beginning with the next chapter, part one of this study takes up Baudrillard's rhetorical theory.

PART I

Appearance, Disappearance, and Jean Baudrillard's Rhetoric of Symbolic Exchange

At first glance, Baudrillard's theory of simulation and simulacra appears to be his most significant contribution to rhetorical theory. Dilip Parameshwar Gaonkar references this theory at the conclusion of "The Idea of Rhetoric in the Rhetoric of Science," writing, "No one doubts that rhetoric functions as the mixer, sometimes as the sweetener, but can one argue that science is a simulacrum (in Baudrillard's sense), a rhetorical construction without reference?" (77). Gaonkar draws on Baudrillard's theory of simulacra to interrogate rhetoric's relationship with reality and also to help rhetorical studies scholars better understand rhetoric's function. Similarly, Frank D'Angelo has argued that Baudrillard's theory of simulation, although a "nontraditional concept" in rhetoric, enables rhetorical studies scholars to understand the production of discourse in a novel way (31). And, in his exploration of reality, representation, and simulation "as rhetorical devices," Barry Brummett describes Baudrillard as "one of the preeminent theorists of simulation" and makes wide reference to his theory of simulation and simulacra (*The World* 1, 6). Moreover, the book that arguably offers the fullest exposition of this theory—Baudrillard's 1981 collection of essays titled *Simulacra and Simulation*—has been listed by Michelle Ballif and Diane Davis in their 2010 contribution to *The Present State of Scholarship in the History and Theory of Rhetoric* as a "must read" in the subarea of rhetoric and poststructuralist studies (Ratcliffe, "The Twentieth" 186). Indeed, Baudrillard's theory of simulation and simulacra has been applied widely across rhetorical studies in subfields including rhetorical criticism (cf. D'Angelo), digital rhetoric (cf. Carolyn R. Miller's "Writing in a Culture of Simulation"), rhetorical hermeneutics (cf. Gaonkar), materialist rhetoric (cf. Dana L. Cloud's "The Materiality of Discourse as Oxymoron"), and even rhetorical pedagogy (cf. Lester Faigley's *Fragments of Rationality*; Richard Marback's "Here and Now"). While any theory that addresses the relationship between an appearance and reality has rhetorical import, Baudrillard's theory of simulation and simulacra emphasizes the way in which a rhetorical construction can turn, or trope, independently of perceived reality. As such, his radical rethinking of this relationship can both complicate and challenge rhetorical theory.

Part one of *Jean Baudrillard: The Rhetoric of Symbolic Exchange* offers a full exposition of Baudrillard's rhetorical theory, of which simulation and simulacra compose only one half. Baudrillard's rhetorical theory stretches the concept of invention so that invention is positioned as the relationship between, on the one hand, the art of appearance and, on the other hand, the art of disappearance. Simulation and simulacra are associated with an extreme version of the former (appearance), which can only be challenged by an extreme version of the latter (disappearance). According to this theory, rhetorical invention becomes the relationship between appearance and disappearance. Invention serves as a kind of fulcrum for Baudrillard's rhetorical theory, a fulcrum on which appearance and disappearance pivot. Rhetorical invention engages appearance and disappearance in exchange, and the back-and-forth movement of exchange is the *telos*, or goal, of his rhetorical theory. Baudrillard argues that "[e]xchange must never have an end" (*PW* 16),[1] and, indeed, his theory of rhetoric seeks to initiate and sustain exchange in perpetuity. Put differently, rhetorical invention is the means to the end that is exchange, but the movement of exchange must not cease or otherwise end.

By considering the effects of disappearance—essentially, what is other than, or what remains outside, the making of appearances—Baudrillard's rhetorical theory challenges traditional rhetorical theories that understand rhetorical invention as an unconditionally productive capacity. His rhetorical theory can be understood as mapping the ways in which thought, discourse, and perception are invented, and as part one demonstrates, this theory positions rhetorical invention as a capacity to sustain practices that are not, at root, productive. Accordingly, this part of the present study examines Baudrillard's departure from more traditional rhetorical theories by grounding his ideas in discussions that have been of central concern to rhetoric for millennia.

By way of illustration, each of the chapters of part one—chapters 3, 4, 5, and 6—concludes with a section titled "Illustration" that applies Baudrillard's theory to Rebecca Skloot's *The Immortal Life of Henrietta Lacks* and to the events captured in the book—events involving Henrietta Lacks, her cells, and her family. While these illustration sections are intended to promote an applied understanding of each part of Baudrillard's rhetorical theory, they also work together as a piece of rhetorical criticism that mobilizes a Baudrillardian perspective to better understand textual and phenomenological rhetoric.

CHAPTER 3

Rhetoric, Sophistry, and Appearance-Making

Baudrillard's rhetorical theory depends on a continued exchange between two subspecies of arts—appearance and disappearance—and a full understanding of Baudrillard's rhetorical theory begins by situating the art of appearance in rhetorical history. At first glance, the whole of rhetoric might be viewed as an appearance-making enterprise, in which a rhetor produces discourse in order to achieve a goal. A rhetor uses discourse to make an argument appear a certain way to an audience and, thereby, persuades the audience, wins its assent, or forges a sense of identification with the audience. In short, a rhetor makes appearances.

Among classical sources that address the relationship between appearance-making and rhetoric, no source is more important to an understanding of Jean Baudrillard's rhetorical theory than Plato's *Sophist.* Most often classified as one of Plato's late dialogues and presumed to be written after 367 B.C.E. (Cooper xiii), the *Sophist* attempts to define a group of itinerant teachers of rhetoric known collectively as Sophists and, in doing so, offers a treatment of both rhetoric and appearance. The dialogue is a continuation of Plato's *Theaetetus* and a precursor to Plato's *Statesman*: The four characters present in the *Theaetetus*—Theodorus, Theaetetus, young Socrates, and Socrates—are, in the *Sophist* as well as the *Statesman*, joined in discussion by a fifth character—a visitor from Elea. The Eleatic visitor and Theaetetus are the primary interlocutors in the *Sophist* dialogue, and they pose a series of questions about the nature and art of the Sophist in an attempt to distinguish the Sophist from the philosopher. The dialogue is widely considered to be one of the best examples of Plato's method of division (*diaresis*), in which one central question (e.g., What is a Sophist?) is consequently divided and subdivided into smaller component parts until the question is resolved. Largely on account of this continuous division, the dialogue is considered difficult and has been subject to widely varying commentaries. Reviewing these commentaries, Gordon C. Neal observes that Plato's *Sophist* allows for a "bewildering range of interpretations" (12). Indeed, little critical consensus exists as to the scope of Plato's text.

Despite the lack of consensus concerning the scope of Plato's text, Baudrillard studies scholars consistently recognize that the terrain of appearance-making, which Baudrillard's theory traverses, was ground first mapped by Plato. In fact, William Merrin, Gary Genosko, and William Pawlett resolutely connect Baudrillard's theory of simulation and simulacra to Plato's *Sophist*. Merrin, Genosko, and Pawlett understand Baudrillard as following in a line of thinkers who grapple with simulation and simulacra, thinkers including Gilles Deleuze, Pierre Klossowski, Martin Heidegger, Friedrich Nietzsche, and Plato. In large part, Merrin reads Plato's *Sophist* and its discussion of simulacra through the work of Deleuze (*Baudrillard* 34). This approach differs from the approaches of Genosko and Pawlett, who more directly associate Baudrillard's theory with Plato's *Sophist*—though their views differ with respect to the closeness of this association. On the one hand, Genosko argues that Baudrillard "displays no strong need to turn Platonism on its head," suggesting that Baudrillardian thought—including his theory of simulation and simulacra—might well be read as being compatible with Platonic thought (*Baudrillard* 29). Pawlett, on the other hand, asserts that "Baudrillard entirely rejects [a] (Platonic) understanding of simulacra" ("Simulacra" 196). Pawlett, thus, understands Baudrillard's theory of simulation and simulacra as influenced most strongly by the notions of simulation and simulacra offered by Nietzsche and Klossowski, which are nonetheless indebted to Plato's *Sophist*. Importantly, the arguments offered by Genosko and Pawlett are, for their differences, both arguments that ignore the rhetorical connections between Baudrillard's work and Plato's. These rhetorical connections, however, are perhaps the most important connections to an understanding of Baudrillard's work and his rhetorical theory.

Curiously, though, among rhetorical studies scholars—arguably the scholars best suited to articulate the rhetorical connections between Plato's *Sophist* and Baudrillard's theory of simulation and simulacra—the *Sophist* has received scant attention. Indeed, scholars including John Muckelbauer, Ellen Quandahl, and Edith Hamilton have outlined no fewer than four quite plausible reasons as to why rhetorical studies scholars might be reluctant to examine the connections between rhetoric and Plato's *Sophist* and, more specifically, between Baudrillard and Plato. As Muckelbauer observes in *The Future of Invention: Rhetoric, Postmodernism, and the Problem of Change*, "very few and very brief rhetorical engagements exist with the Platonic dialogue 'The Sophist'" (82). Muckelbauer is one of the few scholars in rhetorical studies to substantively discuss Plato's *Sophist*; however, he treats the dialogue in a way that "responds" to Deleuze's *The Logic of Sense* and, consequently, omits any reference to Baudrillard (cf. 173 n. 1). When discussing the *Sophist*, Muckelbauer speculates that rhetorical studies scholars fail to engage with it because either they anticipate that the dialogue "contains yet another indictment of sophistry" or they consider the dialogue to be "too philosophical, too concerned with the abstract questions of being and nonbeing" (82). Here, Muckelbauer's speculation as to why rhetorical studies scholars do not more prominently and frequently engage with the *Sophist* might also be understood as a recapitulation of the two dominant ways in which the dialogue has been treated by the small number of rhetorical studies scholars who have studied it. As for reading the dialogue as an "indictment of sophistry," Edward Schiappa's *Protagoras and Logos: A Study in Greek Philosophy and Rhetoric* understands Plato's *Sophist* as sketching the figure of the Sophist as a "rather reprehensible character" (5). As for reading the dialogue as an overly philosophical treatise on "questions of being and nonbeing," Michelle Ballif's reading of Plato's *Sophist* emphasizes the dialogue's ontological argument, specifically its attack on the Parmenides's thesis claiming that there is no such thing as *not* being (42).

Besides the two reasons that Muckelbauer suggests for the scant attention paid to Plato's *Sophist* by rhetorical studies scholars, two other plausible reasons exist. One reason, supplied by Ellen Quandahl, is that rhetorical studies scholars simply prefer more literary Platonic dialogues that uphold an opposition between Plato and the Sophists. Quandahl contends "that for many rhetoricians 'Plato' means *Phaedrus*, *Gorgias* and perhaps portions of the *Republic* and *Symposium*," and Quandahl further argues that the *Sophist* dialogue disturbs the opposition between Plato and the Sophists by positing meaning as "contextual and not absolute" (338, 339). Quandahl's reasoning here is both conceivable and compelling. Still, one final reason as to why rhetorical studies scholars have largely overlooked Plato's *Sophist* relates to the difficulty of following the dialogue's structure. A number of commentaries from scholars of classics and philosophy, alike, bluntly assert that the hard-to-follow dialogue never answers its central question: What is a Sophist? Indeed, Edith Hamilton views Plato as using "figure of the Sophist quite arbitrarily," as nothing more than a means to demolish Parmenides's theory (958). As a result, Hamilton concludes that, throughout the dialogue, "[n]o real picture is given of the men who were the professional instructors of Greece for many years" (958). If Hamilton's understanding of the *Sophist* is to be accepted, it is no wonder that rhetorical studies scholars have not fully engaged with the dialogue.

Amid these four reasons why rhetorical studies has not fully engaged with Plato's *Sophist* nor inquired into the foundations it lays for Baudrillard's own rhetorical theory, three compelling arguments can be made for the relevance of the dialogue to rhetorical studies and, more specifically, to rhetorical studies of Baudrillard. These three arguments build upon one of the more recent interpretations of the *Sophist*, Noburu Notomi's *The Unity of Plato's* Sophist, which convincingly argues that Plato's dialogue pursues the question of the Sophist throughout the entire dialogue. Notomi contends that the *Sophist* maintains a focused scope—one concentrated on defining the nature and art of those itinerant teachers of rhetoric who are called Sophists. As a result of the dialogue's focused scope, the definition of the Sophist it proposes is, as Notomi reveals, much more palatable to rhetorical studies scholars because the definition emphasizes the processes and products of thought and discourse. Notomi builds this interpretation by viewing the dialogue as a unified whole. According to Notomi, the dialogue adheres to a "pedimental structure" (172; cf. Bluck 55–57), in which specific questions concerning what is, what is not, falsehoods, images, and appearances must be answered before answering the text's central question: What is a Sophist? By reading the dialogue's structure as such, Notomi parts company with a majority of other interpreters, who only emphasize the dialogue's middle part (236d–264b) and who understand the dialogue as relevant primarily to questions of ontology, methodology, and logic.

To be sure, Notomi advances a novel interpretation characterized by reviewers as "interesting," "valid," and "plausible" (Sprague 585; Michelini 95; A. Walker 520); he makes "a well-argued and persuasive case" that is "basically sound" (Sprague 585; A. Walker 521). The novelty of Notomi's reading, as reviewer Zina Giannopoulou explains, is that Notomi offers "the first scholarly attempt" to elevate the dialogue's treatment of appearance over and above the dialogue's treatment of what is not, falsehood, and image. Thus, when approached as a unified whole, the dialogue stresses the processes used by and the products made by the Sophist. In short, a unified view of the dialogue homes in on a definition of the Sophist as a maker of appearances, and this definition underlies the first of three arguments holding that the *Sophist* is not only amenable to rhetorical study but is particularly germane to rhetorical studies of Baudrillard.

The Relevance of the Theory Explored in the *Sophist* Dialogue

First, the *Sophist* dialogue remains relevant to rhetorical study and rhetorical studies of Baudrillard for the theoretical issues foregrounded by the definition of the Sophist that it advances. In the closing lines of the dialogue (268c8–d5), the Eleatic visitor proposes a definition of the Sophist, which suggests that the Sophist is distinguishable only through reference to some divine truth and that the Sophist makes appearances through processes that involve imitation, contradiction, irony, and ignorance. Indeed, this definition echoes throughout each of the following four English language translations:

> (1) The art of contradiction making, descended from an insincere kind of conceited mimicry, of the semblance-making breed, derived from image making, distinguished as a portion, not divine but human, of production, that presents a shadow play of words. (Cornford 1016–17)
> (2) Imitation of the contrary-speech-producing, insincere and unknowing sort, or the appearance-making kind of copy-making, the word-juggling part of production that's marked off as human and not divine. (White 293)
> (3) The imitative artist of the contradiction-making art of the dissimulative part of the art of opinion, which belongs to the appearance-making kind of the image-making art that is not the divine but the human part of the productive art defined as the art of conjuring in words. (Ambuel 247)
> (4) The art of contradiction-making, belonging to the ironical part, of the opinion-accompanying type of imitation, belonging to the apparition-making kind, derived from the image-making art, not divine but human, belonging to the art of making, is separated in argument as the wonder-making portion. (Notomi 296)

Variously translated, this definition of the Sophist proves agreeable to both of the interlocutors in Plato's dialogue. And while the characterization of sophistical rhetoric as "a shadow play of words" (Cornford 1016–17), a "word-juggling" (White 293), and a "conjuring in words" (Ambuel 247) might be less agreeable to rhetorical studies scholars, the definition emphasizes issues central to Baudrillard's rhetorical theory.

The definition of the Sophist articulated by Plato stresses issues of reference and truth that foreshadow similar issues central to rhetoric and to Baudrillard's own rhetorical theory. To be sure, recent work on Plato's *Sophist* by Robin Reames suggests that this dialogue most fully articulates Plato's own rhetorical theory, a theory wherein the referential nature of the spoken word—that is, the representational nature of *logos*-as-statement—allows for statements to be either true or false. The dialogue's emphasis on representation and truth are encapsulated in the definition's claim that the art of the Sophist is a uniquely human art. Both the Eleatic visitor and Theaetetus agree that the art of the Sophist is not to be associated with the divine. This distinction is a point about reference, wherein the human distinguishes itself through reference to the divine. The definition of the Sophist depends, therefore, on reference to the divine. Without reference to the divine, defining the Sophist proves an impossible task. Notomi concludes that, without reference to the divine and more specifically a divine truth, the Sophist and the philosopher become indistinguishable (288). The philosopher, of course, uses thought and discourse to pursue divine truth and virtue, while the Sophist might deploy thought and discourse to any number of ends—some of which may not be true or virtuous.

Understood differently, sophistical rhetoric confuses auditors to such a degree that reference to divine truth is perhaps the only way by which auditors can evaluate truth claims and distinguish the Sophist from the philosopher. The confusion that results from the Sophist's shadow play, juggling, and conjuring results from the Sophist's art, which receives description in the Eleatic visitor's definition. The definition depicts the Sophist's processes, which involve imitation (i.e., mimicry, copying), contradiction (i.e., contrary-speech-producing, contradiction-making), irony (i.e., pretense, concealment), and ignorance (i.e., a relational degree of knowledge or expertise), as well as the Sophist's products, which involve the making of appearances, the vast majority of which might be categorized as false appearances (Notomi 270–301). It is through processes that rely on imitation, contradiction, irony, and ignorance and the production of false appearances that the Sophist confuses auditors and obscures truth. The Sophist deploys rhetoric that dissolves the distinction between the true and the false. As Notomi notes, "the sophist takes everything to be true" (200). As such, the Sophist necessarily makes even the false appear to be true. Thus, the Sophist's auditors become incapable of perceiving a difference between the false and the true and, likewise, between the Sophist and the philosopher. In the first place, then, the dialogue's definition of the Sophist and its emphasis on issues of reference, truth, and production offer scholars, especially those interested in studying Baudrillard as a rhetorical theorist, a compelling argument for the relevance of Plato's *Sophist* to rhetorical studies.

The Relevance of the Terminology Introduced in the *Sophist* Dialogue

Second, the *Sophist* dialogue introduces terminology pertaining to image-making and appearance-making that is crucial to rhetorical studies and to studies of Baudrillard's work. To be sure, the dialogue and the definition of the Sophist advanced in it create what might be described as a semantic field connecting terms related to image and appearance; likeness, similitude, and semblance; copies and apparitions; and, most important for the present study, the terms *phantasia* and *simulacra*. As Plato's interlocutors attempt to parse specific questions concerning what is, what is not, falsehoods, images, and appearances, they distinguish between two types of images: likenesses or copies, on the one hand, and apparitions or appearances on the other hand (cf. Notomi 147–55; Ambuel 70–75; Heidegger 277–79). In brief, the first kind of image (εἰκών or *eikōn*) is in true proportion to an original and to an original model regardless of how it is seen by a viewer, while the second kind of image (φάντασμα or *phantasma*) only appears to be like an original to a viewer and achieves its effect on account of dissimilitude and dissemblance (cf. Notomi 148–49). This distinction emphasizes the importance of perception to an appearance, and, as such, it stresses the importance of the term *phantasia* (φαντασία) to the dialogue, the practice of rhetoric, and the study of rhetoric.

To be sure, rhetorical studies scholars have noted the importance of *phantasia* to rhetoric. For instance, Ned O'Gorman observes that the concept of *phantasia* unites rhetorical theories with both psychological theories and phenomenological theories (16), and Debra Hawhee positions "*phantasia* as potentially one of the most important critical faculties for the art of rhetoric" ("Looking" 143). José M. Gonzáles, Deborah K. W. Modrak, Michele Kennerly, and Sara Newman, among other scholars, have also examined the intersections between *phantasia* and rhetoric, and these examinations most often reference Aristotle and his rhetorical theory. Yet, *phantasia* proves especially important to the present study because the term was, as Notomi recognizes, "first introduced in Plato's dialogues" (250). Notomi's study of the word *phantasia* documents that "there is no example of this word extant in Greek literature before Plato" and counts seven instances in Plato's work where the word *phantasia* is used (250; cf. Ambuel 73–74; Crivelli 260). These seven instances occur in three dialogues—the *Republic*, the *Theaetetus*, and the *Sophist*—and, of these three dialogues, *phantasia* appears most frequently in the *Sophist*.

Plato's uses of *phantasia* in the *Sophist* are clustered in a section of the dialogue with particular rhetorical significance. The significance of this section becomes apparent when the aim of the entire dialogue is kept in mind. According to Notomi's interpretation, the dialogue is concerned with the processes and the products of discourse and thought that are associated with the Sophist. Further, both the Eleatic visitor and Theaetetus are participating in processes of discourse and thought about the Sophist, and these processes result in certain products—namely, judgments about the Sophist. To be sure, the dialogue does not present its readers with two speakers who maintain an objective perspective from which they can arrive at the true nature and art of the Sophist; the interlocutors are not, in other words, outside the subject of the discussion. Rather, each speaker is complicit with the production of the appearance of the Sophist. Indeed, the problem here might be understood as analogous to what could be described as the paradox of rhetorical study: in explaining how the production of discourse works, no rhetor is ever outside that production, as the explanation is itself rhetorical. Thus, before they arrive at and agree upon a definition of the Sophist, the Eleatic visitor and Theaetetus must recognize their involvement in this paradox and their complicity in making the Sophist appear.

Plato deploys the concept of *phantasia* as a means by which the interlocutors can work through this paradox of judgment and appearance. Indeed, the Greek for *phantasia* appears in four lines (260c9, 260e4, 263d6, and 264a6) that are each located in the section of the dialogue that considers how judgments are formed through thought and discourse. This section is also the same one in which the Eleatic visitor and Theaetetus begin to recognize their complicity in producing appearances of the Sophist. Among commentators on the *Sophist*, debate exists as to whether Plato uses the word *phantasia* to mean "imagination," "appearing," or "perceptual appearance" (cf. Notomi 250–53). Notomi arguably offers the most detailed reading of the word as meaning a "perceptual appearance" (253) or a "judgment [reached] through perception" (259) and, subsequently, provides the most convincing argument as to the term's importance to the *Sophist* dialogue. According to Notomi, Plato resolves the issue of his interlocutors' complicity in producing appearances by drawing a distinction between three types of judgments, of which *phantasia* are one type. The typology is as follows: Thought is an individual process that produces judgments. Discourse is a process that relies on an individual and another to produce stated judgments, or statements. *Phantasia* constitute a third kind of judgment that are based on perceptions. Schematically, then, thoughts kept to oneself are judgments, judgments that are externalized toward another are statements, and judgments that are based on perceptions are *phantasia.*

Here, Notomi's understanding approximates Martin Heidegger's understanding of *phantasia*, and both commentators understand *phantasia* as a kind of work-around that Plato uses to refute Parmenides's thesis—a thesis holding that there is only being and that there is no such thing as nothing. Heidegger, in fact, views *phantasia* as the "equivalent to λόγος [*logos*] as λεγόμευου"—or, speech or discourse as spoken—and further observes that "Plato interprets φαντασία [*phantasia*] as δόξα [*doxa*]," which, itself, is "*based on* αἴσθησις [*aisthesis*]" (421). Like Notomi, then, Heidegger reads Plato's *Sophist* as defining *phantasia* as an opinion or view based on sense perception. This third kind of judgment or perceptual appearance enables Plato to overturn Parmenides's thesis, since perceptions can be either true or false, regardless of the ontological status of what is being perceived. Accordingly, a thing (in this case, an appearance based on perception) can be (as in exist) and, at the same time, not be (when perception is erroneous). Since *phantasia* admit that perceptions can at times be false, they focus attention on the effects of judgment, statement, and perception. *Phantasia* further allow the Eleatic visitor and Theaetetus to assess the appearance of the nature and art of the Sophist—that is, by way of the effects of sophistic rhetoric as judged, stated, and perceived. The *Sophist* dialogue thus maps new terrain for rhetorical invention as it maps conclusive ground on which a rhetor can produce false appearances—or, appearances that are perceived to be true in contrast with their ontological status.

The *Sophist* dialogue's focus on the processes and products of discourse, thought, and perception advances a rhetorically grounded concept of appearances that has been taken up by theorists—Baudrillard among them—over the past two millennia. Baudrillard's own use of the term *simulacra* fits into the semantic field marked by the term *phantasia*, for *simulacra* "derives from the Latin *simulare*," which means "to 'make like' or simulate" (Pawlett, "Simulacra" 196). Indeed, discussions about simulacra and simulation—discussions about making, perceiving, and evaluating likenesses—are deeply rooted in the semantic field marked by *phantasia* (cf. Brummett, *The World* 7). This semantic field is one that extends from Plato to Aristotle, Quintilian to Augustine, Martin Heidegger to Pierre Klossowski, Xavier Audouard to Gilles Deleuze (cf. Durham; O'Gorman 17). Moreover, as Jean-François Lyotard observes, this semantic field is one that is centrally invested in language (67–69). Lyotard's reading of the way that Plato, Augustine, and Klossowski treat phantasms and simulacra holds that the differences among these three treatments ultimately have to do with communicability and exchangeability (76–77). Thus, Lyotard makes the point that the semantic field marked by *phantasia* is a field concerned with rhetoric. Importantly, though, the terms encompassed by this field—namely, the cognates of *phantasia* and *simulacra*—have become almost indistinguishable in the work of contemporary thinkers, including Klossowski and Deleuze, both of whom Baudrillard read. As Daniel W. Smith notes, the terms *phantasm* (*phantasme*) and *simulacrum* (*simulacrum*) "are perhaps the most important terms in Klossowski's vocabulary," with *phantasm* referring "to an obsessional image produced instinctively from the life of the impulses" and *simulacrum* referring to "a willed reproduction of a phantasm (in a literary, pictorial, or plastic form) that simulates this invisible agitation of the soul" (x). For Klossowski, the only difference between a phantasm and a simulacrum is the presence or absence of will, volition, or intent (133, 140). Deleuze, for his part, weds the two terms together even more so, referring to the first kind of image delineated by Plato in the *Sophist* dialogue as "*copies-icons*" and the second kind of image as "*simulacra-phantasms*" (256). Deleuze hardly distinguishes between *phantasia* and its cognates and *simulacra* and its cognates. Likewise, Audouard—whom Deleuze references (cf. 361 n. 5)—repeatedly uses appositive constructions to rename phantasm as simulacrum (Audouard 58, 63, 70). Accordingly, the terminological and conceptual affinity between *phantasia* and *simulacra* provide a second argument as to the relevance of the *Sophist* dialogue to the present study, for the dialogue begins to map simulacra onto rhetoric.

The Relevance of the Approach Suggested by the *Sophist* Dialogue

Third, the *Sophist* proves relevant to studies of rhetorical theory and, in particular, the present study of Baudrillard because it suggests an approach by which scholars might deductively evaluate the sophistical characteristics of a rhetor such as Baudrillard. Rhetorical studies scholars often classify Baudrillard, either through juxtaposition or through label, as a Sophist. For example, in *Seduction, Sophistry, and the Woman with the Rhetorical Figure*, Michelle Ballif views Baudrillard as a practitioner of "[s]ophistic rhetoric"—that is, someone who presumes "that language resists logic" (5). Additionally, in *Gorgias and the New Sophistic Rhetoric*, Bruce McComiskey refers to Baudrillard as one of four "postmodern sophists" and contends that the "descriptions of how language derives meaning" offered by the classical-era Sophist Gorgias and Baudrillard "are remarkably similar" (89). In fact, the categorizations of Baudrillard as a Sophist offered by both Ballif and McComiskey compare Baudrillard to Gorgias, a figure who is often hailed as the prototypical Sophist. Ballif understands Gorgias, like Baudrillard, as practicing sophistic rhetoric (5), and McComiskey argues that Baudrillard and Gorgias both share the perspective that reality has an uncertain influence on language due to "the interpretive processes of perception" (88). Taken together, the readings of Baudrillard offered by both Ballif and McComiskey unequivocally categorize Baudrillard as a Sophist and also establish strong connections between Baudrillard and other Sophists, namely Gorgias. While the juxtaposition of Baudrillard with Gorgias steers these studies toward close readings of Gorgias's own works and Plato's dialogue *Gorgias*, it stands to reason that Plato's *Sophist*—a dialogue aimed at defining Sophists more generally—might allow rhetorical studies scholars to work toward a different understanding of Baudrillard through a more deductive approach. In other words, the *Sophist* offers rhetorical studies scholars a broad definition of a Sophist that can be applied to an individual theorist like Baudrillard. As such, the *Sophist* dialogue provides perspective on the sophistical tendencies of Baudrillard's rhetorical theory.

When the definition of the Sophist outlined in Plato's dialogue is applied to Baudrillard, he might well appear to be a Sophist—that is, an individual associated with the processes and products of thought, discourse, and perception that are also characteristic of the Sophist, as defined by the Eleatic visitor and Theaetetus; or, put differently, a rhetor who works "in the domain of the human art of image-making" and who is "an apparition-maker," "an imitator," "an ignoramus," "an ironist," and "a contradiction-maker" (Notomi 296). Indeed, part two of the current study examines a good many of these appearances and assesses the basis for considering Baudrillard to be this kind of sophistic rhetor—that is, someone who excels at making appearances, especially at goading audiences into perceiving false appearances as ontologically true. But for now, the point must be made that understanding Baudrillard only as a sophistic appearance-maker is to lose sight of his overarching rhetorical theory. Although his rhetorical theory does examine the production of false appearances by rhetors, Baudrillard's overarching rhetorical theory stretches the concept of invention such that his theory more generally examines the ways in which thought and discourse can be used to create perceptual appearances (both false and true) and can be used to challenge perceptual appearances.

For Baudrillard, rhetorical invention provides the foundation upon which perceptual appearances—what Plato calls *phantasia* and what contemporary rhetorical studies scholars might well call *simulacra*—are created as well as challenged, since rhetorical invention gives way to the thought and discourse that both construct *and* destruct appearances. Baudrillard's rhetorical theory operates in the realm of what are described in the *Sophist* as a third type of judgment—judgments based on an audience's perception of the appearance of thought and discourse: in short, judgments based on perceptual appearances. Baudrillard's theory considers the way such judgments can be made through rhetorical invention and also challenged through rhetorical invention. Throughout his work Baudrillard refers to the construction of perceptual appearances as the art of appearance, while he refers to the destruction of perceptual appearances as the art of disappearance. Thus, his rhetorical theory uses an expanded notion of rhetorical invention to relate the art of appearance to the art of disappearance. The relationship between these two arts—a relationship grounded in the invention of perceptual appearances that lead to very particular effects—constitutes Baudrillard's most significant contribution to rhetorical theory and is outlined in the following two chapters.

Illustration: Baudrillard's Treatment of Henrietta Lacks and Her Immortality

Henrietta Lacks died on October 4, 1951. At the time of her death, Henrietta was a thirty-one-year-old mother of five children. She was a black woman, married and living in segregated Baltimore, Maryland. She died from cervical cancer that had—despite the radiation treatment she received in the public ward at Johns Hopkins Hospital—metastasized throughout her body. Eight months prior to her death, Henrietta had visited Dr. Lawrence Wharton, Jr., to undergo her first cancer treatment (Skloot, *The Immortal Life* 33). Without asking for Henrietta's permission and just prior to beginning the cancer treatment, Wharton procured two tissue biopsies, each about the size of a dime, from Henrietta and sent them to a laboratory inside Johns Hopkins (33). The laboratory was attempting to grow cells in culture, and the cells biopsied from Henrietta's tumor grew better and lived longer than any others. In fact, Henrietta's cells have since been described as "growing with mythological intensity" (40). The degree to which her cells thrived allowed for them to be packaged and shipped to and, eventually, sold and bought by medical researchers around the world.

Named by combining the first two letters of Henrietta's first name and last name, HeLa cells enabled Jonas Salk to discover a vaccination for the polio virus, they laid the foundation for gene mapping, and they were the first cells ever to be cloned. Henrietta Lacks's family was, however, unaware that her cells were being used for research—not to mention for profit—until the 1970s, when Henrietta Lacks was publicly identified in the December 1971 issue of the journal *Obstetrics and Gynecology* as the individual from whom the HeLa cells originated (Skloot 180, 193, 172, 175–76). For twenty years the name *Henrietta Lacks* was not publicly associated with the *HeLa* moniker. Rather, as early as 1953, publications ranging from popular magazines to scholarly journals erroneously reported that the label *HeLa* referred to individuals named *Henrietta Lakes*, *Helen L.*, *Helen Lane*, or *Helen Larsen* (105, 175). Confounded by misinformation about the HeLa cells and the person from whom they originated, and further complicated by shifts in the ethical protocols governing medical research, the story of Henrietta Lacks, her cells, and her family was largely obscured for six decades, until science writer Rebecca Skloot published *The Immortal Life of Henrietta Lacks* in 2010. Skloot's book, which secured wide critical praise (Skloot, "About") and has been selected as a common reading book on over 150 college campuses across the United States (Skloot, "Community"), would familiarize countless readers with the woman and the family behind the HeLa cells.

Having passed away some three years before its publication, Baudrillard never read Skloot's book. Nonetheless, he was familiar with Henrietta Lacks. He discussed her and her cells in two of his writings: "The Final Solution, or the Revenge of the Immortals," which was published as part of his 1999 collection *Impossible Exchange*, and "The Final Solution: Cloning beyond the Human and Inhuman," which was published as part of his 2001 collection *The Vital Illusion*. Despite their staggered print publication dates, both pieces were composed at roughly the same time, for Baudrillard had delivered the latter essay as a May 1999 English-language lecture for the Wellek Library Lectures in Critical Theory at the University of California, Irvine (Rowe). On account of their contemporaneous nature, these essays borrow liberally from one another as they discuss immortality, cloning, and Henrietta Lacks.

To be sure, Baudrillard did not craft two identical pieces; however, both texts open with a conspicuous use of the word *fantasy*, and this mention of *fantasy* might well be understood as a nod toward the semantic field that is indispensable to an understanding of his rhetorical theory—that is, the semantic field that unites the term *phantasia* with the term *simulacra*. For instance, Baudrillard begins his May 1999 lecture by stating,

> The question concerning cloning is the question of immortality. We all want immortality. It is our ultimate *fantasy*, a *fantasy* that is also at work in all of our modern sciences and technologies—at work, for example, in the deep freeze of cryonic suspension and in cloning in all its manifestations. (*VI* 3; emphasis added)

These remarks reverberate with similar remarks from Baudrillard's 1999 essay that equate "our deepest *fantasy* and the *fantasy* of our science" with the "*fantasy* of immortality" (*IEx* 26; emphasis added).[1] Baudrillard's use of the word *fantasy* makes the point that fantasies are constantly "at work," and it seems quite clear that, for Baudrillard as for Plato, fantasies are constantly doing rhetorical work. Fantasies, or what might be called *phantasia* or *simulacra*, are perceptions constructed by thought and discourse. As perceptions based on thought and discourse, fantasies are rhetorical, in that rhetoric can invent an appearance that is perceived to be true in contrast with its ontological status. Thus Baudrillard, like Plato, rebukes Parmenides on rhetorical ground. And, it is on this same rhetorical ground that Baudrillard questions perceptions involving immortality. For Baudrillard, immortality is a fantasy; it is a judgment based on perceived appearances, and, like all judgments from perception that belong to the semantic field marked by *phantasia*, immortality is ontologically suspect. Immortality is, in short, a rhetorical construct: immortality is a perceptual appearance that has been judged to exist and to be valuable; so valuable, in fact, that it drives the work of science researchers who attempt to clone cells.

Within this rhetorical context—a context of fantasy and the perceived appearance of immortality as it is produced through thought and discourse—Baudrillard discusses Henrietta Lacks. Like Baudrillard's introduction to each piece, his discussion of Henrietta Lacks in each piece is quite similar, though not identical. Because these two discussions span a relatively brief paragraph, they are reproduced here in full with the first passage taken from Baudrillard's May 1999 lecture and the second taken from his 1999 published essay:

> (1) Ordinarily, a cell is destined to divide a certain number of times and then to die. If, in the course of its divisions, something happens to disturb this process—for example, an alteration in the gene that prevents tumors or in the mechanisms governing cellular apoptosis—then the cell becomes cancerous. It *forgets to die*; it forgets *how* to die. It goes on to clone itself again and again, making thousands of identical copies of itself, thus forming a tumor. Normally the subject dies as a result, and the

> cancerous cells die with him or her. But in the case of Henrietta Lacks, the tumor cells sampled from her body were cultured in a laboratory and will continue to proliferate endlessly. They constitute so remarkable and virulent a specimen that they have been circulated throughout the world and even sent into space, on board the U.S. satellite *Discoverer 17*. So it is that the disseminated body of Henrietta Lacks, cloned at the molecular level, makes its immortal rounds. (*VI* 5; emphasis original)
>
> (2) Normally, these cells are destined to divide a certain number of times, then die. If, during these divisions, a disturbance occurs (an impairment of the anti-tumour gene, or of the function of apoptosis), the cell becomes cancerous: *it forgets to die*, it forgets how to die. It will clone itself in billions of identical copies, forming a tumour. Usually, the subject dies and the cancerous cells die with him. But in the case of Henrietta Lacks, tumour cells removed during her lifetime were grown on in the laboratory, and continued to proliferate endlessly. Because they were particularly virulent, remarkable specimens, these cells were sent to all parts of the world, and even into space on *Discoverer 17*. Thus the disseminated body of Henrietta Lacks, cloned at the molecular level, continues on its immortal rounds many years after her death. (*IEx* 27; emphasis original)[2]

In these two passages, Baudrillard advances an argument about the rhetorical construction of immortality by discussing Henrietta Lacks. Importantly, his discussion of Henrietta Lacks notes tensions between her body and her cells, her life and her death, as well as her mortality and immortality. These tensions, or challenges, involve various processes, products, inventions, and accidents, and they exemplify the kind of challenges for which Baudrillard's theory has novel import. Although he never discussed Henrietta Lacks in any detail subsequent to the publication of these two pieces, the illustrations in the following chapters show how his rhetorical theory can be leveraged to better understand the events involving Lacks, her cells, and her family as they are captured in Skloot's book. Moreover, these illustrations promote a better understanding of the roles that appearance, disappearance, and symbolic exchange play in Baudrillard's rhetorical theory.

CHAPTER 4

Baudrillard's Art of Appearance: The Construction of Perceptual Appearance

This chapter dissects the half of Baudrillard's rhetorical theory that he calls the art of appearance. The art of appearance is fundamentally a productive art, and it is further indebted to Plato's *Sophist* dialogue. Indeed, Baudrillard's writing reveals his indisputable familiarity with treatments of perceptual appearances—otherwise called *simulacra*—both ancient and contemporary, and he often invokes this familiarity when outlining his own rhetorical theory. In written works and published interviews, Baudrillard repeatedly references the concepts of simulation and simulacra forwarded by Plato. For instance, in an interview with Aude Lancelin concerning the intersections between the 1999 movie *The Matrix* and his own work, Baudrillard contends that "[t]he most embarrassing part of the film is that it confuses the new problem raised by simulation with its arch-classical, Platonic treatment" (*CA* 202).[1] Likewise, in the essay "The Spiraling Cadaver" published in *Simulacra and Simulation*, Baudrillard declares that "we are simulacra (not in the classical sense of 'appearance')" (152).[2] In both of these references, Baudrillard signals his familiarity with Plato's discussion of simulation, a discussion that quite prominently occurs in the *Sophist*. The interview transcript suggests that Baudrillard views Plato's work on simulation as chief among classical works that might otherwise treat issues of reference, truth, and production, while the parenthetical reference in the essay suggests that Baudrillard, like Notomi, interprets classical discussions of simulacra as emphasizing appearance—that is, as emphasizing a kind of discursive product rather than a kind of discursive process, such as appearing or imagining, which is more akin to simulation.

Such references allow Baudrillard to distinguish his own work from that of his predecessors. Indeed, his mention of the "Platonic treatment" of simulation and the "classical sense" of simulacra are contrastive points used to advance his unique understanding of simulation and simulacra, as well as his rhetorical theory. As previously noted, Baudrillard studies scholars including Gary Genosko and William Pawlett debate the degree of affinity between Baudrillard's thought and Plato's. Genosko and, even more so, Pawlett acknowledge differences between the two thinkers, and Baudrillard's use of contrast substantiates these differences. Viewed from a rhetorical studies perspective, the differences between Baudrillard's understanding of simulation and simulacra and Plato's understanding of them emerge when Baudrillard begins to consider the processes associated with simulation together with the products known as simulacra. He shares Plato's understanding of simulacra as perceptual appearances, and he works—albeit loosely—within Plato's typology of three distinct kinds of judgments (judgments as thoughts kept to oneself, judgments as statements articulated to another, and judgments as perceptual appearances of thought and discourse). However, Baudrillard recalibrates the rhetorical aim of this last type of judgment and, more generally, the art of appearance when he articulates two claims that detail the specific ways in which simulation and simulacra construct, maintain, and effect judgment through perception. In brief, these claims contend that

1. simulation is a process that (a) opposes representation and (b) works circularly;
2. simulation produces simulacra, which are models that (a) self-proliferate irrespective of human agents and (b) function tropologically.

The remainder of this chapter elaborates each of these claims; however, three aspects about the approach this study takes in its elaboration of Baudrillard's art of appearance deserve mention.

First, in order to best explain each of Baudrillard's claims for rhetorical studies scholars, this chapter draws widely from Baudrillard's published texts but makes a specific effort to reference the discussion of simulation and simulacra offered in his collection of essays *Simulacra and Simulation*. This collection is commonly cited by scholars—both inside and outside rhetorical studies—for its description of his notion of simulation and simulacra and, thus, serves as a seminal work for scholars. Second, in order to note the sophistical tendencies embedded within Baudrillard's notion of the art of appearance as well as to delineate the ways in which his rhetorical theory moves beyond Plato's work on sophistical rhetoric, this chapter approaches Baudrillard's claim about simulation and simulacra by making ample reference to Plato's *Sophist.* Throughout Baudrillard's work, and especially in the lead essay of *Simulacra and Simulation*, the claims that he articulates speak to the proximity between his notion of simulation and simulacra and rhetorical studies. Arguably, this proximity can best be understood by considering the ways in which he advances, alters, and abandons arguments articulated in the *Sophist.* Third, in order to best reflect Baudrillard's attitude that simulation and simulacra "prevail over history" (*SED* 56),[3] this chapter approaches his discussion of simulation and simulacra with minimal reference to the loose genealogy of simulacra that he outlines in some of his writings, including *For a Critique of the Political Economy of the Sign* (123–63), *The Mirror of Production* (111–67), *Symbolic Exchange and Death* (50–86), *Simulacra and Simulation* (1–42; 121–27), and *The Transparency of Evil: Essays on Extreme Phenomena* (5–9). This genealogy is frequently excerpted, widely read, and often interpreted as arguing that simulation and simulacra are strictly historical phenomena: contemporary processes and products are built upon the industrial era's reproductive processes and automatic products, which are themselves built upon the classical era's imitative processes and representational products. Some debate exists among Baudrillard studies scholars as to the status of this genealogy with respect to Baudrillard's thinking, since he does not consistently invoke the genealogy nor is the genealogy consistent when he does. By deemphasizing Baudrillard's genealogy, the approach taken in this chapter aligns with the views of rhetorical studies scholars Sonja K. Foss, Karen A. Foss, and Robert Trapp, who recognize that this genealogy is important insofar as it offers readers a "sense" of the "dominance" that Baudrillard attributes to simulation and simulacra (312). This same sense of dominance drives the following exegesis of Baudrillard's conception of simulation and simulacra. However, in place of the genealogical reading of his art of appearance, the approach taken here seeks to investigate the rhetorical dimensions of his art of appearance based on the novelty of his claims. In particular, the approach aims to illustrate the ways in which the two overarching claims that Baudrillard advances about the art of appearance contribute to his rhetorical theory.

Claim 1: Simulation Is a Process

An understanding of Baudrillard's notion of simulation and simulacra begins with the premise that simulation is a process. This premise proves important because it speaks to those inventive strategies that rhetors use to produce texts and it illustrates Baudrillard's indebtedness to and departure from Plato's *Sophist.* It stands to reason that an inquiry into Baudrillard's art of appearance-making begins with an examination of the process by which he understands appearances to be made. According to Baudrillard, the process of simulation involves dislocating reference to reality by disregarding truth and time.

Perhaps the best way, initially, to understand Baudrillard's first claim about simulation is through the relationship between a question and an answer. Indeed, the relationship between a question and answer assumes a high degree of importance in Plato's *Sophist,* as the question and answer relationship is viewed as a process that adjudicates truth and falsehood—that is, Plato views question and answer as an evaluative process used to determine fidelity. In the *Sophist* dialogue, Plato's typology of the three kinds of judgments—internalized judgments, externalized statements, and perceived appearances—explicitly positions two of those judgments as products that result from processes of dialogue: judgments are the products of internalized thought processes or dialogues with oneself, and statements are the products of externalized discursive processes or dialogues with others (cf. Notomi 256–61). Understood rhetorically, dialogue constitutes a strategy of invention behind the production of judgments and statements. For Plato, the process of dialogue is, as Notomi observes, "a process of inquiry, which consists of questioning and answering" (260–61). Thus, the relationship between questions and answers is central to an understanding of how judgments and statements are produced. However, Plato's *Sophist* does not explicitly address the process of dialogue that produces the third type of judgment. As Notomi recognizes, although the *Sophist* skips or leaves "empty" such a discussion, Plato suggests that perceptual appearances are judgments reached "through perception" (Notomi 260, 261). The process behind perceptual appearances, or *phantasia,* might otherwise be thought of in terms of a dialogue analogous to the questioning and answering involved in the first two kinds of judgment. Accordingly, dialogue—that is, questioning and answering—functions to adjudicate truth or evaluate fidelity with respect to all three types of judgment: judgment, statement, and *phantasia* alike. Notomi observes that, in Plato's *Sophist,* "dialogue is the place in which truth and falsehood occur" (261). In sum, the *Sophist* does not explicitly address the process by which perceptual appearances are produced, although, by analogy, the text does suggest that the process involves a dialogue in which questioning and answering sort true appearances from false ones.

Baudrillard, at places in his work, follows Plato by framing the process that produces perceptual appearances in terms of a question and answer. To be sure, his treatment of the process is explicit. Throughout the majority of his work, he uses the word *simulation* to refer to the process that produces perceptual appearances. At times, his discussion of simulation might be understood to be backfilling the discussion of process left empty in Plato's *Sophist.* Nonetheless, Baudrillard outlines a radically different approach to the questions and answers that are so central to appearance-making in Plato. According to Baudrillard, simulation involves a process that reconfigures the relationship between questions and answers. No longer are they distinct things, nor even are they distinct activities; rather, question and answer are merged into a question/answer configuration. Baudrillard writes that simulation is "a gigantic operational game of question and answer" (*MP* 126–27)[4] and that the merger of question and answer into "question/answer" constitutes "the new operational configuration" (*SED* 57).[5] For Baudrillard, questions and answers are rearranged in a way that is circular, if not tautological. He explains that the question/answer configuration proves to be one of the "perfect forms of simulation" for "the question induces the answer" (62).[6] Alternatively, he observes that simulation inaugurates a "circular response" in which "the answer is included in the question" (*SS* 75).[7] Baudrillard discusses this circularity by describing simulation as "cycles of question/answer," in which "the unilateral question is precisely not an interrogation any more, but the immediate imposition of a meaning which simultaneously completes the cycle" (*SED* 62).[8] Questions, for Baudrillard, work to impose meaning as a given answer rather than interrogate meaning by searching for an answer. The imposition of answer as question, and question as answer, is, moreover, widespread. According to Baudrillard, "question/answer circularity runs through every domain" (67).[9]

Declaring that the newly arranged "question/answer schema is of incalculable importance," Baudrillard argues that simulation is a process that functions by "[d]islocating all discourse" and by short-circuiting the relationship between "a representative and a represented" (*SED* 64).[10] Here, then, Baudrillard's radical shift away from Plato becomes quite clear. For Plato, questions and answers constitute an important process because they adjudicate truth. However, for Baudrillard, the question/answer configuration constitutes an important process because it opposes representation. Whereas Plato views questions and answers as a process of inquiry used by humans to discern truth from falsehood, Baudrillard views the process of simulation as "networking questions/answers through us" (58).[11] He contends that the process of simulation, on account of its rearrangement of questions and answers, effects the "[e]nd of the theatre of representation" (58).[12] Here,

Baudrillard drives his point home: simulation and its new configuration of question/answer ends practices of representation and challenges Plato's dialectical method.

Juxtaposing Plato's treatment of questions and answers with Baudrillard's treatment of questions/answers helps to unpack the initial claim, upon which Baudrillard's understanding of simulation and simulacra is premised, into two points about simulation. Simulation is, first, a process that dislocates, unsettles, or opposes reference; second, it is a cyclical, circular process. For Baudrillard, the process that produces perceptual appearances obliterates reference and opposes representation. In doing so, the process reveals that it operates according to a logic, which disregards distinctions predicated on truth and time. By treating simulation explicitly, Baudrillard places the process—and its oppositional logic and its circularity—under greater theoretical and rhetorical scrutiny.

Point 1A. Simulation Is a Process That Opposes Representation

Baudrillard's view that simulation collapses questions and answers into a questions/answers configuration suggests, first, that distinctions involving truth are not germane to the process of simulation. In his scheme, no true answer exists; thus, neither the accuracy nor the fidelity of answers or questions can be assessed. In short, Baudrillard's treatment of simulation proves unconcerned with adjudicating the truth of perceptual appearances because he positions simulation as opposed to representation: "Such is simulation," he writes, "insofar as it is opposed to representation" (*SS* 6).[13] In "The Precession of Simulacra," Baudrillard argues that "[r]epresentation stems from the principle of the equivalence of the sign and the real" and that "[s]imulation, on the contrary, stems from the utopia of the principle of equivalence" (6).[14] His discussion, here, generally outlines the major divide between representation and simulation with respect to equivalence, difference, and reference. The divide between the two processes with respect to fidelity is, ultimately, a divide rooted in the logics that accompany each process.

According to Baudrillard, understanding the logic behind the process of representation necessitates an understanding of its main purpose—that is, representation's attempt to equate an appearance with reality. The process of representation produces a text, sign, or representation that attempts to capture, re-create, or encapsulate reality in a way that is equivalent to reality. The chief illustration that Baudrillard invokes in "The Precession of Simulacra" is that of a map. Conventionally, the mapmaking process is executed according to a principle of equivalence. A representative map, Baudrillard explains, is rendered in such detail "that it ends up covering the territory exactly" (*SS* 1).[15] However, Baudrillard points out that the rendering of such a map is a "fable" (1)[16] and that representation's constant attempt at exact representation—that is, equivalence—is always a vain attempt, for reality forever remains the point of reference for representation. The process of mapmaking will never produce a map that is the equivalent of the territory it tries to represent, for that map will always be secondary to, dependent on, or different from the primary, original, real territory. Baudrillard explains that, for all of its attempts to equate an appearance with reality, the process of representation always maintains a division between representation and reality. Put differently, some difference is inherent to the process of representation, as some distance will always exist between the representation and reality.

Baudrillard understands the distance inextricably bound to the process of representation as an operative logic—that is, a logic of distinction that, in spite of representation's attempt at equivalence, abets the difference between the representation and the real, between the copy and the original. The logic reveals that, when a point of reference exists, so too does difference exist. The logic of distinction harbors differences in fidelity that plague any representation. With respect to fidelity, the process of representation and its unsuccessful attempts at equivalence preserve the concept of truth so that the representations can be assessed by their truth, accuracy, or fidelity with respect to reality. Reality, in effect, becomes the measuring stick by which representative processes are judged. Thus, reference allows for representations to be evaluated—as process and products—in comparison to the point of origin for, or the reality behind, the representation. The logic of distinction operates within these comparative judgments as it divides reality (or, the standard of measurement) from representation (or, the unsuccessful attempt at meeting the standards of reality). The logic of distinction further allows for the judgment of representational products as being more or less realistic, more or less true to reality. Baudrillard notes that, within a representational paradigm, an individual can apply the logic of difference to evaluate the degree to which a representation is "true" or "false," "real" or "imaginary" (*SS* 3).[17] The process of representation thereby invites comparative evaluations of its products, whereby one product may be judged poorer than or better than another product. In this way, one map could be more accurate than another map. But even these comparisons between products depend on some orienting reference to reality. Reality becomes the basis for distinction, and, therefore, equivalence proves impossible. As a result of the logic of distinction, which emphasizes differences in time and truth, Baudrillard understands the process of representation to be a thoroughly utopian process.

In contrast, the process of simulation moves beyond the process of representation by taking attempts at equivalence as vain and impossible. The process of simulation further erases distinction based on fidelity because the process of simulation ignores reference. Indeed, Baudrillard emphasizes this point about the process of simulation, stating that "simulation is inaugurated by a liquidation of all referentials" (*SS* 2).[18] Simulation is, metaphorically, a kind of mapmaking without reference to any territory. There is no antecedent to anchor the process of simulation; thus, there is no basis for evaluating the product of simulation (cf. Brummett, *The World* 11). According to the process of simulation, the real must be taken as the imaginary and the imaginary must be taken as the "real"; likewise, the true must be taken as false and the false must be taken as "true." In other words, the process of simulation operates by a logic of radical equivalence, or what Baudrillard describes as "a lack of distinction" or a lack of the logic of difference (*PC* 43).[19] Without the logic of difference, there is no difference—by any terms, temporality and fidelity included—between products of thought and discourse. Therefore, products of thought, discourse, and perception are not obligated to reference reality. Without a point of reference or of truth, products are equivalent to one another and, thus, free to build upon each other: signs build upon other signs, words upon other words, images upon other images, questions upon questions, answers upon answers, models upon other models. "Simulation," says Baudrillard, "is characterized by a *precession of the model*" (16; emphasis original),[20] and from the analogy of mapmaking it might be said that simulation enables any one map to be modeled on any other map—again, irrespective of reference to territory.

Point 1B. Simulation Is a Process That Works Circularly

Second, Baudrillard's description of simulation as a process involving questions/answers alters the temporality implied in the configuration of questions and then answers. Indeed, the precession of models is not a linear one, and Baudrillard's description of simulation positions the process as one that logically obliterates reference to time in addition to truth. The process of simulation is a cyclical, circular, and therefore nonlinear process. For Baudrillard, questions are not necessarily antecedent to answers, and it becomes impossible to trace a linear sequence of questions and answers. Instead, as he explains in *Simulacra and Simulation*, simulation proves to be both a "circular arrangement" as well as "an irreversible process" (80, 35).[21] The process of simulation remains distinct from the process of representation in its temporal orientation: simulation does not look back to a point of origin in reference, nor does it proceed like a historical process.

On the one hand, the logic of distinction that separates representation from reality positions the process of representation as always looking backward in reference to reality. In other words, the logic of distinction manifests itself with respect to temporality as well as fidelity. Baudrillard observes that reality comes first and processes of representation follow after. Reality serves as an antecedent or a reference point to which the process of representation looks as it attempts to achieve equivalence. The result of this back-glancing is that representation becomes a linear process or a historical chronology that always leads away from a singular point of origin. For instance, conventional mapmaking must follow the reality of the territory it attempts to chart. So, inevitably, a temporal difference exists between the territory and its map, as the territory was prior to the process of representation.

On the other hand, simulation, which lacks the logic of distinction, does not look backward in reference, nor can it be measured against or retraced to a point of origin. The process of simulation is, in other words, untraceable and circular. Simulation cannot be backtracked because there is nothing prior to the process, except for the extermination of all reference. The process of simulation is circular because, unlike the process of representation, it does not move outward from one point. Simulation cannot be followed linearly because no point of origin anchors or orders the process. Baudrillard explains that, when examining the process of simulation, it is "[u]seless to ask which is the first term, there is none, it is a circular process—that of simulation" (*SS* 81).[22] In short, the process of simulation is opposed to the process of representation insofar as simulation lacks the anchor of reference to reality and its temporal distinctions. To return to the example of mapmaking, removing the logic of distinction with respect to time provides context for Baudrillard's assertion that the "territory no longer precedes the map" (1).[23] According to his description of simulation, the process enables a situation wherein it is "the map that precedes the territory" or the answer, the question (1).[24]

In describing the process by which reference is abandoned, fidelity disregarded, and temporality ignored, Baudrillard all but launches into a description of the products he associates with simulation. These products, called simulacra, are the focus of his second claim.

Claim 2: Simulation Produces Simulacra

Baudrillard's second claim complements his first: If simulation is the chief process in the art of appearance, then simulacra are the chief constructs forged by that process. These products are judgments from perceptual appearances; they are effects of thought, discourse, and perception. Baudrillard names these products, in plural, *simulacra*. When discussing one product, he uses the singular *simulacrum*. Simulacra, for Baudrillard like *phantasia* for Plato, comprise appearances that can be made, produced, or manufactured. But whereas Plato's description of *phantasia* attributes agency to human actors and evaluates appearances against reality, Baudrillard's treatment of simulacra does not. Rather, he views appearances—not humans—as possessing a degree of agency, and he also views simulacra as substituting for—not being evaluated against—reality.

The difference between Plato's *phantasia* and Baudrillard's simulacra can be again glossed according to each thinker's commentary on dialogue, or the relationship between questions and answers. For Plato, dialogue—that is, the process of questioning and answering—ultimately produces an answer, and answers enable rhetors and audiences alike to calibrate thought, discourse, and perception with truth (cf. Notomi 230). The prominence that answers assume in Plato's understanding of appearance-making implies a high degree of agency for both the rhetor and the rhetor's audience. Plato suggests that the philosopher-rhetor might use dialogue to lead interlocutors to the truth, steering them towards virtue, while the Sophist-rhetor might use dialogue to mislead interlocutors, goading them into accepting false appearances as true. "Question and short answer is," Notomi reminds, "the predominant method of Socrates as well as the sophists" (62). Nonetheless, Plato positions interlocutors as quite capable—at least when given the time to pursue dialogue—of sorting through all kinds of appearances to arrive at the truth. For Plato, interlocutors make judgments appear as answers, and these answers must, in good time, answer to the truth. Thus, his discussion of *phantasia* as rhetorical products emphasizes time, or temporality, and also truth, or fidelity, in a way that reflects the fact his theory works within a representational paradigm.

Baudrillard, of course, does not work within a representational paradigm, and, insofar as he views simulation as a process opposed to representation, his version of simulacra forgoes any allegiance to time and truth. Answers, for Baudrillard, do not allow individuals to uncover truth, nor are answers neatly ordered to follow questions. In fact, he does not conceptualize answers as separate from questions. Rather, his description of a question/answer configuration—which is established in his argument about the process of simulation and which erases the distinction between answers and questions—proves to be characteristic of simulacra. The question/answer configuration might, in other words, be understood as the simulacrum writ large. The products associated with this configuration possess radically reoriented answers and questions with respect to time and truth: answers become capable of preceding questions and exercising a degree of agency over humans (whether rhetors or audiences) and over reality (whether taken as an objective truth or as a subjective construct). As such, Baudrillard's version of simulacra reveals a rhetorical function that far exceeds the function of an appearance under the representational paradigm. He argues that simulacra short-circuit human agency and reality. In other words, his claim that simulation produces simulacra is supported by two additional points: that simulacra are self-perpetuating and that simulacra function tropologically.

Point 2A. Simulation Produces Simulacra, Which Are Models That Self-Proliferate Irrespective of Human Agents

The first point that Baudrillard articulates about simulacra is that these products self-perpetuate, grow, and escalate independently of human agents. This point reveals Baudrillard's commitment to studying discursive effects and perceptual appearances as general systems of circulation rather than discrete communicative exchanges between rhetors and audiences. In keeping with the analogy of question and answer, this point becomes clear through the juxtaposition of Plato and Baudrillard. Plato places the human agent—whether Sophist, philosopher, or statesman—as the impetus behind the dialogue that occurs between his interlocutors. In the case of the *Sophist* dialogue, Theaetetus and the Eleatic visitor exchange questions and answers to communicate the truth about the communicative practices of, and perceptual appearances produced by, human agents known as Sophists. On the contrary, Baudrillard focuses primarily on the effect of perceptual appearances, extracting the human agent from most all of his discussions of simulacra. He writes little of human agents, or those Sophists, rhetors, or interlocutors who pose questions and answers and produce perceptual appearances. Rather, he writes more of the configurations and systems of circulation that perpetuate simulacra. This particular point explains why, within rhetorical studies, Baudrillard has often been categorized as a theorist who attributes very little agency to the rhetor. Sharon Crowley, for example, considers Baudrillard to be emblematic of rhetorical theorists who view individual human agency as impossible or inconsequential ("Response" 5). Baudrillard's discussion of simulacra supports Crowley's observation as it shifts agency from rhetors to discursive effects and, in doing so, positions simulacra as increasingly defiant toward communication.

Baudrillard positions simulacra as defiant toward communication, for they are neither instrumental nor pragmatic. Whereas conventional, and perhaps simplistic, views of communication position humans as rhetorical agents who use discourse to accomplish some end or produce a pragmatic effect, Baudrillard attributes agency to the discursive effects, in aggregate, and not to any individual rhetor. For Baudrillard, discursive effects assume an agency over and above a discrete act of communication or a particular communicator. In fact, he writes that simulacra "short-circuit in advance any possibility of communication," suggesting that simulacra are in no way instrumental or pragmatic (*SS* 81).[25] Indeed, simulacra are effects that do not lead to an end.

Baudrillard glosses the difference between the effects of communication and simulacra using the analogy of the interview (cf. *BL* 200–01). Communication is a conventional interview, in which an interviewer poses a question to elicit an answer from a respondent. Here, the interviewer approximates the rhetor by assuming the agency to ask certain questions for some particular purpose, while the respondent approximates the audience upon which the rhetor works. The conventional interview is, therefore, instrumental or pragmatic in that it uses communication toward an end, and the effects are derived from the agency of the rhetor. Simulation is, by comparison, the "nondirective interview" (*SS* 80),[26] in which the interviewer merely invites the respondent to speak about whatever the respondent chooses. The nondirective interview proves "a circular arrangement" that stages communication by allowing audience-respondents to participate in the question/answer configuration by supplying "phantom content" (80).[27] Note, here, Baudrillard's invocation of the word *phantom*, a cognate of *phantasia*, to describe simulation and simulacra through comparison with the nondirective interview. In the nondirective interview, the rhetor cedes agency to the interview method, assuming that the unstructured configuration of the interview will produce something. Accordingly, no result is produced by any particular rhetorical agent in the nondirective interview. Rather than yielding an answer in the manner of its communicative counterpart, the nondirective interview merely reproduces itself as a configuration, form, or model into which more phantom content can be poured. More participation in this kind of interview configuration yields more phantom content, all of which amounts to further propagation of the nondirective interview. This new interview configuration assumes agency as it self-proliferates; it becomes a model built upon a model—models in precession, an "integrated circuit," a simulacrum (80).[28] Thus, unlike the effects of instrumental or pragmatic communication, simulacra endlessly proliferate in ongoing circulation.

As Baudrillard's interview analogy shows, the defining characteristic of simulacra—and, also, the characteristic that imbues these perceptual appearances with agency—is the endless circulation and proliferation of models. Simulacra are, simply put, models. Simulacra are models that never rest and that freely associate with other models; they are perceptual appearances that detach from points of reference and accumulate; they are effects compounded by other effects to no end. Ultimately, Baudrillard views simulacra as forming "an uninterrupted circuit without reference or circumference" (*SS* 6).[29] He describes "the logic of simulacra," which he calls "powerful" and "inexorable," as "that of the precession of models" (56).[30] Here, his use of the word *precession* (*précession*) invokes precedence—as in coming before; it also invokes motion—as in geophysical motion ("Precession," entry 2). Indeed, Baudrillard plays on the word *precession* in order to attribute agency to simulacra. Invoking the notion of precedence that is connected to the word *precession*, he argues that "the models come first" in simulacra and that models beget other models (*SS* 16–17).[31] Put differently, the agency of simulacra starts and ends with models in pure circulation. By dissolving reference to time and truth, the process of simulation effects this "state of pure circulation" (*TE* 4).[32] Baudrillard describes this state of pure circulation as an orbit (*TE* 4)[33] and refers to the circulation of models as "orbital" (*SS* 16).[34] These references to geophysical motion invoke the second sense of the word *precession* and position simulacra, not only as effects that take precedence over other people and things, but also as effects that have pull. Simulacra can thus be understood as exercising pull—or agency—over communication and over humans. Indeed, Baudrillard studies scholar Chris Rojek notes that Baudrillard's work, at times, documents the "incapacity" of humans, despite their efforts, "to break out of the orbit of simulation" (108).

Baudrillard understands the pull of simulacra over communication as diminishing instrumental or pragmatic communication. "Messages," he writes, "no longer have any informational role"—that is, when they are within the pull of simulacra (*SED* 63).[35] Within that pull, communication that seeks to transmit information for some instrumental purpose or pragmatic use is, according to Baudrillard, relinquished to an "orbital" state: "Information circulates, moves around, makes its circuits (which are sometimes perfectly useless—but that is the whole point: the question of usefulness cannot be raised)—and with each spiral, each revolution, it accumulates" (*TE* 32).[36] The point, as Baudrillard notes, is that the circulation and proliferation characteristic of simulacra results in bloated, overproduced communication that defies instrumental use or pragmatic ends: "So many messages and signals are produced and disseminated that they can never possibly all be read" (35).[37] Not surprisingly, he understands the relationship between communication, which produces instrumental or pragmatic effects, and simulation, which produces simulacra, to be an inverse relationship. When simulacra proliferate, instrumental and pragmatic effects of communication diminish. Remarking on this inverse relationship, Baudrillard declares, "It is useless to ask if it is the loss of communication that produces this escalation in the simulacrum, or whether it is the simulacrum that is there first" (*SS* 80).[38] The inverse relationship between instrumental ends and simulacra is, in other words, not a relationship that can be parsed with reference to origins, causes, or first terms. For Baudrillard, the pull of simulacra is ever expanding. Simulacra pull communication into orbit and, once in orbit, communication is rendered useless.

What is more, Baudrillard sees simulacra as exerting a similar pull over humans. He warns that "we are being dragged into an orbital motion which threatens to become perpetual" (*TE* 34).[39] He issues this warning, however, less for preventive purposes and more for predictive purposes. Indeed, Baudrillard's discussion of the art of appearance leaves little space for human agents to resist the compounded effects that are simulacra (cf. *SS* 26–27). His statement about the threat simulacra pose for humans seems like a premonition of the escalating status and never-ending expansion of simulacra. According to Baudrillard, "the human universe" has already been "reduced to a vast orbital machine" (*TE* 31).[40] Humans, like instrumental and pragmatic communication, circulate without the means to achieve an end. In brief, when humans are confronted by the built-up effects of perception, thought, and discourse, they lack agency. This lack of human agency under the pull of simulacra is no different, however, from the lack of agency attributed to anything caught up with simulacra. Baudrillard writes that "everything," which is either preceded or pulled by simulacra, "has subtly altered its aim so that it can go into orbit" (32).[41] Here, he suggests that simulacra fundamentally alter the aims or purposes of everything within their pull. Multiple purposes, diverse aims, varied uses, and different valuations are all short-circuited by simulacra, which aim only for free circulation, prolific production, and vast accumulation. Accordingly, simulacra short-circuit the communicative agency of humans in order to redirect all things toward this singular aim.

Given that simulacra self-proliferate irrespective of human agents, the absence of the mapmaker in Baudrillard's well-known comparison proves all the more pointed. No human agent can control the simulacrum that is the map. In Baudrillard's configuration, maps further become useless to humans: Maps are not used by humans for an instrumental purpose, such as orientation or demarcation. Instead, they retain the agency in that they use humans as they produce and reproduce the concept of some territory and, concomitantly, the concept of reality. The map that is the simulacrum covers over a void of human agency and reality—or, what Baudrillard refers to as "[*t*]*he desert of the real itself*" (*SS* 1; emphasis original)[42]—and this function of covering over, or concealed substitution, leads to Baudrillard's second point about simulacra.

Point 2B. Simulation Produces Simulacra, Which Function Tropologically

Besides short-circuiting the communicative agency of humans, simulacra also have the effect of short-circuiting judgments based on the perception of reality. Baudrillard's observations about simulacra short-circuiting the perception of reality constitute his second point about the appearances produced by simulation. This second point serves two purposes for him. First, this point follows up his assertion that simulation is a process that dislocates reference to reality. Baudrillard explains that, whereas imitation of reality proves the key rhetorical move within a representative paradigm, within a simulative paradigm, substitution for perceived reality becomes the dominant rhetorical move. As explained below, the effects of such substitution amounts to a short-circuiting of human perception. Second, Baudrillard's point about simulacra substituting for perceived reality reveals the way in which simulacra wrest communicative agency away from humans. When simulacra substitute for perceived reality—that is, when simulacra create the appearance of reality—they manage to pull off an act of substitution, which is familiar to rhetorical studies scholars for its manipulation of audience. By stressing the way in which simulacra substitute for perceived reality, Baudrillard positions simulacra as appearances that can be interpreted as thoroughly rhetorical appearances.

As process and as product, respectively, simulation and simulacra further distinguish themselves from one another on the basis of their relationship to reality. Whereas the process of simulation dislocates any reference to reality and enables the free circulation of models, the products produced by simulation begin to substitute for perceived reality. Put differently, the process of simulation brings about, or effects, the conditions—that is, dislocation, "irreference" (*SS* 3),[43] and circulation—under which simulacra operate. Simulacra, then, operate in a substitutive manner in order to conceal; or, their function can be understood as substitution, and their effect can be understood as concealment. Thus, simulacra are defined by Baudrillard in resolutely rhetorical terms: "It is no longer a question of imitation," he declares in the opening pages of "The Precession of Simulacra" (2).[44] "It is," he clarifies, "a question of substituting the signs of the real for the real, that is to say an operation of deterring every real process via its operational double, a programmatic, metastable, perfectly descriptive machine that offers all the signs of the real and short-circuits all its vicissitudes" (2).[45] With reference to imitation and substitution, Baudrillard describes how his notion of simulacra alters the questions—and, necessarily, the answers—typically associated with perceptual appearances. Here, again, Baudrillard can be understood as invoking Plato's discussion of *phantasia* in the *Sophist* in order to better articulate his own conspicuously rhetorical understanding of simulacra. Whereas Plato understood perceptual appearances to function mimetically, according to imitation, Baudrillard switches the question/answer, so as to understand perceptual appearances as functioning tropologically, according to substitution. Baudrillard's distinction between imitation and substitution as two different rhetorical functions emphasizes what is arguably the most rhetorically unique facet of Baudrillard's art of appearance.

Plato, in his *Sophist* dialogue, stresses the connection between *phantasia* and mimetic function, going so far as to list imitation among the defining characteristics of the Sophist. Indeed, the Eleatic visitor and Theaetetus both agree that the Sophist is defined by a kind of mimesis in which a speaker attempts to mimic the wise (265a10–b3; 268c1). The two interlocutors thereby discuss imitation with reference to some original presentation of the thought or discourse imitated—for instance, the original presentation of wisdom by a wise speaker. By anchoring the kind of imitation practiced by the Sophist to a point of reference, the two interlocutors draw an important distinction between the imitation practices of the philosopher and the Sophist. Both the philosopher and the Sophist imitate thoughts and discourse to make themselves, as rhetors, appear a certain way to their audience. The difference between the two can only be judged according to the type of imitation each rhetor uses to create *phantasia*. Sophists imitate the wise, while philosophers imitate the gods. Notomi offers this succinct summary: "While the philosopher becomes as much like a god as possible, and thus becomes 'divine,' the sophist *appears* to be wise like a god, but is not really a likeness" (288; emphasis original). In order to judge a speaker as either a philosopher or a Sophist, the audience must assess the degree to which the speaker references the gods. Evidently, imitation, as described by Plato in the *Sophist*, proves a practice that falls under the representational paradigm and that also depends on reference to an original or antecedent. Thus, for Plato, the status of judgments derived from perceptual appearance (i.e., *phantasia* and, by extension, simulacra) depend on the kind of imitation exercised by a speaker.

Baudrillard, for his part, forgoes any concern about reference or representation. His version of perceptual appearance does not depend on any one speaker's imitation of thought or discourse; instead, it depends on the ability of a perceptual appearance to execute a concealed substitution. Whereas Plato's discussion of perceptual appearances entrusts audience members to question the origins of a speaker's imitation in order to reach a final judgment about that speaker, Baudrillard's discussion of perceptual appearances pays little attention to the speaker and assumes that audience members will unquestioningly accept an appearance as reality. In *The System of Objects*, Baudrillard addresses the distinction between the mimetic function of perceptual appearances and the tropological function of perceptual appearances through a brief story. The story involves an eighteenth-century illusionist who shares a stage act with an automaton that is indistinguishable from the illusionist. Because the audience members "would eventually chafe if they were left in doubt as to which of the two figures was 'real,'" Baudrillard explains that the illusionist "finds himself obliged to make his own gestures mechanical, and—in what is really the pinnacle of his art—to alter his own appearances slightly so as to give his show its full meaning" (59).[46] Meaning thus depends on a distinction, and the story approximates the Platonic treatment of perceptual appearances, in that an audience relies on imitation and reference to both perceive and judge art.

Moving from this allusion to Plato's work on perceptual appearances to his own work on perceptual appearance, Baudrillard provides additional commentary on this brief story. Noting that the story is "a good analogy for society with a technical apparatus so highly perfected that it appears to be a 'synthetic' gestural system superior to the traditional system," Baudrillard asserts that "there is no reason to assume that the unceasing forward march of *techne* will not eventually achieve a mimesis which replaces a natural world with an intelligible artificial one" (*SO* 59–60; emphasis original).[47] Here, Baudrillard gestures toward the most novel aspect of his own art of appearance—namely, that the production of an appearance, which imitates reality through mimetic function, turns into a replacement for perceived reality. This turning into a replacement, or substitution, proves key to Baudrillard's art of appearance. He suggests that simulacra, which are effects of thought and discourse in their own right, lead to secondary effects wherein simulacra substitute for reality. Elsewhere in his work, Baudrillard explains that simulacra have been "substituted for all other value," including the value placed on reality (*SS* 47–48).[48] He understands simulacra as replicas that perpetuate the singular aim of production, and he sees the effect of this singular aim in the "eternal substitution of homogenous items" that characterize the precession of simulacra (*CS* 30).[49] Further stressing the ability of simulacra to serve as substitutes, replacements, or stand-ins for reality, Baudrillard writes that "the information-replica stands for, stands *in* for, the definitive absence of that real" (*VI* 50–51; emphasis original).

The kind of substitution that Baudrillard attributes to simulacra constitutes the kind of substitution that rhetorical studies scholars attribute to tropes. Tropes are often associated with rhetorical figures such as metaphor, metonymy, synecdoche, and irony (cf. Burke, *A Grammar*), but more generally a trope can be defined as an "artful substitution" (Crowley and Hawhee 438). Accordingly, substitution constitutes the crucial function of a trope, and this tropological function departs markedly from any mimetic function. Indeed, rhetorical scholars, including Phillip Arrington and Krista Ratcliffe, associate tropes with invention. Arrington, for instance, sees tropes as allowing rhetors to invent relationships (325). Ratcliffe understands tropes as designating "the very movement of language itself," as perpetually circulating in "a chicken-and-egg cycle" involving language and bodies, and as possessing the ability to turn reception processes into invention processes (*Rhetorical* 111, 46). Thus, when Baudrillard describes simulacra as substituting for reality, he suggests that simulacra function tropologically—that is, simulacra are an inventive turning; they rhetorically turn effects of thought and discourse in such a way that the effects are taken for reality.

To be sure, the tropological function of Baudrillard's version of simulacra depends on a degree of concealment, in which the artful substitution of the simulacra for reality is effectively hidden from the audience. Baudrillard acknowledges as much in his short story, when he recognizes that "in the case of modern reality we do not awake to the applause of an audience delighted to have been so thoroughly duped" (*SO* 59).[50] Again, his comment draws a distinction between Plato's treatment of classical appearance and reality and his own treatment of contemporary appearance and reality. According to Baudrillard's work on perceptual appearances, the audience does not applaud because the audience does not perceive that they are being "duped" by simulacra. The audience, to be sure, accepts simulacra on account of well-concealed and seamless substitutions. Baudrillard explains that simulacra work at "concealing the fact that the real is no longer real, and thus saving the reality principle" (*SS* 13).[51] Moreover, he defines simulacra, in general, according to concealment, writing, "*the simulacrum is not that which hides the truth, but that which hides the absence of truth*" (*LP* 32; emphasis original).[52] Here, the hiding undertaken by simulacra equates to concealment. According to Baudrillard, the simulacrum, writ large, might be understood as "merely an effect of the ruse" that "consists in its having concealed the end from us" (*VI* 44). Baudrillard's description of the way in which simulacra effectively conceal their tropings stresses the strong rhetorical nature of simulacra, for rhetoric, as Carolyn R. Miller documents, has been often judged to be "more effective, more useful, and more powerful, if it remains concealed" ("Should" 21). As Baudrillard surmises, "it is simulation that is effective, never the real" (*SS* 56).[53]

The concealed turning that defines the tropological function of simulacra also works to explain the way in which simulacra exert agency over human communicators. In his short story and in other places across his oeuvre, Baudrillard describes the way in which the tropings of simulacra begin to control and manipulate humans. Commenting on the story of the illusionist and the automaton, Baudrillard muses, "If the simulacrum is so well designed that it becomes an effective organizer of reality, then surely it is man, not the simulacrum, who is turned into an abstraction" (*SO* 60).[54] This statement not only focuses on a turning—that is, a troping or turning into—effected by simulacra, but the statement also reinforces the notion that simulacra wrest agency away from humans. Elsewhere, Baudrillard explicitly depicts simulacra as controlling. The "simulacra of simulation," he says, maintain the "aim of total control" (*SS* 121).[55] Indeed, as William Pawlett recognizes, Baudrillard's version of the simulacra leads to an "ultimate system of control because instead of exerting control over the world it attempts to jettison it and produce a substitute, a double or clone of the world" ("Virtual" 237). Baudrillard positions the operation of simulacra as control akin to sovereignty, and he describes culture as complicit with this control. Culture, for Baudrillard, consists of "the collective sharing of simulacra," and it begets complicity: "Sovereignty lies only in the mastery of appearances, and complicity lies only in the collective sharing of illusion and secret" (*FS* 74).[56] Baudrillard's description of the concealed tropological function of simulacra ultimately positions his art of appearance as a manipulative art, in that it involves "the manipulation of these models at every level" (*SS* 122).[57] Thus, what is perhaps the most distinctive aspect of Baudrillard's theory of simulation and simulacra—the concealed tropings of simulacra—positions the art of appearance as a manipulative art.

In sum, simulacra are manipulative tropes that compound the effects of simulation. Simulation dislocates the references of thought and discourse to a perceived reality, while simulacra substitute for reality. Baudrillard warns that the tropings of simulacra should not be understood as filling up the space of reality with some positive value but rather as marking the absence of the reality principle (*SED* 219). The effects of simulacra are not, in other words, positive. Baudrillard often describes simulacra as effecting "a hyperreal," which he defines as "the generation by models of a real without origin or reality" (*SS* 1).[58] Escalated—or what Baudrillard often describes as ecstatic—simulacra produce the hyperreal. Hyperreality, as he explains, is "[m]ore real than the real," in that hyperreality is a perfectly concealed substitution and "more 'complete'" than simulacra (*SS* 81; *PW* 39).[59] Baudrillard sometimes calls this state of hyperreality a virtual reality, and, in doing so, he plays upon the adjective *virtual* (*virtuel*), for which the French connotes "possible" or "potential" (*IEx* 115 n. 1). Some debate exists among Baudrillard studies scholars as to whether Baudrillard views virtual reality as categorically different from hyperreality and whether both hyperreality and virtual reality are different from simulation (cf. Pawlett, "Virtual" 237). From a rhetorical studies perspective, however, these debates are beside the tropological point: Simulacra lead to hyperreal or virtual effects; they are the substitution of all possibilities for reality without respect for truth or time; in their precession, they pull at humans, communication, and the world, turning and controlling all toward the singular aim of production and appearance-making. By analogy, simulacra comprise Baudrillard's map, a map that not only "precedes the territory" but that "engenders the territory" (*SS* 1).[60] It is a map that, when viewed in comparison to Plato's discussion of perceptual appearances, cuts a new path through rhetorical theory. Baudrillard's map of this hyperreal territory—itself an effect of ecstatic thought and overproduced discourse—leads to a radical art that rhetorically challenges the art of appearance. That radical art is the art of disappearance, and it receives treatment in the next chapter.

Illustration: The Appearance of HeLa

Baudrillard's rhetorical theory depends, in the first place, on what he terms the art of appearance. According to Baudrillard, the art of appearance involves, first, a process of simulation that both opposes representation and prolifically copies itself and, second, a product of a simulacrum that proliferates irrespective of human agents and functions tropologically. As this chapter's illustrative section shows, the art of appearance gains some clarity when it is understood in terms of Henrietta Lacks's experience and Rebecca Skloot's book *The Immortal Life of Henrietta Lacks.* Likewise, Lacks's experience and Skloot's book can be uniquely understood when Baudrillard's art of appearance is applied to them. Accordingly, this illustration begins by briefly outlining Baudrillard's discussion of Lacks in terms of the art of appearance. Then it proceeds to analyze the events involving Henrietta Lacks, her cells, and her family from the perspective of the art of appearance.

Baudrillard's discussion of Henrietta Lacks in his May 1999 lecture on the rhetorical construction of immortality views Lacks, in part, as emblematic of the art of appearance. Two lines from his paragraph-long discussion are particularly germane to a discussion of the art of appearance. First, he observes that "in the case of Henrietta Lacks, the tumor cells sampled from her body were cultured in a laboratory and will continue to proliferate endlessly" (*VI* 5). Second, he opines that the cells "constitute so remarkable and virulent a specimen that they have been circulated throughout the world and even sent into space, on board the U.S. satellite Discoverer 17" (5). Important, here, are Baudrillard's assertions that Lacks's cells "proliferate endlessly" and that "they have been circulated throughout the world and even sent into space" (5). With these assertions Baudrillard stresses the function of endless proliferation and ceaseless circulation in his art of appearance, and he also suggests that the perceived immortality of Henrietta's cells might be best understood through the art of appearance.

To understand the way that Henrietta's cells make the perception of immortality appear, the events involving these cells require further scrutiny according to the first component of Baudrillard's rhetorical theory—the art of appearance. Baudrillard argues that the art of appearance-making involves a process called simulation and that simulation opposes representation by obliterating reference. Given that Baudrillard associates proliferation and circulation with Henrietta's cells (not Henrietta herself), rhetorical studies scholars must consider the way in which the cells oppose reference. Quite obviously, the biopsy excised two slivers of tissue from their point of origin—that is, Henrietta's body—and, as a result, the physiological reference of cells to body was severed. More subtly, however, thought and discourse were mobilized in a way that worked to obliterate any link between the cells and Henrietta. The cells were given a "code name" and "simply called HeLa" (Skloot, *The Immortal Life* 1). Additionally, references to Henrietta Lacks's real identity—that is, her real name—were obscured for twenty years under a heap of misinformation and a variety of pseudonyms. For instance, articles published in the *Minneapolis Star* and *Collier's* magazine, respectively, reported that the code name *HeLa* referenced *Henrietta Lakes* and *Helen L.* as the cells' point of origin (105–09). Reference was effectively obliterated for two decades with no association made between HeLa and the deceased woman from whom they originated. The importance of the liquidation of all referentiality is aptly captured by one of the research scientists interviewed by Skloot. "Scientists," the researcher explains, "don't like to think of HeLa cells as being little bits of Henrietta because it's much easier to do science when you disassociate your materials from the people they come from" (126). Like Baudrillard, this researcher pinpoints the link between rhetoric and perception with startling acuity: thinking and speaking of *HeLa*—rather than *Henrietta Lacks*—engenders a perception of the cells as cells, and these cells can apparently live forever.

This dissociative or irreferential way of thinking, speaking, and perceiving of HeLa as *HeLa* allowed the cells to proliferate independently of Henrietta Lacks. Freed from the ethical complications that accompany the treatment of humans, research scientists approached the cells as cells. They were growing "the first *immortal* human cells: a continuously dividing line of cells all descended from one original sample, cells that would constantly replenish themselves and never die" (Skloot 30; emphasis original). Although Henrietta Lacks died, the cells grew expansively. And the expansive growth that is characteristic of HeLa effects the perception of immortality.

From one standpoint, the proliferation and circulation of HeLa was physical. As Skloot explains, "HeLa cells weren't limited by space in the same way other cells were; they could simply divide until they ran out of culture medium," which meant that the "bigger the vat of medium, the more the cells grew" (94). After their biopsy from Henrietta, the cells traveled to a laboratory that produced and circulated them widely. HeLa was sent from Maryland to New York, Minneapolis, and Texas and also to India, Amsterdam, and Chile (57, 95). HeLa was eventually mass-produced in a "HeLa factory" at a rate of "6 trillion cells per week" (93, 96). Later, HeLa went into space, as part of "the second satellite ever in orbit, which was launched by the Russian space program in 1960," and also as part of NASA's "*Discoverer XVIII* satellite," which contained "several vials of HeLa" (137). To be sure, HeLa's unchecked proliferation and circulation can be explained through physical, mechanical, or scientific lenses. Baudrillard acknowledges these technical explanations when he observes that HeLa "*forgets to die*; it forgets *how* to die" and that the HeLa cell line "goes on to clone itself again and again, making thousands of identical copies of itself" (*VI* 5; emphasis original). Here, Baudrillard's comments point to a more general disturbance in "the process" that results in endless proliferation or simulative self-copying (5). The disturbance in the physical, mechanical, and scientific processes of cell production is a disturbance that also manifests itself in rhetorical processes involving thought, discourse, and perception.

From a second standpoint, then, the proliferation and circulation of HeLa was rhetorical and can be explained through a rhetorical lens. Just as the HeLa cell culture expanded without limit, so too did the rhetoric that made HeLa appear: The perceived appearance of immortality vis-à-vis thought and discourse about HeLa begot more immortality vis-à-vis more thought and discourse about HeLa. Indeed, popular writings on HeLa have led to more popular writings on HeLa, and scientific articles investigating HeLa have produced more scientific articles investigating HeLa. In fact, Skloot notes that when her "book went to press in 2009, more than 60,000 scientific articles had been published about research done on HeLa, and that number was increasing steadily at a rate of more than 300 papers each month" (312). Thus, the perception of immortality that appears with the physical proliferation, or cloning, of HeLa is reinforced by the rhetorical proliferation of HeLa in thought and discourse.

Having obliterated reference and having rampantly proliferated, HeLa began to assume a concealed agency, secretly wresting agency away from humans. As Baudrillard explains, simulacra function in the same way, in that simulacra aim for total control and begin to organize reality. To be sure, Skloot's book chronicles the way in which certain humans took agency away from other humans. By proceeding without the informed consent of Henrietta and in myriad other ways, the medical doctors and research scientists usurped the agency of Henrietta and her family over her cells. But, importantly, Skloot's book also documents the ways in which HeLa might be understood as wresting agency away from humans. For example, Skloot recounts that, in the mid-1950s, George Gey—who, along with his wife, directed the cell culture lab at Johns Hopkins Hospital and grew the first HeLa culture—would come to lament "the fact that HeLa was now completely out of his control" (Skloot 103). Gey was not the only researcher whose agency was ceded to HeLa. In fact, HeLa exercised a remarkable degree of agency that secretly controlled the thoughts, discourse, and perceptions of a good number of doctors and scientists. Unbeknownst to these researchers, HeLa began contaminating other cell cultures. HeLa floated, traveled, and rode from one culture dish to the next (153). And, as Skloot notes, "if just *one* HeLa cell landed in a culture dish, it took over, consuming all the media and filling all the space" (153; emphasis original). HeLa contaminated many of the cell cultures banked at the American Type Culture Collection without the research scientists' knowledge, and most of these disbelieving scientists initially ignored the contamination (154). HeLa also, as many newspapers voraciously reported, managed to "INVADE" a Russian cell culture (174; emphasis original). HeLa was, in short, an immortal attack agent. "It was this immortality" Skloot acknowledges, "that made it possible for HeLa to take over so many other cultures" (217). Eventually, in the early 1990s, one researcher would even argue that HeLa should be understood as its own species (215). Regardless of whether HeLa is understood as a unique species, as a contaminating invader, or as a strong cell culture, the point remains that HeLa steadily gained agency over time. With this agency, HeLa perpetuated thoughts, discourse, and perceptions of its own immortality. HeLa began appearing as an immortal agent that was able to outgrow, outlast, and outmaneuver humans.

As a product of thought, discourse, and perception, the immortal appearance of HeLa cells ultimately began to substitute for Henrietta Lacks. HeLa cells began functioning as a concealed substitution for the absent Henrietta Lacks, standing in for, turning into, and replacing Henrietta. Put differently, the thoughts, discourse, and perceptions associated with HeLa began to be taken for Henrietta. Consider, for instance, the title of Skloot's book, *The Immortal Life of Henrietta Lacks.* The perceived immortality of HeLa makes the long-deceased Henrietta appear immortal now, too. This artful substitution of immortal cells for mortal human is the tropological function that is characteristic of Baudrillardian simulacra. Skloot's book documents many more examples of this troping. The book quotes from the December 1971 issue of the journal *Obstetrics and Gynecology* as it calculates Henrietta's age, "a combined age of 51 years," by adding her thirty-one years of life to the twenty years HeLa has outlived her (173). As such, the first years of HeLa's immortal life serve as a mathematical substitute for the initial two decades during which Henrietta was dead. Skloot's book also shows Henrietta's family discursively substituting the HeLa cell cultures for

Henrietta. Upon the family's learning about HeLa through an acquaintance, Henrietta's husband thought "*Henrietta's alive?*" and her son Lawrence called Johns Hopkins Hospital, stating, "'I'm calling about my mother, Henrietta Lacks—you got some of her alive in there'" (Skloot 181; emphasis original). Similarly, Susan Hsu, who was a postdoctoral fellow at Johns Hopkins in 1973 and was interviewed by Skloot for the book, also takes HeLa as Henrietta when she encourages Henrietta's family to "be very proud," for "their mother will never die so long as the medical science is around" (189). In each of these examples, HeLa stands in for Henrietta, and HeLa's perceived immortality works to conceal the absence of Henrietta's mortality. Thus, the art of appearance executes a concealed substitution that facilitates the perception of Henrietta's immortality: the art of appearance and its incessant production of HeLa makes Henrietta Lacks appear immortal.

CHAPTER 5

Baudrillard's Art of Disappearance: The Destruction of Perceptual Appearance

The previous chapter examined the claims that Baudrillard advances about the art of appearance, as that art is exemplified by simulation and simulacra. Those claims lead Baudrillard to argue that the art of appearance, when allowed to proliferate in excess, becomes a manipulative and controlling art. The art of appearance produces simulacra that multiply and come to substitute for the reality principle, effecting a state of hyperreality. Marked by an excess of models, hyperreality steers humans toward the perception that there is value in production, or meaning-making. The perception engendered by the art of appearance—that is, the perception that production, alone, retains value—depends on the substitution of simulacra for the reality principle. Baudrillard explains that simulacra not only mark "the absence of a profound reality" but that they have "no relation to reality whatsoever" (*SS* 6).[1] Indeed, the substitution of simulacra for the reality principle not only accelerates the production of meaning by obliterating reference to reality, but this substitution also conceals the absence of reality. Thus, the substitution, turning, or troping that is indicative of hyperreality amounts to an act of concealment, in which models generate the appearance of reality to hide that there is no reality (1–2). In a state of hyperreality, Baudrillard writes, "[i]t is no longer a question of a false representation of reality (ideology) but of concealing the fact that the real is no longer real, and thus saving the reality principle" (13).[2] Elsewhere, he describes hyperreality as the "[h]allucination of the real" (124),[3] explaining that hyperreality entails the "[p]anic-stricken production of the real" (7).[4] Hyperreality is, in other words, the ecstatic production of perceptual appearances that, according to Baudrillard, reach their full potential—wherein potential (or *potentia*) connotes a "power of things longing to appear" (*IEx* 136)[5]—beyond human control. Thus, in hyperreality, perceptual appearances are realized or fulfilled.

For Baudrillard, the fulfillment of perceptual appearances by way of an ecstatic or extreme version of the art of appearance simultaneously gives way to a different art—he calls it the art of disappearance (cf. *FF* 118). He writes that "everything disappears by excess of reality," describing disappearance as the artistic counterpart to appearance—that is, as a reverse movement "by which concepts and ideas (but also phantasies, utopias, dreams, and desires) vanish into their very fulfillment" (*WD* 12).[6] Baudrillard's mention of phantasies, here, can be understood as a deliberate invocation of the art of appearance, as the word *phantasy* is an etymological cognate of the Greek *phantasia* and circumscribed in the same semantic field as the Latin *simulacra*. All of these terms—*phantasy*, *phantasia*, and *simulacra*—connote the perceptions produced by the art of appearance. As Baudrillard's comments make clear, once these perceptions reach, or perhaps exceed, their potential through fulfillment, they give way to a new art—that of disappearance. He suggests that, given the contemporary world and its drive toward production, disappearance occurs after appearances become excessive or after a state of hyperreality has taken effect. He straightforwardly writes that "only that which has appeared can disappear" (*HD* 126), and this assertion is supported by his often-used analogy, which compares the art of appearance to a map. In *Simulacra and Simulation*, Baudrillard writes that "*when the map covers the whole territory, something like the principle of reality disappears*" (123; emphasis original).[7] By way of this analogy, he suggests that the fulfillment of appearance (i.e., the map covering over the entire territory) is concomitantly a disappearance (i.e., the vanishing of the reality principle). Indeed, disappearance is a complementary foil to appearance. The art of disappearance mounts a radical challenge to the art of appearance. Pushing past analogy, this chapter argues that Baudrillard theorizes the art of disappearance by advancing three claims about disappearance—namely, that

1. disappearance is a process that can be figured through (a) the trope of metaphor and (b) the trope of metastasis but that can best be figured through (c) the trope of metamorphosis;
2. disappearance is characterized by (a) radical alterity and (b) ambivalence;
3. disappearance is often framed as (a) a fatal strategy or (b) a seductive game.

Each of these claims elaborates on the art of disappearance in a much-needed way, as the art of disappearance is, by most accounts, the most theoretically challenging component in Baudrillard's work. As Baudrillard studies scholar David B. Clarke recognizes, disappearance challenges scholars across all disciplines, for "it is not entirely obvious what 'disappearance' is" ("Commentaries" 32). Read, most basically, as a remark on disappearance's theoretical complexity, Clarke's comment suggests that even those scholars who are most familiar with Baudrillard's work continue to debate the precise nature of the art of disappearance. For example, William Bogard calls disappearance an "aim" (319), while Mike Gane refers to it as a "process" ("Disappearance" 52); Zygmunt Bauman views disappearance as a "mode" (32), whereas Douglas Kellner understands it as one half of "a fundamental dialectic" in Baudrillard's work ("Commentaries" 40; "Some" 154). Despite the differences in their understandings of Baudrillard's art of disappearance, Baudrillard studies scholars generally seem to agree on the importance of disappearance to his work. The sentiment seems to follow the appraisal offered by Baudrillard studies scholar John Armitage—namely, that "if we seek to read [Baudrillard's] work accurately, we have to do so in view of its disappearance" (Rev. of *Why*).

Rhetorical studies scholars, however, have been reluctant to view Baudrillard's work in terms of the art of disappearance. Of the rhetorical studies scholars who engage with Baudrillard's rhetorical theory, the majority avoid discussing the art of disappearance as disappearance per se. Instead, these scholars draw from a long list of terms that Baudrillard deploys as synonyms of the term *disappearance*—including, among others, the terms *fatal* and *seduction*—and use these terms in place of the term *disappearance*. That rhetorical studies scholars have largely avoided viewing Baudrillard's work and theory through the term *disappearance* is not surprising, since it might well be understood as incompatible with the discipline of rhetoric. Indeed, disappearance presents an especially difficult challenge to rhetorical studies scholars because the term *disappearance* seems antithetical to rhetoric. Rhetoric remains closely linked to the production of appearances, so much so that the whole of rhetoric is often viewed as an appearance-making enterprise, in which a rhetor invents discourse to make an argument appear a certain way to bring about a particular effect. Since rhetoric is traditionally theorized in terms of appearance production, any attempt at yoking rhetoric with disappearance seems misguided, if not futile. Michelle Ballif recognizes that contemporary rhetorical studies scholars "have been warned against" inquiring into processes other than production, insofar as the "proper realm" of rhetorical studies scholarship has been defined as the realm of production (9). Ballif's observation about the tendency of rhetorical studies scholars to focus their inquiry on the realm of production seems to be a persistent tendency—one that, with few exceptions, continues within rhetorical studies today and marks a term like *disappearance* as, at best, untraditional and, at worst, inappropriate for rhetorical study.

However, this chapter establishes that Baudrillard's three claims about the art of disappearance are, in aggregate, very much compatible with rhetoric and do, in actuality, dispose the art of disappearance to rhetorical study. The art of disappearance is grounded in Baudrillard's expansive notion of rhetorical invention, in which thought and discourse can be used not only to construct perceptual appearances but also to destruct perceptual appearance. To be sure, disappearance operates in the realm of perception, just as appearance does. This realm—the realm of *phantasia*—is the realm of judgments that have been derived from thought and discourse and experience. Whereas the art of appearance uses thought and discourse to construct perceptions of meaningful and value-laden *phantasia*, the art of disappearance mobilizes thought and discourse to destruct perceptions of meaning and value. The art of disappearance is, in other words, an art that depends on the invention of thought and the invention of discourse. Baudrillard admits as much when he writes that the art of disappearance "cannot rid itself of language" (*EC* 90).[8] As this comment suggests, the art of disappearance depends on rhetorical invention to affect perception in a radically different way from the art of appearance. Baudrillard's art of disappearance can, consequently, be understood as a subspecies of the art of rhetoric, for disappearance uses thought and language as a means to approach the goal of his rhetorical theory—namely, symbolic exchange.

Claim 1: Disappearance Is a Process That Can Be Figured through Three Tropes

Baudrillard's first claim about the art of disappearance emerges from his claims about the art of appearance. As was established in the previous chapter, Baudrillard understands simulacra as functioning tropologically—that is, he views simulacra as bringing about artful substitutions, in which simulacra come to substitute for reality. This substitution for reality is concomitantly a disappearance that serves as an entrée, an opportunity, or an exigence for the inventive practice of the art of disappearance. From a rhetorical studies perspective, tropes are inventive turnings or artful figures that invent new relationships and compel new movement within language. It follows, therefore, that a rhetorical understanding of the art of disappearance begins with an understanding of how disappearance is figured as a trope that is other than the art of appearance. Throughout his work Baudrillard suggests that disappearance might be figured as a trope in three major ways—as metaphor, metastasis, and metamorphosis. While each of these three conceptualizations of disappearance maintains some rhetorical significance, Baudrillard argues that the art of disappearance must be understood as metamorphosis. More precisely, he claims that the art of disappearance is a transformative process that is best figured through the trope of metamorphosis. As Baudrillard explains, the trope of metamorphosis (which is used to effect transformation) departs in a radical way from the trope of metaphor (which is used to effect transfer) and the trope of metastasis (which is used to effect transport). Thus, parsing these tropes in terms of disappearance is, arguably, the best initial way to identify the rhetorical dimensions of the art of disappearance—thereby following the novel path that Baudrillard's art of disappearance cuts through the terrain of rhetorical theory.

Point 1A. The Art of Disappearance Is Not Adequately Figured through the Trope of Metaphor

In the first place, Baudrillard contends that the art of disappearance should not be figured as metaphor, since the figure of metaphor perpetuates meaning and value. Metaphor proves one of the most recognizable rhetorical figures inside and outside rhetorical studies, and it can therefore be defined in a wide variety of ways. The word *metaphor* can be traced back to the Greek word μεταφέρειν meaning "to transfer" ("Metaphor," etymology), and this early meaning is evident in many later definitions of metaphor. I. A. Richards, for instance, defines a metaphor as "a borrowing between and intercourse of *thoughts,* a transaction between contexts" (94; emphasis original). Richards's definition of metaphor, which stresses the borrowing and transaction between two terms, anticipates Baudrillard's definition of metaphor as "the *transfer of value from one field to the other*" (*SED* 220; emphasis original).[9] According to Baudrillard's definition, metaphor transfers perceptions of meaning, rather than challenging perceptions of meaning. Metaphor, he argues, is "the possibility of communicating meaning" (*FF* 77; *BL* 102). By this definition, metaphor aligns more closely with the art of appearance than the art of disappearance. The figure of the metaphor is, therefore, not a fitting figure for the art of disappearance, since the art of disappearance is characterized by the destruction of meaning and value. Baudrillard writes of the "danger of the metaphor," observing that metaphors maintain a positive economy that risks "filling" the absence that is disappearance with "additional phantasms," or meaning-laden appearances (*SED* 219).[10] Note, again, his conspicuous invocation of the word *phantasms* and the term's semantic relationship to both *phantasia* and *simulacra*. With reference to Julia Kristeva's work, Baudrillard explains that metaphors not only combine and intertextualize values but that metaphors also absorb a multiplicity of meanings (220).

Baudrillard's problem with conceptualizing the art of disappearance with the figure of the metaphor is that, as Baudrillard studies scholar Victoria Grace notes, "[m]etaphors come to have a positive value" (*Baudrillard's* 178). The art of disappearance, however, strives to challenge and destruct perceptions of meaning and value. Baudrillard, in fact, discusses the effect of using metaphor to conceptualize disappearance in an interview with Sylvère Lotringer, explaining that when disappearance is conceptualized with metaphor, disappearance comes to mean death. Baudrillard states that a "metaphorical form" or figuration of disappearance positions "disappearance as death" (*FF* 78; *BL* 103). The metaphor, thus, transfers the meaning of death onto the art of disappearance and communicates disappearance as death. Rhetorically, however, Baudrillard's art of disappearance does not mean death. The only means that are associated with disappearance are rhetorical means—with disappearance constituting the means to exchange in Baudrillard's rhetorical theory. In contradistinction to its metaphorical figuring, disappearance does not mean death—that is, finality, cessation, or termination ("Death," entry 1). To be sure, disappearance does not *mean* anything. Rather, it is an art that poses a challenge to the art of appearance. Baudrillard's rhetorical theory depends on disappearance to destruct perceptions of meaning and, thereby, sustain symbolic exchange. Disappearance is, in other words, a process that sustains exchange through challenge; it does not bring about a cessation in the movement of exchange, and it certainly does not mean death.

Point 1B. The Art of Disappearance Is Not Adequately Figured through the Trope of Metastasis

In the second place, Baudrillard holds that the art of disappearance should not be conceptualized as metastasis. Although it is less well known than the figure of metaphor, metastasis can be found on the lists of rhetorical figures compiled by Quintilian in *Institutio Oratoria* and Richard Lanham in *A Handlist of Rhetorical Terms*. Quintilian defines metastasis as a "transmutation of time," in which a rhetor invokes the past or imagines the future (bk. 9, ch. 2, sec. 41; cf. bk. 7, ch. 4, secs. 13–14). This particular definition has been taken up by scholars such as Kane X. Faucher and Ruth Webb, who argue, respectively, that metastasis amounts to a "displacement" that transports the audience "to the past or into a hypothetical future" (Faucher 127; Webb 100). Additionally, Lanham discusses two definitions of metastasis. First, Lanham renames metastasis as the "fleeting figure," explaining that the figure can be used by a rhetor who passes quickly over an issue (101). Second, Lanham describes metastasis as a retort in which a rhetor "turn[s] back an insult or objection against the person who made it" (101).

Baudrillard's discussion of metastasis retains some sense of the definitions proposed by Quintilian, Lanham, Faucher, and Webb, in that he views metastasis as a figure of rapid future transport. In particular, he defines the figure of metastasis as "proliferation" (*FF* 78; *BL* 103) or "pure repetition" (*TE* 140).[11] This definition, as Baudrillard makes clear, follows Franz von Baader's work that links metastasis with ecstasy (cf. *FS* 53; Faucher 134–35). The figure of metastasis results in the "production of superfluous meaning"—or the appearance that meaning is too much: overexcited, frenzied (*FS* 53).[12] Like a cancerous cell or a crystalline structure, the figure of metastasis charges into the future by way of "invariant reproduction" and "aggravated redundancy" (*TE* 136, 137).[13] According to Baudrillard, the figure of metastasis is premised on a "voracious positivity" (121).[14] Whereas the figure of metaphor maintains a positive economy by imbuing its transfer of meaning with a positive value, the figure of metastasis does not engage in transfer. Rather, the figure of metastasis transmutes concepts so as to transport them into a total positivity. Put differently, Baudrillard understands the figure of metastasis as advancing the appearance of too much value and superfluous meaning. In fact, Baudrillard observes the figure of metastasis at work in the world and indicates that he is wary of the figure's gross prolificacy. He notes that "[e]verywhere one seeks to produce meaning, to make the world signify, to render it visible" (*EC* 63).[15] He further cautions that "[w]e are not, however, in danger of lacking meaning; quite to the contrary, we are gorged with meaning and it is killing us" (63).[16]

On account of this gorging on the overproduction of meaning, Baudrillard deems the figure of metastasis unfit for conceptualizing the art of disappearance, since the art of disappearance involves challenging values and meaning, not propagating them. Whereas metaphor preserves a difference between two fields to make meaning and value, metastasis invades all other fields. Baudrillard describes metastasis as "deterritorialization"

(*EC* 50),[17] observing that the figure amounts to a "cloning system" (*FF* 78; *BL* 103). The figure of "metastasis affects entire networks" (*TE* 72)[18] in that its effects are widespread and distributed, yet consistent. As the figure of deterritorialization, metastasis is the map that covers over the territory and comes to substitute for reality; it is the figure that effects hyperreality, resulting in what Baudrillard calls the ecstasy of communication. Metastasis, for Baudrillard, constitutes a frenzied kind of repetition that knows no limits: the figure of metastasis gives way to pure simulacra—the ceaseless reproduction of the model. To be sure, metastasis brings about a kind of disappearance but not the art of disappearance on which Baudrillard's rhetorical theory depends. Instead, metastasis brings about disappearance insofar as the excessive and ecstatic production of appearances make whatever is not a meaningful value-laden appearance disappear. As Baudrillard explains, metastasis is a figure "given over to the pure promiscuity of its relationship to itself" (8),[19] and that relationship excludes any other relationship, making what is other disappear. The disappearance brought about by metastasis is the "disappearance of the other" (*FF* 78; *BL* 103). Metastatic disappearance is, in other words, the troping or turning of simulacra, in which the proliferation of the one functions as the substitute for the other. Thus, metastatic disappearance amounts to the pinnacle of the art of appearance; it is the vanishing effect of superfluous appearance.

Point 1C. The Art of Disappearance Is Best Figured through the Trope of Metamorphosis

In the third place, Baudrillard considers the figure of metamorphosis. Whereas Baudrillard rejects conceptualizing the art of disappearance through the figure of metaphor (because metaphor merely transfers meaning from one to the other) as well as through the figure of metastasis (because metastasis merely transports or displaces the other through overproduction of meaning), he endorses conceptualizing the art of disappearance through the figure of metamorphosis because the figure challenges the logic of meaning-making. Unlike the theorization of metaphor and metastasis as rhetorical tropes, theorization that has been ongoing for millennia, the theorization of metamorphosis as a rhetorical trope is, according to Kai Mikkonen, "a rather recent phenomenon" that is indebted to key twentieth-century thinkers including Roman Jakobson and Paul de Man (309). Acknowledging that rhetors as far back as Homer and Ovid used metamorphosis as a *theme* in their texts, Mikkonen draws on the work of

Jakobson and de Man—one of whom Baudrillard references in his work (*CPS* 178–79; *SED* 214–18; *UB* 71)—to argue that metamorphosis is a *figure* that is used to "stand for the transformative change or 'correction' of the subject positions and (inter)relationships between the subjects and their others" (329). In other words, the transformation that characterizes the theme of metamorphosis is used, Mikkonen argues, to bring about a rhetorical effect wherein relationships between one and another are changed or corrected. Here, the distinction between the figure of metamorphosis and the figure of metastasis becomes clear: metastasis constitutes a relationship between one and the same, while metamorphosis constitutes a relationship of one into another. Mikkonen further understands the figure of metamorphosis as spurring an examination of "the logic of reference" and also encouraging "an (alternative) logic for representing change" (330). Thus, the figure of metamorphosis considers the relationships between rhetoric and reality, as well as language and reference. Of course, these relationships are the ones upon which Baudrillard builds his rhetorical theory. Moreover, Mikkonen understands the figure of metamorphosis to be especially applicable when "the principle of verisimilitude is taken to its limit" (324). Metamorphosis is, therefore, a figure that lends itself to the art of disappearance—an art that emerges from metastatic appearance-making that has fast approached its limit.

Conceptualized through the figure of metamorphosis, Baudrillard's art of disappearance can fittingly be understood as an attempt to change, correct, or challenge superfluous appearance. In particular, the art of disappearance attempts to challenge the perceptions of meaning made by the art of appearance. Declaring that metamorphosis "abolishes" the potential to make and communicate meaning (*FF* 77; *BL* 102), Baudrillard uses the figure of metamorphosis to conceptualize the art of disappearance as a rhetorical means to challenge the metastatic construction of meaningful and value-laden perceptual appearances. He locates the figure of metamorphosis "at the radical point of the system" and describes the figure as "a process" involving "only the rules of the game of forms" (*FF* 77; *BL* 102). Thus figured as metamorphosis, the art of disappearance can be understood as a process that is initiated at the radical point of the meaning-making system. When the metastatic production of appearances desperately needs a corrective or a challenge, the art of disappearance provides it through an alternative logic, replete with its own perspective and strategies. Indeed, Baudrillard defines metamorphosis as a transfiguration of oneself into another (*EC* 45–46). "Metamorphosis," as Baudrillard understands the figure, "moves from form to form without the intervention of value" (*CA* 73).[20] Furthermore, he contends that "[n]o meaning, either ideological or aesthetic, can be drawn from [metamorphosis]" (73).[21] With its ability to move without preserving the appearance of meaning or value, metamorphosis fittingly conceptualizes Baudrillard's art of disappearance. As he recognizes, "passing from one species to another, from one form to another is a means of *disappearing*" (*EC* 47; emphasis original).[22] Indeed, the figure of metamorphosis conceptualizes the movement that the art of disappearance seeks to initiate with the art of appearance—a movement where "all that has been produced must be destroyed, and that which appears must disappear" (71).[23] The art of disappearance depends, in other words, on "this metamorphosis of effects" (87).[24]

Claim 2: Disappearance Is Characterized by (A) Radical Alterity and (B) Ambivalence

Baudrillard's second claim about the art of disappearance builds upon his first claim. By figuring the art of disappearance through the trope of metamorphosis, Baudrillard's first claim stresses that disappearance transforms effects by way of challenging appearance. As he sees it, the challenge is that of response: "Challenge," writes Baudrillard, "is that to which one cannot avoid responding" (*EC* 57).[25] The art of disappearance seeks to goad the art of appearance into response—that is, to initiate and sustain a back-and-forth movement of challenge and response, of perceptual destruction and perceptual construction—and it does so by mobilizing alterity and ambivalence. Baudrillard's second claim details these two characteristics of the art of disappearance. The first characteristic of disappearance, which imbues the art with the capacity to issue a strong challenge, is alterity. Baudrillard associates the art of disappearance with a perspective of radical alterity, and the first point below details this perspective of radical otherness. The second characteristic of the art of disappearance, which allows the art to issue a strong challenge, is ambivalence, or a radical questioning of value. Together, alterity and ambivalence are the characteristics of the art of disappearance that allow it to radically challenge the art of appearance.

Point 2A. Disappearance Is Characterized by Radical Alterity

By conceptualizing the art of disappearance through the figure of metamorphosis, Baudrillard defines disappearance as a transformation that occurs at the limit of appearance-making. Once the making of perceptual appearances exceeds its limit, it moves, passes, or turns into another form—namely, the art of disappearance. Disappearance can be understood as following from appearance but also as remaining apart from appearance. In other words, the art form of disappearance is other than the art form of appearance, and, on the basis of its position as other, the art of disappearance is capable of challenging the art of appearance. The difficulty in this figuration, however, is locating a place for disappearance in relation to the overproduced appearances characteristic of metastasized simulacra. On the one hand, Baudrillard argues that the making of perceptual appearances proves an all-encompassing process that eradicates all others through self-proliferation. Here, the implication is that a metastasized art of appearance, which has reached its productive limit, would leave disappearance no place from which to stand as other. On the other hand, Baudrillard's entire rhetorical theory emphasizes the exchange that occurs between the art of appearance and that of disappearance. The implication, here, is that disappearance must be located someplace from which it can stand against appearance as other, challenging appearance and facilitating the movement of transformation. The question of placement confronts the art of disappearance: Where does the transformation take place, if metamorphosis depends on a challenge between one form and another and if metastasis eradicates the other through the hyperrealization of one? Put differently, from where does the challenge of the other emerge? From what perspective can disappearance-as-metamorphosis emerge from appearance-as-metastasis? Baudrillard answers these questions by associating the art of disappearance with a perspective of radical alterity—that is, a perspective of radical otherness. Arguing that the art of disappearance embraces a perspective of alterity, Baudrillard locates the form of the art of disappearance at a distance from that of appearance. Since his art of disappearance is located outside entrenched value systems and threadbare dialectical positions, the art of disappearance is able to challenge the art of appearance by seizing on the perspective of alterity.

To be sure, Baudrillard's move to associate disappearance with radical alterity is one that affirms disappearance's role in his rhetorical theory. He locates his notion of disappearance in alterity, and a number of rhetorical studies scholars have increasingly called attention to the role that alterity plays in rhetoric. For instance, in *Inessential Solidarity: Rhetoric and Foreigner Relations*, Diane Davis observes that radical alterity amounts to an "interruption" or "a rupture in the tropological field" (84). According to Davis, rhetorical studies scholars "have mostly elected not to" engage with the interruption that is radical alterity (85). Rather, as Davis observes, rhetorical studies scholars largely concentrate on the work of subjects that "get things done in the world" through "appropriation and assimilation"—in short, through "the play of the same that [rhetorical studies scholars] are content to call 'successful communication'" (84). Davis, however, views radical alterity as an "opening for the field of rhetorical studies" and urges scholars to attend to alterity and engage with the interruption (85). Davis's remarks, which draw most heavily on the work of Emmanuel Levinas, in many ways parallel the argument that Baudrillard advances about the art of disappearance: his art of disappearance occurs on account of a tropological rupture—when metastasis gives way to metamorphosis—and it also keeps itself at a distance from communication—that is, the reproduction of the same through appearance-making and simulation. Thus, Baudrillard's work on disappearance might assist rhetorical studies scholars who take up Davis's call to attend to the rhetorical dimensions of radical alterity.

Like Davis, Baudrillard suggests that radical alterity is an interruption of established systems—namely, systems of communication that make perceptions, meaning, and value appear. In fact, he identifies two kinds of alterity—accidental alterity and affective alterity—both of which embrace the perspective of radical otherness to interrupt the art of appearance. The first kind of alterity is indicative of what he calls "the perspective of accidental alterity" (*RA* 116).[26] The perspective of accidental alterity embraces those anomalies and those aleatory vulnerabilities that interrupt the function of systems. "All of the accidents, breakdowns, slips, skids, madness," writes Baudrillard, "is our alterity" (116).[27] Accidental alterity would, for him, be an unexpected glitch in the communicative system. Given two interlocutors, the perspective of accidental alterity is the radical other perspective from which a hiccup, belch, or blurt by one interlocutor might interrupt the communication of the pair. In short, accidental alterity is the perspective from which something other than communication occurs by happenstance. Baudrillard, however, also identifies what he terms as "another, more positive perspective" on alterity (116),[28] and he associates this second kind of alterity with affectation (117).

The perspective of affective alterity holds that a play "on the manipulation of signs" brings about an otherness in language use (*RA* 117).[29] "Affectation," as Baudrillard explains, "is the quality of something that plays with artificiality" (117).[30] Thus, the perspective of affective alterity embraces manipulation, artificiality, and play in such a way that the perspective gains distance from the established system. The perspective of affective alterity "lets signs be signs when others think they are handling substances and being" (117).[31] According to Baudrillard, this perspective brings about a metamorphosis or a transformation in the system itself, for affective alterity is the ability "to play well in an operational system, so well that it discreetly changes it into a system of signs and illusion" (117).[32] Given two interlocutors, the perspective of affective alterity would transform their relationship. No longer would these individuals engage in interlocution. Instead, they would engage in something like contralocution, whereby one individual might maintain the goal of successful communication while the other maintains a goal of play. The incommensurate goals of play and communication effectively position communication as other or foreign. Moreover, the play of affectation results in a transformation of the entire system of communication. When the perspective of affective alterity is leveraged against the productivist perspective of systematic communication, the making of meaning becomes impossible and communication is, in effect, transformed. Affective alterity is, therefore, the perspective from which something other than communication is strategically mobilized to interrupt and transform communication. As such, affective alterity provides the best perspective from which the art of disappearance can be deployed, by playing the other against the play of the same.

Indeed, Baudrillard associates the art of disappearance with radical alterity because the perspective of alterity allows language to do something other than produce perceptual appearances. Baudrillard, like Davis, connects alterity to foreignness. While Davis advocates "for a kind of foreign policy in the field" of rhetorical studies (85), Baudrillard weaves the foreignness of alterity into his rhetorical theory by way of the art of disappearance. As Baudrillard studies scholar David Teh recognizes, "radical alterity lurks throughout [Baudrillard's] *oeuvre*," in that Baudrillard "proposes that we find a way of appreciating what is foreign" ("Radical" 177). In works that include *Radical Alterity*, *The Transparency of Evil*, and *The Intelligence of Evil*, Baudrillard builds upon the work of Victor Segalen to argue that "[t]he other must be maintained in its foreignness" (*TE* 169).[33] The foreignness that Baudrillard attributes to radical alterity is an argument about language. He argues that the perspective of alterity is characterized by both "foreignness and incomprehensibility" as these two principles are manifested in "cultures, manners, faces, languages" (168, 167).[34] With respect to language, Baudrillard observes that every language "obeys the laws of communication" but concomitantly follows "its own rules, its own arbitrary determinants, its own implacable logic" (160).[35] The rules of language—namely, its arbitrariness, its internal logic, and its fundamental foreignness—are, according to Baudrillard, "ineluctable," "irreducible," and "indestructible" (160).[36] Every language, he declares, is "fundamentally untranslatable into any other language" (160),[37] and all languages prove foreign to the goal of communication. The otherness that is inherent to language is "why all languages are so 'beautiful'—precisely because they are foreign to one another" (160).[38] Baudrillard writes that, at the "most radical level," every language abides by the rule of alterity—the rule that allows languages to "be *other* than" what can be communicated (144; emphasis original).[39] Thus, the perspective of alterity positions language as fundamentally incomprehensible, and this "incomprehensibility" serves as a cornerstone of the art of disappearance (158).[40]

By associating the art of disappearance with the perspective of radical alterity, Baudrillard enables a comparison between traveling and the process of disappearance. "Travel," he says, "is comparable to relationships with others" (*TE* 171).[41] Since disappearance is located as other in its relationship with appearance, travel and disappearance are indeed comparable. To begin with, both travel and the art of disappearance assume a degree of otherness, foreignness, and strangeness with respect to meaning. Incomprehensibility, or what could be considered other than meaning or the absence of meaning, is characteristic of both disappearance and travel. In fact, Baudrillard describes the art of disappearance as "a fascination through absence" and as a process that always has "to travel," for "absence is always on the move" (*RA* 85).[42] Likewise, he observes that travelers follow absence, too: "What we seek in travel," writes Baudrillard, is "to be taken over by the journey—in other words by absence" (*TE* 170).[43] He argues that both the art of disappearance and travel are ways "to 'stroll' through the Other, the foreign, and to test its strangeness" (*RA* 75).[44] The strolling constitutes a kind of voyage, and Baudrillard understands this "voyage as metamorphosis" (*TE* 171).[45] Evidently, he finds grounds to compare the art of disappearance to travel because both are types of transformations by way of another. For both disappearance and travel, the perspective of radical alterity proves crucial: the stance of foreignness preserves distance, facilitates thinking from the outside, and retains inventive potential (*RA* 70, 69, 89). In particular, this perspective enables the art of disappearance to travel outside the territory controlled by metastatic appearance. Indeed, the radical alterity of disappearance positions the art as beyond or "behind appearance" (*AA* 31). By occupying that radically foreign place beyond appearance, disappearance locates itself beyond and apart from the systems of meaning-making and value propagated and perpetuated by the art of appearance.

Point 2B. Disappearance Is Characterized by Ambivalence

To elaborate on Baudrillard's analogy that likens radical alterity to travel, the art of disappearance might be said to rely on the perspective of radical alterity as traveling relies on a passport: the passport provides access to another territory, just as the perspective of alterity provides access to the territory of disappearance—that is, the territory that is radically other than the one consumed by the map of appearance-making. However, once access to the territory has been granted, the focus shifts from access to the actual practice of travel or, by analogy, the practice of the art of disappearance. As Baudrillard makes clear, traveling in the foreign territory of disappearance does not amount to an aimless drifting. Rather, the travel of disappearance necessitates the strategic use of ambivalence to challenge perceptual appearances.

The territory that is the art of disappearance is an ambivalent one in which no meaning or value exists. It is a territory of absence—one "beyond the end, beyond the subject, beyond all meaning," and Baudrillard contends that "the first fruits of an art of disappearance" begin to "emerge only from the disappearance of all added values" (*WD* 21).[46] Put differently, the art of disappearance emerges from the absence of values and the incomprehensibility of meaning; disappearance is enabled by ambivalence. According to Baudrillard, when values and meaning disappear, "the possibility of an art" arises (22).[47] He describes the art of disappearance as a kind of "strategy" and as a kind of "game" (21, 22),[48] and both of these descriptions will be examined below. For the moment, however, it is important to note that, regardless of whether the art of disappearance is better characterized as a strategy or a game, disappearance involves the play of ambivalence. As Baudrillard studies scholar Marcus A. Doel recognizes, Baudrillard conceives of disappearance as an ambivalent form ("Commentaries" 36). The emphasis that Doel places on Baudrillard's categorization of disappearance as an ambivalent form resonates with work by other scholars who specialize in the study of Baudrillard. Marc Schuster, for example, reads Baudrillard as mobilizing ambivalence to "question the legitimacy of value" ("Ambivalence" 9). Schuster, paraphrasing Baudrillard, notes that the ambivalence that informs Baudrillard's work signals "the incessant potential for the destruction of the illusion of value" (10). As Schuster makes clear, ambivalence possesses a destructive potential that is leveraged against illusions (or what might otherwise be described as false perceptions) of value. The art of disappearance relies on ambivalence to challenge the perceptions or illusions produced by the art of appearance. In other words, ambivalence occupies a rhetorical role in Baudrillard's theory, for it mobilizes thought and discourse to challenge the production of perceptual appearances. Indeed, David Teh acknowledges the rhetorical role that ambivalence occupies in Baudrillard's theory, arguing that the ambivalence Baudrillard champions must be understood as functioning on "a rhetorical level" ("Baudrillard"). According to Teh, ambivalence is both a "position" and a "device" for Baudrillard, simultaneously "poetic and logical, aesthetic and structural" ("Baudrillard").

Arguably, ambivalence epitomizes Baudrillard's art of disappearance and imprints itself on the whole of his work—so much so that Gary Genosko labels Baudrillard a "theorist of radical ambivalence" (*Undisciplined* 6). Nonetheless, rhetorical studies scholars should not let ambivalence get out ahead of Baudrillard's rhetorical theory. He takes care to position ambivalence within the art of disappearance, and he remains cognizant that the art of disappearance is, itself, a subspecies of his art of rhetoric. In other words, ambivalence must be understood as serving the purpose of the art of disappearance. It is through the use of ambivalent thought and ambivalent discourse that the art of disappearance accomplishes its purpose—namely, the destruction of perceptions that appear to have meaning and value. To the point, Baudrillard stresses the role that ambivalent thought and discourse play in the art of disappearance. In *The Vital Illusion*, after he instructs readers to approach "disappearance as an art form—to exercise it, to perform it, to create an art of disappearance" (68), he addresses ambivalent thought. He couples his instructions with a warning that the thought required by such an art is difficult: "the most difficult thing," Baudrillard writes, is "to remain on the enigmatic, ambivalent, and reversible side of thought" (68). Ambivalent thought is, therefore, a very difficult part of practicing the art of disappearance. In *For a Critique of the Political Economy of the Sign*, Baudrillard also discusses ambivalent discourse, explaining that it challenges perceptions of value, not by negating that value, but instead by nullifying the perception of value (209). In no uncertain terms, Baudrillard stipulates that "[a]mbivalence is not the dialectical negation of value" (209).[49] Thus, ambivalence proves crucial to the art of disappearance, so crucial that the art of disappearance can be defined as the mobilization of ambivalent thought and ambivalent discourse to destroy the perception that certain appearances have value or meaning.

Claim 3: Disappearance Is Often Framed as (A) a Fatal Strategy or (B) a Seductive Game

Foregrounding the role that ambivalent thought and discourse occupy in the art of disappearance, Baudrillard's third claim characterizes disappearance in two dominant ways: (1) as strategy and (2) as game. These characterizations configure the art of disappearance in slightly different ways, as both the frame of *strategy* and the frame of *game* emphasize certain characteristics of disappearance. A robust examination of the art of disappearance, therefore, considers both of these configurations. In what follows, the art of disappearance, its radical perspective of otherness, and its mobilization of ambivalent thought and discourse are examined, respectively, as strategy and as game.

Point 3A. Disappearance Is Often Framed as a Fatal Strategy

Baudrillard regularly frames the art of disappearance as a strategy; as such, the alterity and the ambivalence that are characteristic of disappearance become strategic moves. In his early work, Baudrillard declares that "disappearance itself can also be a strategy" (*FS* 113).[50] This assertion is bolstered in his subsequent writing and interviews. In one of his final writings, *Why Hasn't Everything Already Disappeared?*, Baudrillard contends that the art of disappearance is "another strategy" (21).[51] Here, his use of the word *another* can be understood as a deliberate reference to alterity, and his use of the term *strategy* can similarly be understood as a very deliberate choice. As he explained to interviewers Caroline Bayard and Graham Knight, "[t]he term *strategy* represents an opportunity because it is apt" (*HD* 81; emphasis added). Baudrillard explains that the term *strategy* "has form" and "it speaks to the imaginary" (81). From his perspective, moreover, the term *strategy* can be readily applied to illusions and indicates a "crazy logic" that manifests itself "in the unfolding of things" (82). Perhaps for want of a better term to describe disappearance, Baudrillard declares, "Let us call it strategy" (82). Calling it *strategy* allows him to distinguish the art of disappearance from the art of appearance. Whereas the term *manipulation* captures the control exerted by the production of appearances, *strategy* captures the destructive potential of disappearance: "manipulation," Baudrillard writes, "can never be, or take the place of, strategy" (*FS* 66).[52] His distinction here is familiar to rhetorical studies scholars, who, for decades, have distinguished between rhetoric as the manipulative use of language and rhetoric as the strategic use of language (cf. Kuypers and King, "What" 4). When configured as a strategy, the rhetorical dimensions of the art of disappearance prove quite evident: the art of disappearance seizes on the opportunity to mobilize the perspective, logic, and form of what is other than meaning-making—namely, ambivalence—in order to "aim at the hollow spot of appearance" (*EC* 69).[53]

Quite often Baudrillard discusses the art of disappearance by labeling its constituent parts—alterity and ambivalence—as *strategy*. He discusses alterity as a strategy, for instance, when he argues that we should count affective alterity among "the strategies for escaping artificiality" (*RA* 118).[54] He further discusses ambivalence as a strategy, contending that, once the status of communication (as a metastatic paradox that overproduces perceptions of meaning) is accepted, there are only "ambivalent strategies" (*BL* 150). However, even more frequently Baudrillard discusses what he calls *fatal strategies*. Within rhetorical studies, Sonja K. Foss, Karen A. Foss, and Robert Trapp have emphasized the importance of fatal strategies to Baudrillard's work, arguing that these strategies connote "the creative possibilities embedded within" the contemporary "rational paradigm" (325). Foss, Foss, and Trapp explain that the term *fatal* opens up the possibility of "alternative worlds"—namely, those dominated by "fate" (326). Here, Baudrillard's use of synecdoche—his substitution of the part (fatal strategies) for the whole (the art of disappearance)—seems to have confounded rhetorical interpretation. The importance of fatal strategies is not so much a reliance on fate but rather a strategic use of the fatal as a form by which the art of disappearance and its characteristic alterity and ambivalence can be practiced.

In fact, Baudrillard is explicit about his use of the term *fatal*, explaining that "[t]he term 'fatal' has nothing fatalistic or apocalyptic about it"; rather, it implies bringing "things to a point of no return, in a spiral which is no longer that of their production, but of their disappearance" (*EC* 87–88).[55] Baudrillard explains that a "fatal strategy" is, therefore, "an expression which describes a process, a reversibility that is in the order of things, and this is, at the moment, truly delirious, fatal" (*HD* 82). Key to his discussions of fatal strategies is his point that the fatal is the symbolic challenge to the banal. As strategy, the fatal is other than and ambivalent toward the value-laden productivity that is the banal. For Baudrillard, the perception of the banal—the perception that there is value and meaning in production—is a dominant perception that plagues the contemporary world. He associates the banal with "the relay of information" that is characteristic of communication and the unchecked art of appearance (*Telemorphosis* 48).[56] Subsequently, the fatal offers a perspective, a line of thought, and a kind of discourse that is other than this banal perception of the contemporary value system (cf. *RC* 17–18; *BL* 50). By way of "its fatal strategy," the art of disappearance "envelopes the subject," that is, the banally productive human subject who operates according to systematized perceptions of meaning and value (*FS* 144).[57] To be sure, strategy informs Baudrillard's focus on the fatal, which is, according to Gary Genosko, "the most symbolically effective, theoretically violent form available" (*Undisciplined* 6), and this form symbolically pivots "on the border between life and death" in order to destabilize the opposition between life and death (46).

In the end, then, the fatal strategically attacks the banal perceptions that accompany the subject. Fatal strategies are other than and ambivalent toward perceptual appearance. In short, they are one way that Baudrillard frames the art of disappearance; as he declares, these strategies bring about a "metamorphosis of effects" (*EC* 87).[58] To be sure, his work embraces the metamorphic effects of fatal strategy. As Alan Cholodenko and Edward Colless note, Baudrillard's theory does not just describe fatal strategies; rather, it "fatally" exemplifies metamorphosis ("Envoi" 9). This metamorphosis is a "passing [. . .] from one form to another," and Baudrillard is emphatic that such a passing "is a means of *disappearing, not of dying*" (*EC* 47; emphasis original).[59] The strategy is, as he makes clear, subservient to the art.

Point 3B. Disappearance Is Often Framed as a Seductive Game

Baudrillard also frames the art of disappearance as a game, in which otherness and ambivalence become a kind of play. In using the term *game* to conceptualize disappearance, Baudrillard emphasizes the symbolic obligations or challenges forged by the rule-based play of disappearance. "Games," he argues, "create obligations like those found in challenges" (*S* 132),[60] and "[o]ne cannot opt not to respond to a challenge" ("Please" 80).[61] The parallels between the art of disappearance and rule-based games are, as Baudrillard elucidates, many. Both disappearance and games initiate obligatory play: in "the sphere of play" established by both, players are symbolically compelled to engage in game play (*S* 132).[62] He observes that "one just doesn't leave a game," in the sense that "one cannot refuse to play" (132, 132–33).[63] Instead, a pact or an obligation akin to sportsmanship binds the players of the game in a rule-based relationship (133). Rules are, therefore, indispensable to both disappearance and games. According to Baudrillard, game players exhibit "a passion for rules" and "a giddiness born of rules" (132).[64] The rules of the game institute an order that "creates a symbolic pact which compels one to observe the rules without reserve, and to pursue the game to the end, as one pursues a challenge to the end" (133).[65] As Baudrillard studies scholar William Pawlett notes, the symbolic set of obligations forged by rules "does enable the play and metamorphosis of appearance and disappearance" ("Illusion" 100). From Pawlett's perspective, the radical, metamorphic transformation facilitated by disappearance depends on a set of gamelike rules, and Baudrillard's writing describes the play that constitutes the art of disappearance as operating "according to the rules of the game of disappearance" (*AA* 28).

Indeed, the game that is disappearance can be understood as abiding by two predominant rules: alterity and ambivalence. Premised on the notion that "[o]nly that which comes from the domain of disappearance" proves "truly other" (*AA* 28), the first rule of the game of disappearance—the rule of alterity—eschews the product-focused goal of appearance so "that everything can be put into play" (*S* 135).[66] As Baudrillard explains, the art of appearance strives to craft a perception that appears as reality, imbuing it with an unchallengeable meaning and value. Thus, the products of appearance-making are made to seem beyond play, as the perception of reality creates a fantasy that places appearances outside the game. However, the rule of alterity invigorates the challenge posed by the game that is disappearance. Taking everything generated "in the domain of production" as a mere "extension of the same" (*AA* 28), the rule of alterity by which the game of disappearance is played challenges the very possibility that anything can remain outside the game. This perspective—that all things are in play—serves as a rule for the game of disappearance, in that this perspective of alterity engenders the challenging play characteristic of disappearance. The game of disappearance adheres to a rule of alterity that allows disappearance to play its game from a position other than appearance (*BL* 138). Consequently, Baudrillard asserts that games, like that of disappearance, "do not belong in the realm of fantasy, and their recurrence is not the repetition of a phantasy" (*S* 148).[67] Baudrillard's invocation of *phantasy*, here, underscores the positioning of the art of disappearance as what is other than the art of appearance and the perceptual appearances, *phantasia*, or simulacra that it produces.

In addition to the rule of alterity, the game of disappearance adheres to the rule of ambivalence. The rule of ambivalence requires disappearance to challenge the notion of value or meaning. The rule of ambivalence holds that "ambivalence is definitive" (*LP* 51)[68] and that all appearances of value and meaning constructed through perception are capable of being destructed—that is, these perceptions, *phantasia*, and simulacra are capable of being played until they disappear. As Baudrillard explains, the game of disappearance is "where one plays with value" (*S* 153).[69] He explains the rule of ambivalence as a play toward "worthlessness" (*SA* 29).[70] Again, he is deliberate in his choice of terms, explaining that "the term 'worthlessness' is ambivalent" and that the rule of ambivalence forces the game of disappearance to be played on "a field of discourse that can no longer be fully explained" (24, 29).[71] Thus, the rule of ambivalence disturbs perceptions of value and meaning that are propagated through discourse. Interrogating perceptions of value and meaning—that is, putting perceptions of value and meaning into play—constitutes the second rule by which the game of disappearance is played, and, as Baudrillard instructs, "we've got to play the game" (29).[72]

When Baudrillard configures the art of disappearance as a game, he frequently uses the term *seduction.* The term connotes for him "a great game" (*PW* 22),[73] or a form "that allows the playing out of a rule" (*FS* 129).[74] At places in his writing, he declares that seduction not only plays out rules but that seduction "*IS* the fundamental rule" (*EC* 67; emphasis original).[75] Seduction, Baudrillard writes, "is an art of disappearing" (66).[76] Indeed, he deploys the term *seduction*, at times, as a synonym for, and at other times, as a synecdoche for the game that is disappearance. He explains that *seduction* "expresses the fundamental rule that *all that has been produced must be seduced*" (*FS* 166; emphasis original).[77] He clarifies that being seduced means being "initiated into disappearance after having been initiated into existence" (166).[78] Put differently, the game of disappearance commences as a challenge to metastatic appearances. Baudrillard remains careful to note that "[s]eduction is not that which is *opposed to* production"; but rather he emphasizes that seduction is what is other than production (*EC* 58; emphasis original).[79] Seduction, in other words, emphasizes alterity, and it is on this alterity that rhetorical studies scholar Michelle Ballif focuses. Ballif notes well that, within the game that is seduction, "no player can be greater than the challenge" (12).

The challenge of seduction—that is, the art of disappearance—is manifested in bodies as well as language. Baudrillard acknowledges that "the body" consistently is first to be caught in the game of seduction (*EC* 46).[80] This acknowledgment explains his frequent use of the seduction frame when he discusses the art of disappearance in relation to subjectivities and psychologies of genders, sexes, and identities (cf. *S*; *TE* 22–27). However, he also discusses the challenge of seduction as one that is manifested in language use. Baudrillard contends that "the symbolic equilibrium of the world is founded on these relations of seduction and playfulness" in which there is continuous play of "the game of mutual seduction" between forms (*EC* 59).[81] The form of language that is meaningful and value-laden communication is, therefore, challenged by an ambivalent form of language that melts "the polar circuits of meaning" (58).[82] He refers to this second form of language as "a seductive theory of language" (58),[83] and he ultimately sees this form of language as crucial to the metamorphic transformation that characterizes disappearance. According to Baudrillard, seduction and the eradication of meaning "go together," for "to seduce things is to put them back into their cycle of appearance and disappearance, of incessant metamorphoses" (*FS* 202–03).[84] Thus, as one of the dominant ways that he configures the art of disappearance, the game of seduction attempts to use language to challenge the meaningful and value-laden art of appearance and to bring about metamorphosis. In fact, Baudrillard states that "metamorphosis is at the root of all seduction" (*EC* 46).[85]

Whether understood as a game or as a strategy, the art of disappearance challenges the art of appearance by using alterity and ambivalence to transform perceptual judgments based on appearances. The challenge that the art of disappearance initiates results in a movement that Baudrillard calls symbolic exchange. Symbolic exchange is the ultimate goal of Baudrillard's rhetorical theory, and it is the subject of the next chapter.

Illustration: The Disappearance of Henrietta Lacks

Baudrillard's rhetorical theory depends, in the second place, on what he calls the art of disappearance. He describes the art of disappearance as a transformation, and he conceives of disappearance using the trope of metamorphosis rather than the tropes of metaphor or metastasis. For Baudrillard, the art of disappearance mobilizes ambivalence and alterity to destroy the perceptual appearances produced by the art of appearance. As this chapter's illustrative section shows, the art of disappearance can be applied to the events involving Henrietta Lacks, her cells, and her family captured in Rebecca Skloot's *The Immortal Life of Henrietta Lacks*. Applying this component of Baudrillard's rhetorical theory to the experiential and textual dimensions of Lacks's story enhances understanding of both the story and the theory. Consequently, this illustration opens by revisiting Baudrillard's May 1999 lecture that mentions Lacks and also by considering Baudrillard's comments for what they reveal about the art of disappearance. Next, the illustration analyzes Lacks's experience and Skloot's book from the perspective of the art of disappearance.

HeLa, or what Baudrillard refers to as Henrietta Lacks's "disseminated body" (*VI* 5), is emblematic of both cloning and immortality for Baudrillard. Cloning, as he explains in his May 1999 lecture, is a "collective fantasy of a return to a non-individuated existence and a destiny of undifferentiated life" or a "temptation to return to an indifferent immortality" (14). In such a fantasy, a perceptual appearance substitutes for reality. In Lacks's case, the immortal clone HeLa substitutes for the mortal original woman. Viewed more abstractly, this substitution is one wherein the inhuman substitutes for the human, and Baudrillard discusses the relationship between them at some length in his lecture on immortality and cloning. He explains that "[h]umankind, alone among all living things, tries to build itself a deathless alter ego and at the same time to perfect natural selection through artificial selection—an act that confers on the human being an absolute privilege" (17–18). He positions the appearance-making that is cloning as a productive process, which builds the inhuman and fosters the perception of immortality. He notes, however, that this productive process fundamentally alters the relationship between the human and the inhuman. He cautions that "at the same time and precisely through this action, humankind puts an end to natural selection, a process that implies, according to the laws of evolution, the death of any given species—including its own" (18). Here, Baudrillard argues that the perception of immortality—a perception constructed by cell culture, HeLa cloning, and the production of the inhuman—devalues mortality. In the relationship between immortality and mortality, the mortal form is perceived as less valuable than the immortal one. This perception further alters the relationship between the inhuman and the human in a way that devalues and fundamentally threatens the human form. "By ending natural selection," Baudrillard concludes, "humankind contravenes symbolic law, and in so doing effectively risks its own disappearance" (18). For him, then, the appearance-making of HeLa the immortal clone occurs simultaneously with the disappearance of Henrietta the mortal human. With respect to his May 1999 lecture and his reference to the events involving Henrietta Lacks, the art of disappearance encompasses everything that is other than HeLa, everything that escapes the value system monopolized by perceptions of immortality. In short, the art of disappearance mobilizes thought and discourse in a way that destroys perceptions of immortality's meaning and value.

Disappearance, as Baudrillard discusses, can be figured in one of three ways—as metaphor, metastasis, or metamorphosis—and all three of these figurations appear in Skloot's book as it maps the relationship between the immortal inhuman HeLa and the mortal human Henrietta. At places in the book, Skloot uses metaphor to figure the relationship between the appearance of HeLa and the disappearance of Henrietta. In these figurations the trope of metaphor maintains the meanings and values associated with the deceased mortal human and merely transfers these same meanings and values to the thriving immortal clone. Accordingly, the trope of metaphor depends on the physiological death of the mortal human. By being figured as death, metaphorical disappearance effects a transfer of values from the dead to the living. Metaphorical disappearance operates rhetorically as well. Perhaps the best example of Skloot metaphorically figuring the relationship between HeLa and Henrietta occurs during Skloot's initial meeting with Sonny, one of Henrietta's three sons. Sonny, who was only four years old when Henrietta died, shares a description of his mother: "She liked takin care of people," he explained; "people always say she was really just hospitality, you know fixin everything up nice" (*The Immortal Life* 159). Henrietta, from what Sonny had heard, was valued for her care, her hospitality, and her ability to fix up things. As he describes his mother's values, Sonny proceeds to transfer these uniquely human values to the inhuman HeLa. He remarks that "it make sense what she did with them cells," and the sense to which Sonny refers here is a metaphorical sense. Like the mortal Henrietta, the immortal HeLa takes care of people by creating "medical miracles like polio vaccines, some cure for cancer and other things, even AIDS" (159). Metaphorically, the immortal cells are hospitable to the point of being able to fix up bodies. In such a figuration, the values of the dead human simply transfer to the inhuman. This transfer elides the disappearance or death of the human, as the human values are preserved even though the human has passed away.

At other places in the book, Skloot figures the relationship between the human and the inhuman using the figure of metastasis. Metastasis is the trope of transport, and it displaces the other in order to repeat itself. The trope of metastasis is, for Baudrillard, indicative of simulacra and a state of hyperreality. Baudrillard, himself, likens metastasis to cloning, so it is not surprising that the figurations involving the trope of metastasis advance the immortal inhuman clone over, above, and beyond the mortal human. According to the trope of metastasis, disappearance is displacement, and the mortal human is displaced by the self-proliferating immortal inhuman.

Physiologically, the unbounded repetition of the immortal and inhuman HeLa cells inside Henrietta's body overwhelmed and displaced her human cells. This act of displacement and metastasis brought about her death. Rhetorically, HeLa began metastasizing in a way that overwhelmed the thought and discourse about Henrietta. Skloot quotes one researcher who observes, "Whenever we read books about science, it's always *HeLa* this and *HeLa* that" (266). The researcher acknowledges that HeLa has effectively displaced Henrietta: "Some people know those are the initials of a person, but they don't know who that person is" (266). Skloot further figures the disappearance of the mortal Henrietta in her description of the Internet searches conducted by Henrietta's daughter Deborah, who received a surprising variety of hits when she searched the Internet for the term *Hela*. She learned, Skloot tells us, that "Hela is the native name for the country of Sri Lanka"; that Hela is "the name of a defunct German tractor company and an award-winning shih-tzu dog"; that Hela is "a seaside resort in Poland, an advertising firm in Switzerland, a Danish boat where people gather to drink vodka and watch films, and a Marvel comic book character who appears in several online games" (254). Accordingly, Skloot's book regularly figures disappearance through the trope of metastasis. This figuration depicts the way in which thought and discourse about the immortal inhuman HeLa rhetorically overwhelm Henrietta and displace the thought and discourse about the mortal human. The rapid transport and productive repetition of the selfsame appearance that is the immortal HeLa leaves little space for anything to challenge appearance-making.

Skloot, however, uses a third figuration for disappearance that is most apt: metamorphosis. As a trope, metamorphosis effects transformation of one thing into another and conveys the way which disappearance of the mortal human Henrietta can offer a corrective challenge to the meaning-making monopoly of the inhuman and immortal HeLa. In his 1999 lecture Baudrillard is quite definitive about the role of transformation, stating, "A form—and life is a form—can only be exchanged with another form, never traded for an equivalent" (*VI* 29). He grounds this assertion about transformation in a discussion of the human, asserting that the "human is that which cannot be traded as currency for any given artificial species, such as clones, even if the clones perform better, are a 'better value'" (28–29). Here, Baudrillard explains that the form of the mortal human defies meaning and value, unlike the immortal clone. This defiance toward exchange value is characteristic of his art of disappearance. Similarly, Henrietta defies exchange value. She, the human, could not be traded like the inhuman cells.

Note here that Skloot's book, quoting from Michael Rogers's 1976 *Rolling Stone* article on HeLa, documents that cell cultures can be "traded" (193).

Beyond noting that HeLa cells could be traded, Skloot's book adeptly figures Henrietta's disappearance using the trope of metamorphosis by suggesting that Henrietta, upon her death, was transformed into a supernatural form of life. Skloot's interviews with Henrietta's family members document this transformation. Her family members recount that, as soon as Henrietta's casket was interred, "rain fell thick and fast" followed by "long rumbling thunder, screams from the babies, and a blast of wind so strong it tore the metal roof off the barn below the cemetery and sent it flying through the air above Henrietta's grave, its long metal slopes flapping like the wings of a giant silver bird" (92). This same storm burned fields, uprooted trees, demolished buildings, and even killed one of Henrietta's relatives. One of Henrietta's cousins all but attributed the storm to Henrietta, exclaiming, "We shoulda knew she was tryin to tell us somethin with that storm" (92). Henrietta's daughter Deborah sensed the deceased Henrietta's supernatural or spiritual form, too. Skloot describes Deborah as believing that her mortal mother Henrietta "lived on" and controlled the lives of those who remembered her (7). According to Deborah, Henrietta arranged marriages and divorces (7), and she even orchestrated car accidents and fires (192). In other words, Skloot's book uses the trope of metamorphosis to transform Henrietta's disappearance into an appearance of a different form. By way of transformation, then, the disappearance of a mortal human form challenges the perceptions of value and meaning that are monopolized by the immortal inhuman form.

It is through the trope of metamorphosis that Skloot uses Henrietta to chart a radical position from which to challenge the value-laden appearance of immortality advanced by HeLa. The disappearance of Henrietta Lacks sets Henrietta apart from the appearance-making enterprise that is HeLa. By way of her disappearance, Henrietta occupies a place from which she can stand against HeLa as other and challenge the value of immortality. By thus presenting readers with a transformed Henrietta—that is, with a supernatural or spiritual form that controls human life—Skloot introduces a radically other position that might challenge the production of immortality through the cloning of HeLa. This supernatural and spiritual realm was, as Skloot herself notes, foreign to her (7). But, for Henrietta's family, this radical alterity, this supernatural otherness, this spiritual transformation "was so much more concrete than the explanation offered by science" (296). Through the death of her mortal earthly body, Henrietta had been transformed into an immortal heavenly body (295). Henrietta had disappeared as a physical human form, only to appear as a spiritual one (295). And, as a spiritual and supernatural—if not superhuman—form, Henrietta can challenge the cellular and scientific—if not subhuman—form that is HeLa. In effect, the disappearance and transformation of Henrietta allows her to escape an in/human value system and an in/human understanding of immortality. From the radically other place of the supernatural and spiritual realm, immortality does not mean the same thing for Henrietta as it does for HeLa. The transformed Henrietta is ambivalent towards immortality and, by way of her placement as a radical other, nullifies the value associated with HeLa's immortality. As Baudrillard contends in his May 1999 lecture, "it makes no sense to oppose the immortality of the Same [*sic*], of repetition, of the clone, of the virus, with a morality of values and differences; it is necessary to oppose *immortality* with the superior *immorality* of forms" (*VI* 29; emphasis original). Put differently, the ambivalence of other forms is what matters for Baudrillard, for Skloot, and for Henrietta.

In sum, the experiences of Henrietta Lacks, her cells, and her family, as well as the text of Skloot's book, rhetorically figure Henrietta's disappearance in terms of a transformation. By disappearing as a life form, Henrietta can appear as a supernatural or spiritual form. Thus, disappearance begets appearance. But, it is through this disappearance-turned-into-an-appearance that the transformed Henrietta can challenge the perceived value of immortality that has been affixed to HeLa. And, so begins symbolic exchange: The rhetorical invention of thought and discourse mounts a radical challenge to a perceived appearance and tropes that perceived appearance into a disappearance. The disappearance, in turn, is concomitantly transformed into an appearance. And, the back-and-forth movement of exchange is sustained.

CHAPTER 6

Symbolic Exchange and Rhetorical Invention

The past two chapters—one detailing Baudrillard's claims about the art of appearance and one detailing his claims about the art of disappearance—both note that the goal, or *telos*, of Baudrillard's rhetorical theory is a movement that he names *symbolic exchange.* So far, *Jean Baudrillard: The Rhetoric of Symbolic Exchange* has only offered fleeting descriptions of symbolic exchange and, otherwise, forgone a thorough exegesis of it. Any extended discussion of symbolic exchange has, to this point, been deferred in favor of profiling the two arts that facilitate it. The present chapter, however, takes up symbolic exchange and offers a treatment of Baudrillard's theoretical goal. As this chapter demonstrates, symbolic exchange proves a thoroughly rhetorical goal on account of its theoretical premises about language use and the expansive notion of invention that it embodies. Drawing on a fundamentally agonistic understanding of the relationship between humans and the world, Baudrillard's notion of symbolic exchange uses rhetorical invention to pit the twin arts of appearance and disappearance against one another.

Symbolic exchange constitutes the goal of Baudrillard's rhetorical theory, and he indicates as much when he unequivocally states, "Exchange must never have an end" (*PW* 16).[1] Baudrillard studies scholars have long acknowledged the importance of symbolic exchange to his work; yet, these same scholars also note the perplexing opacity of the concept. Mike Gane, for one, contends that "symbolic exchange is perhaps the most central of Baudrillard's terms and yet the most allusive" ("Symbolic" 210). The allusiveness of symbolic exchange often dominates its interpretations. Baudrillard studies scholars, Gane among them, frequently attempt to explain symbolic exchange by unpacking the concept's allusions to the work of Marcel Mauss and Georges Bataille (211). While tracing these allusions is helpful in historicizing the concept of symbolic exchange, these anthropological allusions are less helpful to the current project, as they do not directly assist in defining symbolic exchange as the goal of Baudrillard's rhetorical theory. Rhetorical studies scholars might, in other words, take a more direct approach to theorizing symbolic exchange as a rhetorical goal. Indeed, the domain of the symbolic and the activity of exchange are familiar to rhetorical studies scholars, especially those who follow Gerard Hauser in understanding "rhetorical communication" as occurring "whenever one person engages another person in an exchange of symbols to accomplish some goal" (3). Despite the resonance between Hauser's definition of rhetoric and what Gane views as Baudrillard's "most central" construct, Baudrillard's notion of symbolic exchange departs from Hauser's definition of rhetoric in that he positions the exchange relationship as the rhetorical goal. Baudrillard's notion of symbolic exchange is, thus, relational: Symbolic exchange is the optimal relationship between thought, discourse, perception, and human beings. Symbolic exchange, according to Baudrillard, is "a reciprocal arrangement" that links the art of appearance with the art of disappearance in a "parallel concatenation" of "signs, events, affects and passions" (*IEx* 84, 85).[2] Symbolic exchange relates the art of appearance to the art of disappearance, and, as Baudrillard states in an interview with Paul Sutton, the "symbolic exchange between appearing and disappearing is the complete symbolic operation" (*HD* 125–26).

The complete symbolic operation that is symbolic exchange depends on a reversibility between the art of appearance and the art of disappearance. As Baudrillard explains, "[e]verything that appears disappears; everything that disappears can reappear—here there is a symbolic exchange" (*HD* 125–26). In other words, the complete symbolic operation—that is, the movement from appearance to disappearance and from disappearance to appearance—is the troping that Baudrillard ascribes to each art individually. On the one hand, the art of appearance metastasizes to the point of effecting disappearance; on the other hand, the art of disappearance morphs in a way that brings about transformation. Viewed in succession as a back-and-forth movement, these tropings and turnings are what Baudrillard describes as reversibility. Broadly, reversibility is a kind of "turnaround," which, as Baudrillard makes clear, is not a dialectical form (*EC* 87; cf. *BL* 185).[3] On the contrary, he argues that reversibility is "the true symbolic form," in that the relationship between appearance and disappearance is aimed at repeatedly achieving "a reversible effect" (*BL* 175).[4] Appearance and disappearance are, in other words, two sides of the coin that is symbolic exchange; appearance and disappearance are radical reversals of one another, and their "general reversibility" is the movement or symbolic exchange toward which Baudrillard's rhetorical theory strives (*FS* 110).[5] Indeed, Baudrillard understands thought and discourse as constructing and destructing perceptions in order to initiate and sustain the reversible movement of symbolic exchange. "The principle of reversibility," he writes, "requires that all that has been produced must be destroyed, and that which appears must disappear" (*EC* 71).[6] Thus, symbolic exchange entangles the processes that construct perceptions with the processes that destruct perceptions through a relationship of reversibility, where the effects of one art can execute a reverse turn leading into the other art. Here, the emphasis that symbolic exchange places on the effects of thought, discourse, and perception—specifically, that symbolic exchange is a relationship, which reverses effects—implies that the theoretical construct of symbolic exchange is, indeed, a rhetorical goal: symbolic exchange is a relationship brought about by a reversal of the effects of thought, discourse, and perception.

The rhetorical dimensions of symbolic exchange become even more pronounced when the reversible relationship is also understood as an agonistic one. By describing symbolic exchange as an agonistic duel, Baudrillard invokes the concept of agon to underscore the rhetorical dimensions of symbolic exchange. Agonism, as rhetorical studies scholars such as John Poulakos, Jeffrey Walker, and Debra Hawhee have observed, aided the theorization of rhetoric in classical times. In *Sophistical Rhetoric in Classical Greece*, for instance, Poulakos offers an overview of the ancient use of agonism, observing that Isocrates casts his text "*Antidosis* in the form of a legal *agon*" in order to "reverse" public opinion of sophistic rhetoric and that Plato uses the term *agon* (ἀγών) to connote both a trial and a competition (135; emphasis original; 37). Walker, in *Rhetoric and Poetics in Antiquity*, glosses the persona of Theognis from the *Theognidea* as framing the "rhetorical encounter" of poetic discourse as an encounter "in which the speaker, as a competitor in an *agôn* with other voices, attempts to persuade/seduce to choose and keep him as a companion, mentor, and ethical model" (148). Walker further notes that "*agôn* does not preclude, either, the arguing of unconventional positions" (158). Hawhee, in "Agonism and Aretê," concludes that "agon, especially during the time of the sophists, produced a style of rhetorical training based on movement" (205). Since agonism—at least as it intersects with rhetoric—is associated with forms, reversals, competition, seduction, and movement, it is no wonder that Baudrillard chose to describe the symbolic exchange relationship as an agonistic one. In fact, he views "radical antagonism" as "the key" to the whole relationship of symbolic exchange (*BL* 140; cf. *PW* 82). Reversibility is, for him, a "supple and antagonistic strategy" (*EC* 89).[7] At places in his writing, he seems to foreground symbolic exchange's agonism over its reversibility, referring to the "antagonistic force" of symbolic exchange (*LP* 193).[8] According to David McFarlane, Baudrillard's writing actually makes theory "*a total agonistic process*" by manifesting symbolic exchange in writing (emphasis original). Baudrillard further connects agonism with duality, arguing, "The dual form, the *agon*, is a symbolic form" (*LP* 161; emphasis original).[9] Here, he plays on the French for the word *dual* (*duel*)—which, as David Teh recognizes, is also the French word for the English *duel*—in order to compare symbolic exchange to an antagonistic battle ("Baudrillard"). Teh, in fact, argues that a crucial component of Baudrillard's symbolic exchange "is best summed up" in the homonym of duel and dual, where *duel* designates agonism and *dual* "is a logical trope, standing for the logic of the double" ("Baudrillard"). Indeed, the dual relationship that Baudrillard associates with symbolic exchange corresponds to the "duel" that, for him, resides "at the heart of language" (*TE* 144).[10] This duel is one in which appearance and disappearance perpetually battle each other by using thought and discourse to construct and destruct perceptions.

Understanding symbolic exchange as a rhetorical goal—and, more specifically, a rhetorical relationship involving the movement of reversibility and the antagonism of the duel—allows rhetorical studies scholars to better understand Baudrillard's position on communication. Of course, chapter 4 of the present study establishes that Baudrillard associates instrumental and pragmatic communication with the art of appearance and also that he detests the overproduction of communication. His views, here, surely support the observation of rhetorical studies scholars Sonja K. Foss, Karen A. Foss, and Robert Trapp, who recognize that Baudrillard prefers "the term *symbolic exchange* instead of *communication*" (303; emphasis original). Baudrillard's terminological preference stresses his theoretical preference, too, in that the goal of his rhetorical theory is symbolic exchange and not communication.

In an essay titled "The Vanishing Point of Communication," Baudrillard explains his disdain for communication on account of what it does to the goal of his rhetorical theory. His rhetorical theory presupposes that communication threatens the relationship that is symbolic exchange to the point of rendering symbolic exchange a failure. Baudrillard writes that the "presupposition" of his theory is that "the failure of speech and symbolic exchange is the basis for the principle of communication" ("Vanishing" 16). The threat of communication is the threat of the overproduced appearance of meaning and value, the effects of which would dominate the relationship that is symbolic exchange, stalling any movement and squelching any agonism between appearance and disappearance. Making perceptions appear to have meaning and value via the art of appearance risks, as Baudrillard cautions, extinguishing exchange and cutting sensory experiences out of the symbolic realm. In fact, Baudrillard argues that communication amounts to an "abduction of all the senses, of looking, of touching, of smelling, of all the potential violence of exchange" ("Vanishing" 17). Communication removes humans from their senses, from their worlds, and from their relations. In other words, Baudrillard understands communication as depending on the failure of the symbolic exchange relationship; as he acknowledges, this failure "has consequences for the failure of all human relations" ("Vanishing" 17). By taking symbolic exchange as its goal, Baudrillard's rhetorical theory takes an optimal relationship—a relationship wherein using thought, discourse, and perception instrumentally (to make meaning and value appear) does not usurp the antagonistic and reversible relationship between humans and their world—as its goal. This optimal rhetorical relationship is, therefore, one in which the alterity and ambivalence of disappearance challenge the meaning-making and value-laden art of appearance. Symbolic exchange is, to be sure, a rhetorical relationship, since both the arts of appearance and disappearance invent thought and discourse to either construct or destruct perceptions. As the next section details, symbolic exchange is a relationship that pivots on Baudrillard's expansive notion of rhetorical invention.

Invention, Perception, and the World

Rhetorical invention sits at the heart of Baudrillard's rhetorical theory. Indeed, he champions invention; he sees processes of invention driving the art of appearance and fueling the art of disappearance. The invention of thought and discourse allows both of these arts to engage one another and to relate to one another in symbolic exchange. The symbolic exchange relationship can, as this section will argue, be understood as a relationship founded on rhetorical invention, and Baudrillard's work positions it as such. By analogy, symbolic exchange is the inventional pivot that relates the art of appearance to the art of disappearance. Baudrillard's rhetorical theory depends on this pivot and its expansive notion of rhetorical invention to sustain the reversible movement and agonistic duel between both arts. The inventional pivot that is symbolic exchange attempts to effect movement between appearance and disappearance, and Baudrillard's work can be understood not only as describing this pivot but also pushing this pivot into movement.

Baudrillard distinguishes invention from discovery, and the distinction he draws between them offers symbolic exchange wide license to relate the construction of perceptions via the art of appearance to the destruction of perceptions via the art of disappearance. Discovery, for Baudrillard, extinguishes possibility and limits perception, whereas invention engenders possibility and emboldens perception. He formulates this distinction when he writes that "what one has discovered, one can never invent" (*PC* 98).[11] For him, discovery and invention are mutually exclusive concepts, with invention preferred over discovery because it allows for more possibility and different perceptions. Baudrillard illustrates the advantages of invention in two understated references—one to the discovery of America and one to the discovery of objective reality. With respect to America, Baudrillard's reference invokes the lines of thought and discourse that advance the perception that some explorer, such as Christopher Columbus, *discovered* America: "We always thought that things were passively waiting to be discovered, in much the same way that America is imagined to have been waiting for Columbus" (*VI* 76; cf. *PC* 98). But, as he notes, the perception that privileges discovery simply "is not so"; instead, "it is actually a sort of invention" (*VI* 76). America, Baudrillard would suggest, is a perception that has been invented. The reference to America allows him to make the point that more possibilities and perceptions are opened up through invention—including the possibility that the appearance of discovery manufactured by human perception is deceiving. Similarly, he observes that the dominant lines of thought and discourse advance the perception that objective reality was discovered—that the principle of reality, like America, is perceived to be an immutable thing, a given. As an alternative to this perception of reality, he suggests that humans might have "invented reality, which remains to be discovered" (*PC* 98).[12] Indeed, as these illustrations show, Baudrillard finds discoveries limiting to human perception. Discovery attempts to separate things from perceptions and then fix the meaning of those things, while invention sees things *as* perceptions and then duels with those perceptions. Baudrillard, for his part, prefers invention—that is, he prefers to duel with perception. In a 1991 interview, he describes his own thought and writing, including his work on simulation and simulacra, as efforts in service of his desire "to invent another game, to talk about something else" (*BL* 205).

As two kinds of art, appearance and disappearance have rhetorical invention in common, and it is on this basis that they relate to one another: "one has to take art as an attempt," Baudrillard states, "to invent" (*BL* 59; cf. *RC* 27).[13] Art, for him, aims to invent new thought and discourse that either produce perceptions or challenge them. Therefore, Baudrillard's art of appearance as well as his art of disappearance can be understood as grounded in invention. The invention of particular perceptions made possible by the art of appearance opens up, in turn, new possibilities for destructing those appearances. Baudrillard understands the art of appearance and the communication it produces as "*invented* structures of relations where humans communicate without passing each other, without touching each other, without looking at each other" ("Vanishing" 17; emphasis added). Here he suggests that the art of appearance is, at root, rhetorical invention. Likewise, he suggests that the art of disappearance is, at root, rhetorical invention when he claims that the art is "an *invention* of strategems" that correspond to alterity and ambivalence (*EC* 75; emphasis added; cf. *S* 98; *FS* 228)[14] or that the art of disappearance consists of "inventing the other" (*PC* 120).[15]

Beyond referring to appearance and disappearance as separate artistic inventions, Baudrillard also makes clear that the relationship between appearance and disappearance is a relationship constituted through a radically expansive notion of rhetorical invention, or what Baudrillard terms symbolic exchange. In short, the reversible relationship between the two art forms is a relationship that is, at root, rhetorical invention. The stress that Baudrillard places on invention as constitutive of symbolic exchange is arguably most pronounced in one of his final writings, *Why Hasn't Everything Already Disappeared?* In its opening paragraphs, he focuses his thought and his discourse on the "art of disappearance," asserting that "[t]he human species is doubtless the only one to have invented a specific mode of disappearance" (*WD* 10).[16] This assertion is important, not only for the emphasis it places on invention—in that it reinforces his view that the art of disappearance is rooted in rhetorical invention—but also for the way it opens up into a broader discussion that links invention to symbolic exchange. The invention of disappearance, as Baudrillard proceeds to note, is concomitantly the invention of appearance: "It is when a thing is beginning to disappear that the concept appears" (12).[17] This statement might also be understood in reverse, so that appearance begets disappearance. Either way, symbolic exchange is the expansive notion of rhetorical invention on which this relationship pivots.

The move from appearance to disappearance, or from disappearance to appearance, depends on rhetorical invention. Baudrillard solidifies this point in *Why Hasn't Everything Already Disappeared?* by building upon the work of Hannah Arendt. "If we look closely," he writes, "we see that the real world begins, in the modern age, with the decision to transform the world, and to do so by the means of science, analytical knowledge and the implementation of technology—that is to say that it begins, in Hannah Arendt's words, with the invention of an Archimedean point outside the world" (10).[18] Baudrillard's mention of Arendt's work here and her discussion of "an Archimedean point" helps him advance an argument about rhetorical invention—namely, that invention mediates the construction and destruction of the appearances produced by human perception. To be sure, he positions this Archimedean point as a rhetorical invention: The point is marked by thought and discourse that construct certain perceptions and destruct others. Viewed from Baudrillard's perspective as a rhetorical invention, the point engenders a paradoxical, perhaps antagonistic, exchange: "the real world begins, paradoxically, to disappear at the very same time as it begins to exist" (11).[19] Thus, invention enables appearance and begets disappearance, or, conversely, invention enables disappearance and begets appearance. In the end, symbolic exchange is the relationship between appearance and disappearance, a relationship rooted in rhetorical invention.

To clarify the point that symbolic exchange is a kind of expansive rhetorical invention—a point crucial to Baudrillard's rhetorical theory—the opening paragraphs of *Why Hasn't Everything Already Disappeared?* merit closer examination. Indeed, its opening lines summon the reader to consider processes of appearance alongside processes of disappearance: "Let us speak," writes Baudrillard, "of the world from which human beings have disappeared" (9).[20] Speaking, of course, is indicative of a process of appearance. Speaking or oratory is the quintessential rhetorical activity, and, traditionally, the human rhetor is central to the act of speech. At the same time, however, the speech that Baudrillard theorizes is speech of a world absent humans. Evidently, this invocation to discourse is inherently paradoxical and radically antagonistic to any notion of subjective agency. The antagonism turns an appearance into disappearance. What is more, this paradoxical summons to discourse follows a four-line epigraph of an altered quotation from Raymond Queneau's poem "The Explanation of Metaphors" (73 n. 4). Thus, the opening lines of this piece move from an epigraph that references metaphor to a turning or troping indicative of metastasis or perhaps metamorphosis. Clearly, the inventive troping—metaphor, metastasis, and metamorphosis—that enables symbolic exchange occupies a prominent place in this piece and stresses the rhetorical dimensions of Baudrillard's work on appearance and disappearance.

Following the summons to discourse in the opening lines, Baudrillard references Arendt's discussion of the Archimedean point, which enables him to contend that invention allows for the movement between the appearance of perception and its disappearance. Baudrillard, in other words, is focused on the rhetorical invention that enables pivoting between appearance and disappearance. Arendt, as Steven Mailloux reminds, attended Martin Heidegger's 1924–25 lectures on Plato's *Sophist* (53–54), and perhaps nowhere in Arendt's work are these lectures more influential than in *The Human Condition.* In *The Human Condition,* Arendt discusses the Archimedean point and Galileo's invention of the telescope, and this discussion can be read as focusing on perception's role in initiating and sustaining relations between humans and their world. Repeatedly Arendt comments on the duality of the telescope invention, which "at once adjusted to human sense and destined to uncover what definitely and forever must lie beyond them" and which "put within the grasp of an earth-bound creature and its body-bound senses what had seemed forever beyond his [*sic*] reach, at best open to the uncertainties of speculation and imagination" (258, 260). Invention, Arendt surmises, constructs perceptions and simultaneously destructs perceptions, and her discussion of invention harbors a sense of the paradox and antagonism on which Baudrillard concentrates. Arendt's point is that Galileo's invention demonstrates "both the worst fear and the most presumptuous hope of human speculation, the ancient fear that our senses, our very organs for the reception of reality, might betray us, and the Archimedean wish for a point outside the earth from which to unhinge the world" (262). For Arendt, invention pivots between the appearance of perception and the disappearance of perception, and it is upon this view of perception—perceptions that pivot on the invention of thought and discourse—that Baudrillard builds his rhetorical theory.

In *Why Hasn't Everything Already Disappeared?* Baudrillard expands Arendt's discussion of the Archimedean point, extending it to the domain of language, representation, and naming. He declares that "[t]he moment a thing is named, the moment representation and concepts take a hold of it, is the moment when it begins to lose energy—with the risk that it will become a truth or impose itself as ideology" (12).[21] Indeed, Baudrillard's declaration here is a claim about invention as it manifests itself as the relationship between appearance and disappearance. He continues, noting that, "[b]y representing things to ourselves, by naming them and conceptualizing them, human beings call them into existence and at the same time hasten their doom" (11).[22] With good reason, many rhetorical studies scholars would be inclined to focus on Baudrillard's comments regarding representation and naming, two processes that have traditionally attracted attention within the field. For example, Baudrillard's view seems to align with Raymie McKerrow's fourth principle of critical rhetorical studies—a principle stressing that "terms are contingently based" and holding that the act of naming constitutes the "central symbolic act of a *nominalist* rhetoric" (105–06; emphasis original). But Baudrillard's point is not so much about naming, representation, technology, science, or even knowledge; instead, he invokes Arendt and then extends her discussion to the domain of language to make a point about the invention processes that create and destroy perception. These invention processes are rhetorical—that is, they are an amalgamation of thought, discourse, and senses—and they enable the movement or pivoting that is symbolic exchange. The Archimedean point and Baudrillard's own point is, in short, all about invention. Invention possesses the power to transform perceptions, by turning an appearance into a disappearance, pivoting between the two, and moving in what Baudrillard calls symbolic exchange.

Advancing Rhetorical Hypotheses

By endorsing an expansive view of invention as the basis for relating appearance to disappearance, Baudrillard erects a theoretical framework that will allow him to argue that symbolic exchange is rhetorical and, likewise, that the reversible arts of appearance and disappearance are expressly rhetorical. Symbolic exchange is, as this chapter has argued, a reversible movement and an antagonistic relationship, which together serve as the goal of Baudrillard's rhetorical theory. The invention-based movement relationship that is symbolic exchange has, to this point, been described as uniting two subspecies of art; but, as Baudrillard makes clear throughout his work, these subspecies of art are thoroughly rhetorical in that they are each hypotheses. Baudrillard contends that when he speaks or writes "it's always a hypothesis" (*BL* 205). Since his work on both appearance and disappearance constitutes particular lines of thought and discourse that embrace possibility related to perceptions of language use, he uses the word *hypothesis* (*hypothèse*) to describe both arts. As the claims he makes about appearance and disappearance show, he invents these two arts and labels them *hypotheses* to signal that his propositions concerning both appearance and disappearance not only depart from past thinkers but also embrace possibility without regard to fact ("Hypothesis," entry 1).

For Baudrillard, the art of appearance, the process of simulation, and the products of simulacra constitute a hypothesis. In *Simulacra and Simulation*, he labels simulation and simulacra as the "most interesting hypothesis" among other hypotheses (80),[23] and he repeatedly asks his reader to consider these hypotheses in relation to other hypotheses (79, 86). Indeed, the hypothesis of simulation and simulacra becomes most interesting when it is understood in relation to the hypothesis of the reality principle. Since reality is often taken as a discovery, the reality principle constrains the invention of hypotheses. Humans, according to Baudrillard, speak of the principle of reality as a limit to particular hypotheses, in the sense that reality is "what all hypotheses run up against" (*PC* 101).[24] He advances his theory of simulation and simulacra in order to test the principle of reality and explore the boundaries of thought and discourse. His work on simulation and simulacra can thus be understood as running "[c]ontrary to what is said about [reality]" (101)[25] in two senses: first, within view of the overproduced appearance of reality and, second, within view of the concealed disappearance of reality. Viewed in terms of the art of appearance, Baudrillard's writings on simulation and simulacra advance a hypothesis that is a means to exchange between appearance and disappearance. He describes the evolution of his own thought with respect to simulation, simulacra, and communication as a series of hypotheses that he "maintained" and "changed" (*BL* 87). Viewing "the hypothesis of manipulation, mystification, and alienation" as "too conventional," Baudrillard felt it necessary "to seek out another hypothesis" (87). He "turned this hypothesis around" and "invert[ed]" the hypothesis so as to make it "more interesting" (87, 88, 88). In effect, he reversed his hypothesis about the art of appearance and turned it into a hypothesis about the art of disappearance.

Like appearance, disappearance is an assertion that embraces possibility, and, subsequently, disappearance can be understood as a hypothesis. Baudrillard admits as much when he claims that "nothing distinguishes the hypotheses from the assertion" (*EC* 101).[26] He also recognizes that, with respect to the art of appearance, "there is nothing to rule out the paradoxical hypothesis" (*IEx* 88).[27] Indeed, since he defines the goal of his rhetorical theory in terms of a reversible exchange, his rhetorical theory seems to necessitate that the hypothesis of the art of appearance be countered by a reverse hypothesis—namely, the hypothesis of the art of disappearance. Baudrillard sums up the hypothesis of disappearance as believing "for a single instant the hypothesis that there is a fatal and enigmatic bias in the order of things" (*FS* 230).[28] This is "the hypothesis of a fatal strategy," which, Baudrillard acknowledges, "must itself be fatal too" (229).[29] Put differently, he understands the hypothesis of disappearance as keeping with the characteristics of disappearance, including alterity and ambivalence. Thus, the hypothesis of disappearance effects a transformation by being radically other than the hypothesis of appearance and by being meaningless and worthless in comparison to the hypothesis of appearance. He explains that the hypothesis of disappearance proves an "enthralling hypothesis" for the way it moves "in the opposite direction" to the meaning-making value-laden hypothesis of appearance (*PC* 53).[30] To be sure, Baudrillard "celebrates" the "changeless character" of the hypothesis of disappearance, suggesting that there is something predictable about alterity and ambivalence with respect to bringing about transformation: "If you are aware of the sign of an appearance, then the hypothesis of fatality," he writes, "allows us to predict the event, the event coming with a sure sign" (194).[31] The event to which he refers here is the event of disappearance, or the destruction of perceptual appearance.

Baudrillard's twin hypotheses are inventions that pivot back and forth in symbolic exchange, and the movement between them is, of course, the goal of his rhetorical theory. Symbolic exchange is grounded in rhetorical invention, for the exchange relationship between the hypotheses of appearance and disappearance depends on the invention of thought and discourse that pivot in accordance with the tropes of metastasis and metamorphosis. Baudrillard, in fact, sees all hypotheses as possessing the potential to pivot between the construction of perceptions and the destruction of perceptions, and this view attests to the expansiveness of his conception of invention. Invention encompasses all possibilities and all perceptions—even those that are fundamentally opposed to one another—allowing hypotheses to move, turn, and pivot. In fact, he describes the relationship between the hypothesis of appearance and that of disappearance as a "situation of two hypotheses which are incompatible" (*HD* 66; cf. *VI* 55). His comments, here, prove that the symbolic exchange relationship is not a dialectical one: No third hypothesis will emerge from the relationship between appearance and disappearance, and no theoretical compromise will take place. For Baudrillard, rhetorical invention is the only link between these two antagonistic hypotheses, and it is only by way of invention that these hypotheses duel. Indeed, the two reversible hypotheses might even be conceptualized as one hypothesis concerning the duality of the symbolic exchange relationship.

Baudrillard clarifies the exchange relationship between the two hypotheses through a comparison to an iceberg. The "iceberg hypothesis" maintains that appearance is the portion of the exchange relationship "showing above the water," while disappearance is "the submerged part" (*IEx* 94).[32] "There is no break between them," he explains, "just a water-line," and the twin hypotheses "are secretly formed of a single substance, of a single mass which, on occasion, flips over" (94).[33] Here, Baudrillard's comparison of an iceberg to symbolic exchange makes four important points about the hypotheses of appearance and disappearance. First, the comparison underscores the notion that appearances are only one half of the exchange relationship he proposes. Second, no break exists between the appearance and disappearance; rather, the two hypotheses depend on invention as a waterline or pivot, which either marks or moves the transformation into the other. Third, the comparison notes occasions during which the relationship flips, turns, or reverses. Fourth, and perhaps most importantly, the comparison in no uncertain terms argues that appearance and disappearance are made of the same substance. The current study—also in no uncertain terms—unequivocally contends that the "single substance" from which the hypotheses of appearance and disappearance are formed is rhetoric, and this contention receives support from Baudrillard's discussion of the reversibility between these two dueling hypotheses.

For all of his tacit presentation of his invented hypotheses as rhetoric, his discussion of the reversibility of hypotheses explicitly positions them as rhetoric. The potential of any hypothesis to flip, turn, or pivot emphasizes what Baudrillard describes as the "reversible continuity of hypotheses" (*SS* 18).[34] He views all propositions as capable of reversal, hence the continuity he finds among all hypotheses. By framing all hypotheses as reversible, he suggests that all thought and discourse are susceptible to symbolic exchange—that is, a radical antagonistic challenge from an opposing rhetorical invention; or, a transformative movement between metastatic appearance and metamorphic disappearance. Just as all invented hypotheses are susceptible to a reversal or an exchange, Baudrillard's own hypotheses are susceptible to reversal and dependent on a fundamental opposition for that movement. To be sure, he describes his writing and speech as "always" consisting of "these 'reversible' hypotheses" (*UB* 97; cf. *DL* 33) that promote exchange.[35]

The reversible, oppositional relationship, which grounds itself in invention and unites Baudrillard's hypotheses is, as he states in a 1996 interview, rhetorical: "Oppositions of this kind still have something rhetorical about them" (*CA* 233).[36] As the original French makes clear, Baudrillard uses the term *rhetoric* (*rhétorique*) to comment on the fundamental reversibility of all invented hypotheses. Within the context of the interview, he deploys the term *rhetoric* to characterize comments he made about the relationship between the writings of Antonin Artaud and those of Alfred Jarry. More specifically, his comments place Artaud's relation to the world and to language in opposition to Jarry's relation to the same. According to Baudrillard, the opposition in how these writers relate to the world and to language is a rhetorical opposition. Artaud "wanted to recreate reality, or attempted to recover a level of reality," whereas Jarry played "morbid games" and wrote in a way that signaled "the end of reality" and "[t]he irruption of a vision of the world" (*CA* 232, 225, 233).[37] Importantly, Baudrillard's comment on the rhetorical nature of this opposition is not restricted to the one opposition between Artaud and Jarry; rather, his comment references a specific kind of opposition that maintains a rhetorical dimension (233). The "kind" of opposition in which Baudrillard finds something rhetorical is, upon closer examination, the same kind of opposition that constitutes the symbolic exchange relationship. In fact, in the opposition that Baudrillard invents between the two writers, Artaud stands in for the hypothesis of appearance and Jarry for the hypothesis of disappearance. Thus, Baudrillard's comments about a kind of opposition maintaining something rhetorical about it are, more precisely, comments about the rhetorical basis of the antagonistic and reversible relationship of symbolic exchange.

Baudrillard's use of the word *rhetorical* in this 1996 interview is but one instance of him presenting the goal of his rhetorical theory as explicitly rhetorical. The "kind" of opposition to which he refers in this statement is a symbolic opposition, and this kind of opposition—a reversible, antagonistic duel between the hypotheses of appearance and disappearance—surely does have something rhetorical about it. The fact that Baudrillard uses the term *rhetoric* as an adjective (*de rhétorique*: i.e., *rhetorical*) to describe the foundational relationship upon which he invents all of his writing, speech, and photography promotes Baudrillard's appearance as a rhetorical theorist and further warrants the study of him as such. In fact, Baudrillard invokes the term *rhetoric* in over forty places throughout his published writings, interviews, and addresses. Heretofore, all of these forty-some occurrences have been overlooked by rhetorical studies scholars. Furthermore, the fact that he used the word *rhetorical* to classify a kind of opposition that he proposed himself directs scholarly attention to the effect of Baudrillard's own words and speech. Put differently, a rhetorical understanding of Baudrillard's own position with respect to his hypotheses necessitates a consideration of the effect of such hypotheses—that is, the ability of such hypotheses to construct or destruct human perceptions and, thereby, sustain symbolic exchange. Such a consideration leads into Baudrillard's final, and most explicitly rhetorical, point about these rhetorical hypotheses—namely, that the effects of his hypotheses are conditioned upon refutation.

Affecting Exchange through Refutation

Since symbolic exchange is the goal of Baudrillard's rhetorical theory, the hypothesis of appearance and the hypothesis of disappearance can both be understood as attempting to invent thought and discourse that bring about and sustain reversibility and movement. Accordingly, the efficacy of either hypothesis necessitates exchange or movement, and Baudrillard contends that the efficacy of either one is conditioned upon disconfirmation or refutation. "The theoretical ideal," writes Baudrillard, "would be to set in place propositions in such a way that they could be disconfirmed" (*PC* 100).[38] In other words, Baudrillard views an effective hypothesis as a proposition that invites refutation. Effective hypotheses—or, effective rhetorical inventions—promote oppositional movement between appearance and disappearance. The oppositional movement, which is made possible by the ability of a hypothesis to be refuted, is the symbolic exchange that constitutes the goal of his rhetorical theory. Thus, in order to be deemed effective, the hypotheses of appearance and disappearance must invite refutation—that is, they must meet the condition of refutability.

The condition of refutability that Baudrillard outlines for his hypotheses indicates that his rhetorical theory encourages a kind of rigorous testing or challenging. Indeed, Baudrillard describes the invention of hypotheses as an attempt at bringing about a refutation. In the essay "Radical Thought," for instance, he reflects upon the aim of his hypothesis of appearance, writing, "you put forward the idea of simulacrum, without really believing in it, even hoping that the world will refute it (the guarantee of scientificity for Popper)" (*PC* 102).[39] Here, his comments clarify that the hypothesis of appearance and the metastasized troping of simulation and simulacra were invented so as to elicit a refutation. By invoking the work of Karl Popper, Baudrillard implies that his hypotheses are propositions that can be tested and refuted—that is, disconfirmed or falsified. Popper, in *The Logic of Scientific Discovery*, articulates the same argument. Popper endorses falsifiability over verifiability as the logical criterion for science, stating, "I shall not require of a scientific system that it shall be capable of being singled out, once and for all, in a positive sense; but I shall require that its logical form shall be such that it can be singled out, by means of empirical tests, in a negative sense: *it must be possible for an empirical scientific system to be refuted by experience*" (40–41; emphasis original). Here, Popper distinguishes the concept of falsifiability from the truth-seeking concept of verification that drives logical positivism. Similarly, Baudrillard contends that all hypotheses are reversible and, therefore, that it remains possible to refute all hypotheses. This contention unseats any singular hypothesis from being perceived as a positive truth. Indeed, Baudrillard contends that "there will never be any way of verifying" his hypotheses, as "[v]erification is practically impossible" (*HD* 66). Since both thinkers avoid making truth claims about hypotheses, Popper's concept of falsifiability bolsters Baudrillard's notion of reversibility. Both Popper and Baudrillard understand a particular hypothesis as capable of being tested until it is falsified—that is, challenged, overtaken, superseded—by another hypothesis.

Key to the falsification described by Popper and the refutation emphasized by Baudrillard is the relationship between perception and experience. Popper's notion of falsifiability not only guards against the perception that any single hypothesis is true, but it also understands that perceptions of hypotheses are falsified by experience. Likewise, Baudrillard's notion of refutation, in addition to unseating truth claims, requires that perceptual appearances be challenged by experience—namely, experience characterized by alterity and ambivalence, or otherwise associated with the hypothesis of disappearance. Importantly, his understanding of refutation is not merely issuing a hypothesis that patently negates or subtly substitutes for an established perception. Such an exchange of perceptions is akin to the rhetoric of the Sophist, as described by Plato in the *Sophist* dialogue, and this kind of trading in appearances would draw only on the resources of the art of appearance. Without challenging perceptual appearances through experiences of ambivalence or alterity, no symbolic exchange would be effected, and the goal of Baudrillard's rhetorical theory would neither be initiated nor sustained. His rhetorical theory is, in other words, not content to produce exchange by manufacturing appearance upon appearance, upon appearance. Such an appearance-making venture would simply mirror the process of simulation that he describes. Rather, an effective hypothesis, for Baudrillard, is a hypothesis that is capable of refutation, falsification, or disconfirmation and is, therefore, capable of promoting exchange between the art of appearance and the art of disappearance. Promoting symbolic exchange between appearance and disappearance necessitates a testing of a perception against experience characteristic of disappearance, and the efficacy of a given hypothesis can be understood as conditioned upon this test. Thus, an effective hypothesis for Baudrillard is one that is tested against experience—more specifically, tested against the experience of the rhetor in the world.

To return to the example of Baudrillard's hypothesis of appearance, it becomes clear that, because the hypothesis advances a proposition that understands the production of discourse and thought as a self-perpetuating, self-proliferating, and controlling endeavor, the proposition presents a barrier for this particular hypothesis to effect exchange. The hypothesis, as Baudrillard explains, might initially be understood as self-confirming. He describes the "idea of the simulacrum" as "a conceptual weapon against reality" (*CA* 171).[40] He views his rhetorical invention as a means to provoke reality, challenge reality, and elicit a refutation from reality. However, he explains that reality never appears to refute the hypothesis (*PC* 102; *CA* 170). Rather, in accordance with the metastasized rhetorical tropings of the simulacra, the hypothesis is taken for reality. Baudrillard writes that "[r]eality absorbed the simulacrum and now adorns itself in all of the rhetoric of simulation" (*CA* 171).[41] Here, with another explicit mention of rhetoric, he explains that, initially, the simulation and simulacra hypothesis forecloses the condition of refutability by playing a game of appearances only. In yet another instance where he uses the term *rhetoric*, Baudrillard stresses the fundamental position of simulacra as the products of rhetoric—that is, "the rhetoric of simulation" (*PC* 102)[42]—and names them as such. As rhetoric, simulacra possess the ability to dupe humans by concealing the absence of reality through prolific substitution or metastasized troping. Troping makes refutation difficult, perhaps impossible, in the sense that it folds the condition of refutation back upon itself: Refuting reality becomes a refutation of simulacra. The refutation of a concealed substitution that marks the absence of a principle, ultimately, implies presence, or the presence of something. Viewed as such, the metastasized tropings of simulacra result in the theoretical equivalent of a double negative, turning the condition of refutation into a kind of impenetrable confirmation and foreclosing the possibility of refutation. Rather than maintaining the condition of refutation, the hypothesis of appearance might very well be understood as guaranteeing confirmation and extinguishing symbolic exchange. The metastasized tropings of the appearance hypothesis threaten the effectiveness of Baudrillard's thought and discourse.

Against these metastasized tropings, Baudrillard manages to offer up two types of experiences. The first type of experience that he offers amounts to a chronicling of his own experiences as a rhetor who sees his hypothesis run in a self-confirming circuit. At a number of places—among them a 1991 interview with Monique Arnaud and Mike Gane and, again, in his 1995 essay "Radical Thought"—Baudrillard describes the paradox in which he, as rhetor, found himself. He writes that seeing his hypothesis confirm itself was an experience where "you are disarmed by the lamentable confirmation of your words by an unscrupulous reality" (*PC* 102).[43] Stating that "the simulacrum hypothesis deserved better than to become a reality" (*CA* 92), he makes it clear that he regrets that the "simulacrum has become reality" (171).[44] Baudrillard further refers to this experience as a "trick" and as a "travesty" (*CA* 171; *PC* 101),[45] in the sense that the hypothesis's rhetorical tropings render the condition of refutation and the goal of symbolic exchange all the more difficult to achieve. Offering a blunt assessment of the efficacy of hypothesis on his own rhetorical practice, Baudrillard states that, "when what you have said becomes true, when it is confirmed by everything around you—then suddenly you find that you have nothing more to say" (*BL* 205). This first type of experience that Baudrillard describes suggests, at first glance, that his simulation and simulacra hypothesis failed to meet the condition of refutation and, therefore, functioned ineffectively as a means to radical exchange between appearance and disappearance. Of course, in keeping with his expansive understanding of rhetorical invention, there is always the possibility that what ostensibly looks like an ineffective failure might be understood as an effective success, and this possibility leads to a different kind of experience that Baudrillard uses to test perception.

The second type of experience that Baudrillard holds up against the metastasized hypothesis of appearance suggests that having "nothing more to say" might be the very strategy he uses to test the perceptions advanced and hyperrealized in his hypothesis. Baudrillard writes that simulacra, having taken up the rhetoric of simulation, mask or conceal "the continuity of nothing" (*PC* 102)[46] or "the continuity of Nothingness" (*CA* 171).[47] Thus, saying nothing and drawing on experiences that reveal the nothingness behind appearances of something offers him a way to satisfy the condition of refutability. Clearly, for Baudrillard's hypothesis to be deemed an effective hypothesis—that is, a hypothesis that invites refutation according to the principle of falsifiability—experiences must be marshaled against the perceptions advanced by the hypothesis. He must locate experiences that seem to align with the hypothesis of disappearance, challenge the hypothesis of appearance, and, thereby, offer grounds for refutation. Indeed, much of Baudrillard's work marshals isolated experiences that test his hypothesis of appearance. In such work he might be seen as presenting test cases—from the attacks on the World Trade Center (cf. *ST*) to the photography of an object (cf. *AA*; *PH*; Bonnal)—that he views as refuting perceptual appearances and, therefore, meeting the condition of falsifiability. These test cases are ones in which the unchecked production of meaning and value disappear through alterity and ambivalence. They are cases through which he challenges appearance-making and, thus, serve as a means to symbolic exchange between appearance and disappearance. These are the experiences wherein seemingly foreclosed systems "end up turning on themselves without intending to, and skidding" (*FF* 120; *BL* 125). These experiences provide Baudrillard with a ground for refutation, and, as such, they preserve the effectiveness of his hypothesis, a hypothesis he once described as "a rather effective one" (*FF* 120; *BL* 125).

Situating Symbolic Exchange

The relationship between the hypotheses of appearance and disappearance, a relationship rooted in invention and brought about through refutation, proves crucial to Baudrillard's rhetorical theory. As this chapter has demonstrated, the symbolic exchange relationship constitutes the goal of Baudrillard's rhetorical theory, and the efficacy of rhetoric, for him, depends on the movement inherent to this relationship. On at least one occasion—a 1995 interview with Roy Boyne and Scott Lash titled "Symbolic Exchange: Taking Theory Seriously"—Baudrillard describes the symbolic exchange relationship as a situation, stating definitively that his theory results in a "situation of two hypotheses" (*HD* 66). This statement is particularly interesting to rhetorical studies scholars, for the study of rhetoric is often grounded in the various situations that provide "the full context of a rhetorical event" (Farrell and Young 35). Indeed, Lloyd F. Bitzer's theory of the rhetorical situation has, for decades, dominated the study of rhetoric. Bitzer's theory defines the rhetorical situation as a complex of a genuine exigence, an authentic audience, and real constraints, which together invite and structure discourse so that discourse can modify the exigence and, thereby, change reality (Bitzer, "The Rhetorical" 5–6). To be sure, Bitzer's theory of the rhetorical situation has been both criticized (cf. Vatz; Consigny) and adapted (cf. Edbauer); nonetheless, the theory arguably serves as a useful lens through which Baudrillard's description of symbolic exchange as a situation might be understood and also with which the current chapter might be concluded.

From the outset, it is clear that Baudrillard's description of symbolic exchange as a situation is not what Bitzer would call a rhetorical situation. Bitzer anchors his theory in an objective reality ("The Rhetorical" 11), and both of Baudrillard's twin hypotheses depart from such a conception of reality. Appearance begins to produce itself as a substitute for reality through metastatic troping, while disappearance reverses the effects of appearance through the trope of metamorphosis and plays with the absence of the reality principle. Unlike the rhetorical situation described by Bitzer, where a "real or genuine" situation means that the "exigence and the complex of persons, objects, events and relations which generate rhetorical discourse are located in reality" (11), the situation described by Baudrillard is not one focused on reality. The differences in how the two theorists understand their respective situations in relation to reality further influences the role of rhetoric in those respective situations. Bitzer views the role of rhetoric as bringing about a change to reality and, more specifically, modifying the exigence, or urgent need, that calls for the intervention of rhetorical discourse (6–7, 9). For Bitzer, rhetorical invention ostensibly allows the production of discourse that will fit the situation well (10). Baudrillard, however, views rhetoric as the means to exchange, wherein invented discourse sustains a back-and-forth movement between his two hypotheses. According to Baudrillard's rhetorical theory, the two hypotheses of appearance and disappearance will not be modified by rhetoric; rather, they are themselves rhetoric and they will simply be flipped, moved, transformed, turned, or reversed by rhetoric. For Baudrillard, rhetorical invention serves as the pivot for this movement between the two dueling hypotheses; exchange, not change, is the goal of Baudrillard's rhetorical theory.

Although Baudrillard's situation of two dueling and thoroughly rhetorical hypotheses does not meet the criteria of what Bitzer terms a rhetorical situation, Bitzer's theory does profile the two hypotheses that constitute the situation of symbolic exchange for Baudrillard. In the course of defining his theory of a rhetorical situation, Bitzer dismisses a number of alternatives to the rhetorical situation. Among these alternatives are two types of situations that he calls sophistic situations and fantasy situations. According to Bitzer, sophistic situations are situations in which "a contrived exigence is asserted to be real," while fantasy situations are situations "in which exigence, audience, and constraints may all be the imaginary objects of a mind at play" ("The Rhetorical" 11). Symbolic exchange seems to use rhetorical invention to unite these two types of situations and lock them in an antagonistic duel. On the one hand, the hypothesis of appearance might be understood as reflective of the sophistic situation. Here, the prolific production of perceptions that appear to have meaning and value amounts to contrivances that come to take the place of reality. Indeed, Baudrillard confesses to working within a sophistic situation when he discusses his experience advancing the hypothesis of simulation and simulacra. Recall that Baudrillard admits to inventing an assertion—namely, that simulacra have taken the place of reality—and, although he hoped that reality would refute the assertion, no such refutation occurred (*PC* 102). Thus, his contrivance asserts itself as real. On the other hand, the hypothesis of disappearance might be understood as reflective of fantasy, or a fantasy situation. Here, the alterity and ambivalence that are characteristic of the hypothesis of disappearance are invented according to imaginary play of the mind. Clearly, Baudrillard proves that his hypothesis of disappearance embraces a pataphysical project contra a metaphysical one. Pataphysics, a kind of thought derived from the work of Alfred Jarry, constitutes an "imaginary solution to the absence of problems," or a "perfection of play" (*CA* 216).[48] Baudrillard's use of pataphysics in conjunction with the hypothesis of disappearance is, thus, indicative of what Bitzer would call a fantasy situation.

Neither adhering nor conforming to Bitzer's definition of a rhetorical situation, Baudrillard's situation of dueling hypotheses—a situation that relates appearance to disappearance, or what Bitzer would call sophistic situations and fantasy situations—is thoroughly rhetorical. Indeed, part one of the present study has argued as much, first, by literally situating Baudrillard's discussion of appearance and simulation and simulacra alongside Plato's *Sophist* dialogue and, second, by describing the pataphysical alterity and ambivalence that characterizes his discussion of disappearance. In spite of Bitzer's definition, appearance and disappearance are rhetorical. Baudrillard labels simulation as "rhetoric" (*PC* 102),[49] and he understands "the techniques of communication," which emerge from appearance-making as encompassing "all the sophistries" ("Vanishing" 17). Disappearance is no less rhetorical, especially in its use of pataphysics to challenge perception. By drawing on pataphysics and the radical invention of alterity and ambivalence, Baudrillard, as Gary Genosko recognizes, "rhetorically employed rhetorical ploys" ("Pataphysics" 151). Indeed, Baudrillard's use of rhetorical invention to advance hypotheses of appearance and disappearance serves his ultimate goal of initiating and sustaining exchange between the twin hypotheses. These hypotheses are locked in opposition, and he notes that there is something rhetorical about this kind of opposition (*CA* 233). The goal of Baudrillard's rhetorical theory is, in other words, to bring about and maintain a dynamic, reversible, and antagonistic "situation of two hypotheses" (*HD* 66).

Such a goal makes Bitzer's dismissal of sophistic situations and fantasy situations all the more curious. The two dismissed situations are, of course, connected, and that connection reaches backward to Plato's *Sophist* dialogue and stretches forward into the work of Baudrillard. The connection between the sophistic and the fantastic is both theoretical and etymological, as the very word *fantasy* is a cognate of *phantasia*—the term birthed by Plato and used most prevalently in his *Sophist* dialogue (cf. Notomi 250–53). Bitzer's elision of this connection proves emblematic of the way in which the field of rhetorical studies has largely avoided engaging with Plato's dialogue and, to some degree, Baudrillard's work—not to mention the field's propensity to overlook hypotheses that fundamentally challenge either the principle of reality or the processes of production. Bitzer's dismissal of these two interconnected situations further speaks to the importance of perception within rhetorical studies, as both sophistic situations and fantasy situations can effect perception in ways that are tangible, material, and very real. Indeed, the emphasis that Plato, Baudrillard, and others place on perception and, moreover, perceptions derived from sophistries or fantasies certainly supports the notion that rhetoric can function in a way that departs from reality. As Baudrillard's rhetorical theory makes clear, perceptions are constantly on the move: Turning, troping, flipping, and reversing, perceptions are constructed and destructed often without regard to any kind of reality. Perceptions appear and disappear on account of invention—that is, the invention of thought, discourse, and sense. To be sure, when Bitzer excludes sophistic situations and fantasy situations from his theory of the rhetorical situation, he is constraining rhetorical invention. Likewise, when Baudrillard advances hypotheses about the art of appearance, the art of disappearance, and the relationship between the two, he is also working to define rhetorical invention. Whereas the theory advanced by Bitzer whittles rhetorical invention down, chipping away at its prowess, the theory advanced by Baudrillard radically expands rhetorical invention, opening it up to an infinite number of possibilities, processes, and opportunities. Indeed, Baudrillard's rhetorical theory might be rounded up to giving rhetoric its full opportunity, wherein the "opportunity to disappear is as important as the chance to appear" (*HD* 126).

Illustration: The Symbolic Exchange between HeLa and Henrietta Lacks

Symbolic exchange is the ultimate goal of Baudrillard's rhetorical theory, and this goal is the focus of this final illustrative section. Baudrillard's brief mention of Henrietta Lacks in two 1999 pieces—each addressing the relationship between appearance and disappearance, immortality and mortality, the human and the inhuman—suggests that the relationship between the immortal HeLa and the mortal Henrietta Lacks that is captured in Rebecca Skloot's *The Immortal Life of Henrietta Lacks* might best be understood as a symbolic exchange relationship. While the illustrative sections of the three previous chapters have established the connection between Baudrillard's rhetorical theory and the events involving Henrietta Lacks, her cells, and her family, this illustration evaluates Henrietta Lacks's experience and Skloot's book so as to consider the degree to which symbolic exchange was initiated and sustained.

For Baudrillard, symbolic exchange is an agonistic relationship brought about by reversing the effects of thought, discourse, and perception. He understands symbolic exchange as a type of relationship that is possible between all forms, including the form of the immortal and the form of the mortal. In his 1999 lecture he describes the "double movement" of the symbolic exchange between the immortal form and the mortal form as moving through three stages: "first the reign of the immortals, then the mortal and sexed beings overtaking the immortals; Today [*sic*], however, the immortals are silently avenging themselves through the processes of cloning, through interminable reduplication, through the obliteration of sex and death" (*VI* 29). Cloning, then, is a contemporary process by which the immortal form gains the advantage in the game that is symbolic exchange. However, as Baudrillard cautions, "the game is not over yet" (29). Indeed, he anticipates a reversal during which "mortal creatures" capitalize on a "vital exigency," mount a "fierce resistance," and refuse "any final solution" (30). According to Baudrillard, such a reversal "is a matter of life and death" (30). Theoretically, then, Baudrillard champions the opportunity for and the ability of the mortal human to challenge the immortal clone. By analogy, he roots for Henrietta Lacks in her symbolic duel with HeLa; he joins Henrietta's family in perceiving her as a supernatural or spiritual form. To sustain symbolic exchange, the perception that the immortal clone, or HeLa, is meaningful and valuable would have to be destroyed by thought and discourse that embraces alterity and ambivalence. And, as the illustrative section in the last chapter demonstrates, Skloot's book advances thought and discourse—figured as metamorphosis and invoking the supernatural or spiritual realm—that might sustain the symbolic exchange between the immortal and mortal forms.

Stepping back from the specific figurations of appearance and disappearance, Skloot's book preserves a tension that pits the thoughts, discourse, and perceptions associated with cellular immortality against those associated with supernatural immortality in a kind of relationship that might well be understood to be a symbolic exchange relationship. In the book, thought and discourse are invented to advance the perception that cellular immortality is meaningful and valuable. Readers can see this same meaningful and valuable appearance in the scientific language that characterizes HeLa. More subtly, though, Skloot's book invents thought and discourse in order to challenge this perception. Readers can detect this challenge in the familial language that characterizes Henrietta Lacks as a spiritual form. Thus, the book locks scientific language in an agonistic duel with familial language. The thoughts, discourse, and perceptions of scientists butt up against the thoughts, discourse, and perceptions of family relations. Perceptual appearances are produced and, then, these appearances are destroyed. Disappearances turn into appearances that turn back into disappearances. Reversal follows reversal ad infinitum.

From a Baudrillardian perspective, Skloot's award-winning and best-selling book appears to have been so successful because it initiates and sustains symbolic exchange. The book invents and maintains a situation of two hypotheses—one that associates immortality with science and cells and one that associates immortality with family and spirit. For the most part, the book avoids verifying either of these hypotheses, keeping both open to refutation. Skloot largely withholds her judgment on the events involving Henrietta Lacks, her cells, and her family, and, instead, keeps the thoughts, discourse, and perceptions surrounding these events in perpetual motion. Skloot's book creates a rhetorical space in which perceptual appearances might be constructed and, just as quickly, destructed. In other words, the book maintains a situation of two hypotheses, and these hypotheses perpetually refute each other, sustaining the back-and-forth movement between appearance and disappearance that is characteristic of symbolic exchange. Here, Skloot's approach to creating a textual space in which the symbolic exchange between appearance and disappearance might be initiated and sustained is epitomized by her depiction of two pairs of agonistic items.

The first pair of items that epitomize the symbolic exchange enacted in Skloot's book are themselves two books, both of which were owned by Henrietta's daughter Deborah. The first book was Henrietta's bible, which was passed down to Deborah and which contained locks of hair from Deborah's mother and sister (*The Immortal Life* 308). The bible was Deborah's only possession that once belonged to her mother, Henrietta (222). The second book was Victor McKusick's textbook, *Medical Genetics*, which McKusick gave to Deborah when she donated blood to Johns Hopkins in 1974 (187–88). The textbook contained McKusick's autograph and a printed picture of

Henrietta that Deborah had never seen before (188). Skloot establishes a tension between the two books, each of which seems to function as a symbolic challenge to the other. Both books contain Henrietta's DNA—the bible in the form of Henrietta's hair and the textbook in the form of a reference to HeLa—but the meaning and value of this DNA depends on the thought, discourse, and perception that envelop it. The bible, of course, stands in for one hypothesis—the hypothesis that privileges spiritual forms and that is articulated in familial language—while the textbook stands in for the other hypothesis—the hypothesis that privileges cellular forms and that is articulated in scientific language. The meaning and value of each text appear in accordance with one kind (whether familial or scientific) of thought, discourse, and perception; yet, this same meaning and value disappear with the other kind of thought, discourse, and perception. By juxtaposing the bible and the textbook, Skloot provides readers with a pair of items that epitomize the ability of her book to create a situation of two hypotheses that initiates and sustains symbolic exchange.

The second pair of items that likewise epitomize symbolic exchange are two pictures, both of which Skloot describes as hanging on the wall of Henrietta's youngest son, Zakariyya. The first picture that hung on Zakariyya's wall was the widely publicized picture of Henrietta Lacks that now adorns many covers of Skloot's book. In this picture Henrietta stands "with her hands on her hips" and smiles confidently (247). This picture is the same one that was published in McKusick's textbook and had not been seen by Henrietta's children until Deborah received the textbook (247). The second picture that hung on Zakariyya's wall was "a fourteen-by-twenty-inch print of Henrietta's chromosomes," which had been painted with "fluorescent dyes" so that the print "looked like a photograph of a night sky filled with multicolored fireflies glowing red, blue, yellow, green, purple, and turquoise" (234). This second picture was a gift to the Lacks family from Christoph Lengauer, who, at the time, was a cancer researcher at Johns Hopkins. Skloot's description of these two pictures conveys the agonism—in this case, between appearance and disappearance, immortality and mortality, the inhuman clone and the human donor—that sustains symbolic exchange throughout *The Immortal Life of Henrietta Lacks.* The pictures symbolize the dueling hypotheses that challenge each other throughout the text. The first hypothesis advances the disappearance of Henrietta the mortal human, whereas the second hypothesis advances the appearance of HeLa the immortal clone. Skloot's book suspends the two hypotheses (like the two pictures) in an unresolved tension, allowing readers to engage with the challenge that is symbolic exchange in a palpable way. These pictures retain value only insofar as the thoughts and discourse that accompany them make them seem valuable. Perceived with other thoughts and discourse, the value of each picture would be nullified. Skloot's book suspends ultimate value judgment and, thus, locks the hypotheses—epitomized here as two pictures hanging on a wall—in symbolic exchange: the disappearance of Henrietta confronts the perceived value of HeLa, just as the disappearance of HeLa confronts the perceived value of Henrietta.

PART II

Provocations: The Many Appearances of Jean Baudrillard

Part one of *Jean Baudrillard: The Rhetoric of Symbolic Exchange* argued that the definition of the Sophist advanced by Plato in his dialogue of the same name was amenable to the study of Baudrillard as a rhetorical theorist, because, among other reasons, this definition suggests an approach by which rhetorical studies scholars can deductively evaluate the sophistical characteristics of Baudrillard. Put differently, Plato's definition of a Sophist allows rhetorical studies scholars to gauge the degree to which particular rhetors and rhetorical theorists conform to classical characteristics of sophistic rhetoric. For the present study, this definition affords rhetorical studies scholars a provocative perspective from which to consider Baudrillard's rhetoric and rhetorical theory. Characteristics that were, in some way, used to define the Sophist in Plato's dialogue might be applied to Baudrillard and his work as an additional approach to assess his status as a sophistic rhetor. In large part, this approach departs from previous readings of Baudrillard's work as sophistical, as these readings conventionally juxtapose Baudrillard with the prototypical Sophist Gorgias (cf. Ballif; McComiskey).

The four chapters of part two employ this uncommon approach to the study of Baudrillard, his rhetoric, and his rhetorical theory by examining Baudrillard's appearances as an aphorist, illusionist, ignoramus, and ironist. Chapter 7 takes Baudrillard's appearance as an aphorist as an invitation to examine the strongly performative aspects of his rhetoric. This chapter shows that Baudrillard was quite cognizant about his choice of genre—especially when it came to his use of the aphorism—and that he was extraordinarily reflective about his writing and his theory. Next, Baudrillard's appearance as an illusionist receives treatment in chapter 8. This treatment leads to an elaboration of the place that fact occupies in his rhetorical theory. To clarify fact's place in Baudrillard's rhetorical theory, this chapter analyzes Aristotle's use of the word *phantasia* in his *Rhetoric* and Baudrillard's use of fact in his *America.* Chapter 9 investigates Baudrillard's appearance as ignorant and suggests that this appearance results, in part, from his use of Ferdinand de Saussure's work on anagrams. This chapter also explores what Baudrillard has to say about being stupid—namely, that stupidity might be a useful strategy in a world that overproduces intelligence. To round out the evaluation of Baudrillard's many appearances, chapter 10 assesses his appearance as an ironist, leading to a comparison between Baudrillard's work on irony and Kenneth Burke's work on the same. While the terms that both Baudrillard and Burke use to articulate their theories of rhetoric are similar, tracing these terms uncovers salient differences between the two theorists. Together, these four chapters consider perceptual appearances of Baudrillard as provocations for a further elaboration of his rhetorical practice and theory. By investigating particular and, in some cases, erroneous perceptions of him, these chapters demonstrate the importance of rhetorically investigating Baudrillard, his work, and his words.

CHAPTER 7

Appearing as Aphorist: Baudrillard, Writing, and Theory

Upon Baudrillard's death in 2007, the *Los Angeles Times* published an obituary by staff writer Elaine Woo. Among the obituaries for Baudrillard, especially those published in the United States, Woo's "Jean Baudrillard, 77; Kept a Sharp Eye on Blurry Reality" is one of the most thorough and probing. Toward the middle of this obituary, Woo lists a number of Baudrillard's appearances, sketching him as a "small, round man," "a caustic polemicist," "a messenger," and a "witty aphorist." While all of these appearances might merit comment, the last one—Baudrillard as aphorist—is the focus of this chapter. Indeed, Baudrillard appears as an "aphorist" in other obituaries (e.g., Poole), and his use of the aphorism receives repeated mention in the work of Baudrillard studies scholars. William Pawlett, for instance, understands Baudrillard as practicing "aphoristic reflection" (*Jean* 108). Moreover, Ryan Bishop and John Phillips note that Baudrillard maintains "a variety of styles" and that "[h]is writing tends to build on an aphoristic way with the sentence and can move quickly from prophetic and analytic statements to classical (humanist) techniques from the ancient arts of persuasion" (33). By focusing on Baudrillard's appearance as an aphorist, this chapter examines one way in which he performed his rhetorical theory—that is, one way he used language to initiate and sustain symbolic exchange. As this chapter will demonstrate, Baudrillard's use of the aphorism genre distinguishes his art from the art of the Sophist.

The central question in Plato's *Sophist* dialogue concerns art—namely, the defining characteristics of the Sophist's art. The dialogue's interlocutors explain that the Sophist is an "imitative artist" who works in "words" (Ambuel 247). The interlocutors, Theaetetus and the Eleatic visitor, conclude that the Sophist plays, juggles, or conjures in words (cf. Cornford; White; Ambuel), and the suggestion, here, is that words are the tools of the Sophist's art.

The suggestion invokes contemporary understandings of rhetoric as instrumental, or of rhetoric as language used to bring about some desired effect or achieve some intended goal. Of course, instrumental language is symptomatic of the meaningful, valued-laden, information-driven communication that Baudrillard sees as proliferating in contemporary society. But as numerous commentators on the *Sophist* dialogue clarify, Theaetetus and the Eleatic visitor actually contend that the instrument of the Sophist's art is the Sophist. According to the Eleatic visitor, "the maker of appearance presents himself as the instrument" by using his body and voice to render an imitation (Plato 267a; Ambuel 245). Stanley Rosen explains that, according to the interlocutors, the Sophist's art is one "in which the producer is himself the tool" (312). Likewise, Noburu Notomi elaborates on this notion by way of analogy: "whereas a painter produces his product, a picture, using external materials, such as a canvas, paints, and a paintbrush, and a sculptor makes a sculpture using bronze and tools, an imitator using *himself* as an instrument creates a product out of himself" (283; emphasis original). Here, Notomi draws on the interlocutors' discussion of painting (Plato 266d), which is used to expound on the Sophist's art and position the Sophist as both "the instrument and material" of sophistic art (Notomi 283). Thus, Plato's discussion of the art, instrument, and material associated with the Sophist exceeds a focus on the words used and, instead, emphasizes the performative nature of the Sophist's imitative art.

The analogy that Notomi deploys to explain the instrument and material of the Sophist's art resonates with a portion of a conversation between Baudrillard and François L'Yvonnet published in 2001 as *Fragments*. During this conversation L'Yvonnet distinguishes "*between the method of the painter, which consists of adding matter, and that of the sculptor, which consists in removing it*" (22; emphasis original).[1] The distinction, as L'Yvonnet frames it for Baudrillard, is a distinction that could be applied to writing, in which one type of written work develops through accumulating, building, and "*adding successive elements*" and the other type of work develops through refining, subtracting, and paring down "*to the fragmentary*" (22–23; emphasis original).[2] Baudrillard agrees with the distinction and calls it "a fine image," before he outlines his view that there are "two different forms of writing, the one which gathers things together and builds up totalized bodies of ideas and the other which, by contrast, scatters things, attentive to the details" (23).[3] Baudrillard then moves into a discussion of the subtractive type of writing, which he associates with writing aphorisms. The aphorism, according to Baudrillard, constitutes "a sacrilege against the canonical form of the well-argued essay" (23).[4] In this discussion, then, the analogies of painter and sculptor are invoked to outline a difference in two artistic methods as they are executed by writers. The analogy suggests that all writers work with the same instruments and materials but that they differ in their execution of their art—with some, who write in long genres, accumulating words, and others, who write in short genres, subtracting words. Notably, the distinction between these two writing methods proves one that Baudrillard associates with the use of writing genres.

When these two discussions of art are viewed alongside one another, the aphorist's reliance on genre as artistic instrument, method, and product differentiates the aphorist from the Sophist, who relies on varied artistic instruments, models, methods, and products. As commentators on Plato's *Sophist* dialogue explain, the art of the Sophist depends on instruments (e.g., the Sophist's body and voice), a mimetic model (e.g., the wisdom of the gods), a method (e.g., short contradictory questions), and a product (e.g., a false appearance), all of which are distinct aspects of the art of imitation (cf. Notomi 282–88). The art of the aphorist, however, depends on one written genre as instrument, method, and product combined. As instrument, the aphorism assembles words to bring about an effect on a reader. As method, the aphorism is subtractive in its approach to writing, in that it pares down its use of words to achieve effect. As product, the aphorism is a fragmentary short form of writing. The aphorist's art is thus encapsulated by a genre—a rhetorical form—that is, in and of itself, a means to exchange. In no way does the genre of the aphorism, whether viewed as an instrument, method, or product, align with the instruments, models, methods, or product of the Sophist's art. Accordingly, Baudrillard's appearance as an aphorist should not be seen as an appearance that classifies him as a Sophist. Still, Baudrillard's appearance as an aphorist is a provocative one—one that invites further study—and the remainder of this chapter examines the significance of Baudrillard's appearance as an aphorist to his writing and his theory.

Style and Genre

For myriad reasons, when critics comment on Baudrillard's writing—that is, comment on Baudrillard's writing as it is written and not for the meaning it conveys—they frequently stress the style of it. The critical preoccupation with his style is, in part, symptomatic of classifying Baudrillard (however misguidedly or erroneously) as a postmodern. The oversimplified view of postmodernity pits style against substance in a false binary and understands the postmodern as elevating style above substance. Thus, this perspective justifies, perhaps even begs for, the study of Baudrillard's style of writing. Treatments of Baudrillard's "style" as "postmodern" (Woodward 170) are quite common in studies of Baudrillard's work. These treatments of Baudrillard's style fall, as Sonja K. Foss, Karen A. Foss, and Robert Trapp note, into two distinct types. One type of treatment understands Baudrillard's style "as undermining his credibility" while the other type of treatment understands his style "as insightful and interesting" (333). Here, the distinction drawn by Foss, Foss, and Trapp is important, as it elides the fact that this style-based distinction can also be understood as a genre-based distinction. Criticism of Baudrillard's style becomes most pronounced when Baudrillard begins to deploy the genre of the aphorism in his writing. However, most discussions of Baudrillard's use of the aphorism occur in the context of style, not genre. References to his "aphoristic style" permeate the criticism and characterization of his writing. David B. Clarke, Marcus A. Doel, William Merrin, and Richard G. Smith, for example, reference "Baudrillard's increasingly aphoristic style" ("Introduction" 4). Furthermore, Richard J. Lane (144), Zoe Thompson (102), and Temenuga Trifonova (172) each make explicit reference to Baudrillard's "aphoristic style." And Mike Gane regularly groups Baudrillard's aphoristic works—the *Cool Memories* series and *America*, among them—classifying them based on the change in Baudrillard's "writing style" that they exhibit (*Baudrillard* 178).

From a rhetorical perspective, however, what critics have predominantly called style could also be investigated as genre. Gary Saul Morson makes the best argument for such an investigation, arguing that the aphorism genre is defined by its brevity as well as its worldview. Morson contends that genres, including the genre of the aphorism, "follow from the sense of experience," which has, in turn, been manifested in an "appropriate form of rhetoric" (*Long* 5). The particular experience that Morson identifies as being conveyed through the genre of the aphorism is that of mystery—namely, that the world remains a mystery to humans ("Aphorism" 413, 415, 419). This worldview is, of course, paradoxical for presuming that the world does not submit to full view. In other words, the mystery of the aphorism emphasizes that humans cannot fully see, sense, or perceive the world. The "dim" world, as Morson notes, "does not give itself away" to humans (421, 413). The aphorism is a genre that reflects the impossibility of the pursuit of wisdom, value, truth, or knowledge by humans. In fact, Morson's emphasis on defining a rhetorical genre in terms of the worldview it effects reveals the way in which his previous work on Mikhail Bakhtin influences his definition of genre, since Bakhtin also defined genre in terms of ideology and human experience (*Long* 5; "Aphorism" 410). Morson's definition of the aphorism genre further resonates with contemporary discussions of genre in rhetorical studies, which share similar roots in Bakhtin's discussions of genre (cf. Devitt, 59–63). Indeed, Morson understands genres as occasioned and as suggesting roles for the writer and for the reader (*Long* 5–6). The aphorism genre is, for Morson, a genre occasioned by human perception of a mysterious world, and writers use the aphorism to convey the unperceivable dimensions of the world to their readers. In this regard, Baudrillard is no different. The aphorism is indeed a rhetorical genre, and, accordingly, Baudrillard's decision to write aphorisms can be understood as both a stylistic choice and a genre choice.

To be sure, discussing Baudrillard's writing in terms of genre as well as style is a discussion that is not without consequence. Three such consequences prove relevant to the study of Baudrillard as a rhetorical theorist. First, discussing Baudrillard's use of the aphorism as a genre choice emphasizes Morson's point that the aphorism's substance drives its style. Indeed, Morson suggests that, because uses of the aphorism convey a similar understanding of human experience—a worldview of mystery—from writer to reader, the written features of the aphorism genre eventually develop similarities, too. He explains that these similarities constitute "sets of tacit but recognized conventions and assumptions" (*Long* 5). No doubt, some of these conventions are stylistic; yet, even these conventions emerge from the substantive purpose behind the writing. In the first place, then, a focus on aphorism as genre does not allow for easy bifurcation of style and substance, and, as a consequence, the focus on genre undermines the reductive notion that rhetors like Baudrillard, who are often and perhaps erroneously classified as postmodern, elevate style over substance or form over content. Here, Barry Brummett's *A Rhetoric of Style* is illustrative. Brummett refers to Baudrillard as one theorist among many whose work "points to an understanding of the essential connection between style and rhetoric" (9). Acknowledging that Baudrillard's work can be read in a way that positions "style as mere surface" (9), Brummett initially suggests that Baudrillard might well be understood as a theorist who elevates style over substance. However, Brummett takes care to clarify Baudrillard's actual position. Recognizing that Baudrillard actually "bemoans" the elevation of style over substance, Brummett groups Baudrillard with a number of theorists whose work details "why it makes less and less sense to think of style as opposed to substance" (12). The consequence of viewing Baudrillard's choice of the aphorism as a genre certifies Brummett's classification of him as a theorist who views style as substantial.

Second, when Baudrillard's use of the aphorism is understood as a choice in genre, this choice associates him with countless other writers across millennia and across cultures. Rather than promoting an understanding of Baudrillard as mimicking the style of an earlier aphorist, a focus on genre suggests that he uses the aphorism as other aphorists have before him—to respond to a similar occasion, despite differences in social settings, and to convey a similar message of the enigmatic world to readers. Baudrillard's discussion of the aphorism makes ample reference to what can only be called an intellectual history of aphorists, which includes Friedrich Nietzsche (*F* 1, 22; *BL* 159; *CM5* 32), Georg Christoph Lichtenberg (*SED* 230; *F* 22, 29; *CM5* 8, 13, 15, 98; *LP* 39, 99, 200, 210), and Chuang-Tzu (*SED* 119–21; *F* 23), among others. This intellectual history shared among aphorists is strong. In fact, Baudrillard acknowledges having been "a great devotee of Nietzsche" early in his education, admitting that "[i]f I come back to him again now, this is doubtless because I'm going back to the aphoristic form" (*F* 1, 2).[5] Indeed, the parallels between Baudrillard's writing and Nietzsche's are many. Both writers are known to be hyperbolic, and their writing style was often linked to their choice of the aphorism genre (Nehamas 22–23, 18). Nietzsche, like Baudrillard, also adapted his use of genre and style to bring about a greater effect on readers (4–5, 37). As with Nietzsche, Baudrillard's use of the aphorism conveys "significant information to his readers" (37). Apart from Nietzsche, Baudrillard associates his thought and writing with the aphorisms of many other aphorists. Thus, the second consequence is one that places Baudrillard's writing into a rich intellectual history of many other writers of aphorisms.

Third, and finally, focusing on the aphorism as a genre, not only as a style, suggests that Baudrillard remains keenly aware of the aphorism's rhetorical function and, moreover, deliberately deploys the genre to bring about a desired effect on his readers. This suggestion finds support in Baudrillard's work. Consonant with Morson, who cites Aristotle's *Rhetoric* to note that "a short genre typically has a longer counterpart" (*Long* 9), Baudrillard explains that his writing of aphorisms initially emerged in tandem with the longer work *Fatal Strategies*. While he was writing *Fatal Strategies*, Baudrillard kept "a sort of journal," which he considered publishing as "a book with parallel entries where you would have the more theoretical part on one side and the journal on the matching page" (*BL* 39).[6] That particular plan was abandoned. However, Baudrillard would eventually publish his journals of aphorisms as the five-part *Cool Memories* series. Although he composed this series while he was writing a number of other book-length pieces and essays, the short aphorisms of the series are not presented alongside the longer works as he had initially envisioned. Baudrillard's statements further reveal that he was not only aware of the relationship between the short-form and long-form genres but that he was also very much aware of the purpose of the aphorism genre. In his conversation with L'Yvonnet, he remarks on the purpose of the aphorism genre, stating, "The enigmatic aspect is at least as essential as the brevity of form" (*F* 29).[7] Here, Baudrillard recognizes that the aphorism genre works to preserve the enigma of the world in a fragmentary way that "defies interpretation" (29).[8] Similarly, when in dialogue with Enrique Valiente Noailles, Baudrillard remarks, "The enigma of meaning is the secret of writing and this is expressed in its concision and its aphoristic form" (*ExD* 12).[9] Baudrillard further understands the genre as one that escapes the closure or finality that is characteristic of the pursuit of knowledge, wisdom, truth, value, or meaning; he writes, "*Aphorizein* (from which we get the word 'aphorism') means to retreat to such a distance that a horizon of thought is formed which never again closes on itself" (*CM5* 31; emphasis original).[10] In the third place, then, focusing on Baudrillard's use of the aphorism as a rhetorical genre underscores his intentional use of it to affect his readers.

From Writing to Performance

Acknowledging that Baudrillard's use of the aphorism constitutes a deliberate rhetorical use of a genre gives new meaning to some of the observations made by Foss, Foss, and Trapp in their profile of Baudrillard's style. After they distinguish between those readers who find that Baudrillard's style undermines his credibility and those who find that his style proves insightful, Foss, Foss, and Trapp note that the readers who receive Baudrillard more amenably "applaud his ability to shock and his unusual writing style as enacting the very conditions about which he writes" (333). If, for the reasons detailed in the previous section, the references to Baudrillard's style are taken as references to his use of the aphorism genre, then the readers who are receptive to his writing are receptive because Baudrillard's writing uses the genre of the aphorism to *enact* his theory. Foss, Foss, and Trapp's choice of the verb *enacting* signals that Baudrillard's writing is well received because it is performative. Indeed, as the present section of this chapter argues, the aphorism genre affords Baudrillard a means by which he can rhetorically act out his theory.

The aphorism, or as Baudrillard sometimes calls it, the fragment, is a performative genre that serves as the instrument, method, and product of his theory, in that it uses thought and discourse to make human perceptions both appear and disappear. Take, for example, the following aphorism from *Cool Memories IV*:

> Our most ordinary perception obeys a kind of aesthetic protocol which states that there must always be something to see and someone to see it. In other cultures, only a few rare things are presented to the gaze. The rest is suprasensible, and eludes both aesthetics and culture. It is when this rule is abolished that the world is given over to a universal protocol of sensibility, in which the very appearance of things is converted into a cultural value. (86)[11]

In keeping with the conventions of the aphorism genre, this four-sentence-long fragment is brief. Moreover, this fragment is performative in that it initiates and sustains symbolic exchange between appearance and disappearance. On the one hand, Baudrillard's deployment of the aphorism genre, here, participates in the production of a perceptual appearance: he communicates his thoughts about perception, sense, and culture using discourse. The meaning of this particular aphorism pertains to the view of perception espoused by contemporary Western culture. As the aphorism suggests, this view holds that the world is transparent—that is, thoroughly perceivable and knowable—and that this transparency is valuable to the culture. The argument here is an appearance. The aphorism performs appearance by constructing a perception about human perception, which is communicated to readers.

On the other hand, this aphorism is also enacting disappearance. As Baudrillard understands it, the genre of the aphorism is a kind of subtractive writing, in which language is pared down or, it might be said, challenged to disappear. This particular aphorism further exhibits the turning and troping that is characteristic of symbolic exchange, as the appearance of one perception transforms into its disappearance. Observe that this aphorism traces two conflicting views of perception—a Western view, in which the world is transparently perceivable, and another, in which the world is fundamentally enigmatic. The aphorism appears to take the perspective of transparency, recognizing that, once the enigmatic aspects of the world are abolished, appearance is fully valued. But Baudrillard never confirms that the rule of fundamental enigma has been abolished. Rather, the aphorism leaves open the possibility that the world maintains its suprasensibility—that is, a fundamental position above human sensibility. To be sure, this particular aphorism turns an appearance into a disappearance by taking a position that embraces both ambivalence and alterity. Thus, this aphorism can be understood as adhering to the conventions of its genre, for it maintains the mystery of the world.

As this example demonstrates, Baudrillard's use of the aphorism genre performs appearance and disappearance at the same time. During an interview with *Le Journal des Psychologues*, Baudrillard admits as much. Commenting on his aim for *Cool Memories*, he states that the project "was an attempt at fragmentation" (*BL* 179).[12] The fragmentation to which he refers is his use of the aphorism genre for his writing, a practice he describes this way: "phenomena appear, we must grasp them as they appear, hardly giving them time to make sense, then steer them immediately into the director of their disappearance" (179).[13] Indeed, the genre of the aphorism enacts symbolic exchange by countering the production of perceptual appearance with the disappearance of those same perceptions. Within the genre of the aphorism, meaningful and value-laden messages are challenged by ambivalence and alterity. Although short in length, the brief form of the aphorism is instrument, method, and product of symbolic exchange. The aphorism genre enacts a constant movement, turning, and troping as it performs transformation.

From Practice to Theory

When Baudrillard's appearance as an aphorist is studied, he reveals himself to be extraordinarily deliberate in his use of the aphorism genre. Clearly, Baudrillard possessed an awareness of the genre, which allowed him to deploy it to purposeful effect on his readers. The same deliberateness with which he approached his use of aphorisms characterizes his approach to writing, in general, and writing theory, more specifically. To conclude this chapter, then, this section examines Baudrillard's work on writing and writing theory.

Baudrillard understands writing as an activity that is both a personal and symbolic challenge. In *The Intelligence of Evil or the Lucidity Pact,* Baudrillard declares that "writing is an activity in its own right" (76).[14] His point, here, is to contrast writing's status as an activity with claims that writing is interactive. Baudrillard, in fact, holds that "writing's never an interaction" (*P* 31; cf. *LP* 76),[15] and his position that writing is an activity preserves the potential for an agonistic exchange between appearance and disappearance. From his perspective, any interaction between appearance and disappearance would weaken their agonistic relationship and thwart symbolic exchange. The activity of writing, however, promotes symbolic exchange and aligns with his rhetorical theory. Baudrillard's work, when writing, "is to make things appear or disappear" in accordance with his rhetorical theory (*BL* 182).[16] More to the point, writing proves a deeply personal activity for Baudrillard. "I just write for myself," he divulges in an interview with Anne Laurent (182).[17] Indeed, Baudrillard views writing as a personal "challenge"—one that he started in accordance with his own wants and one that he is prepared to stop at any time (44).[18] Furthermore, it is through writing that Baudrillard acts politically. "Indeed," he states, "writing is the only political act that I am capable of" (181).[19] It is also through writing that Baudrillard articulates his most radical thoughts. "I express most radically what I think," he explains, "in the written form" (209).

While writing might be said to be conducive to Baudrillard's radical thought, including his theory of symbolic exchange and his hypotheses of appearance and disappearance, he also understands writing as frustrating his theory. Baudrillard explains that, in his writing, he attempts to approach concepts so that he "would no longer be the subject of knowledge, and to remove [him]self from the position of the subject" (*AA* 33). However, Baudrillard notes that these attempts are complicated, since "discourse is something that always replaces you in the position of the subject" (33). Elaborating on "this repositioning within discourse," he suggests that within writing or even with speaking "it's impossible not to be a subjectivity and a producer of meaning" (33). To combat this repositioning, Baudrillard argues that writing must "play the whole game" by making things "appear as well as disappear" (*BL* 45).[20] Playing disappearance against appearance and targeting human perception, Baudrillard describes the way in which writing pushes thoughts, discourse, and perception to the extreme. Writing, for Baudrillard, is "the invention of another, antagonistic, world" (*P* 32).[21] "Writing," he says, "has a more offensive action" (32)[22] and "can take itself to its logical extreme" by following and reduplicating the world (*IEx* 150).[23] The strategy, here, is using writing to invent another world, to describe a perspective of alterity, to introduce ambivalence, and to interrogate the perception that certain appearances are meaningful and laden with value. Thus, while Baudrillard concedes that writing is a productive art, he contends that rhetorical invention, which is so integral to writing, enables his writing to challenge perceptions of appearance. A radical notion of rhetorical invention allows him to deploy writing in a way that mobilizes disappearance to antagonize the appearances characteristic of a perceptive subject.

Baudrillard's discussion of writing leads directly into his discussion of theory. Both writing and theory play the same game of metamorphosis, turning disappearance against appearance and turning appearance against disappearance. "Writing," exclaims Baudrillard, "is nothing but that [game], and theory as well" (*BL* 204). Theory, for Baudrillard, is inextricably bound to writing. Like writing, theory is innately rhetorical as it aims for symbolic exchange. He describes the purpose of theory as baiting meaning into disappearing and as inverting systems to challenge reality. He argues that "theories do not consist of having ideas (and thus flirting with the truth), but consist of setting up traps into which meaning naively falls" (*AA* 18). The traps that theory sets are, indeed, for meaning—the perception of meaningful appearances. Theory traps these perceptions by becoming what it addresses. Baudrillard describes theory as "autodestruction," suggesting that theories work from within things in order "to wrest things away from their condition" in reality (*EC* 98).[24] "The status of theory," Baudrillard asserts, "could not be anything but a challenge to the real" (98).[25] He describes the process by which theory challenges the real as an acceleration of systems: "The object of theory is to arrive at an account of the system which follows out its internal logic to its end, without adding anything, yet which, at the same time, totally inverts that system, revealing its hidden non-meaning, the Nothing which haunts it, the absence at the heart of the system, that shadow running alongside it" (*IEx* 149).[26] Theory, in short, demonstrates the way in which systems produce artful substitutions as the real. Rather than critiquing the tropological function of systems, Baudrillard understands theory as turning those systems once more in an ambivalent reversal.

Ultimately, Baudrillard understands theory in much the same way as the aphorism genre. Like the aphorism, theory attempts to defend the fundamental enigma of the world through offensive action. Theory, states Baudrillard, "seeks to preserve the enigma of the object through the enigma of discourse" (*EC* 97).[27] According to Baudrillard, thinking and writing maintain enigmatic qualities, qualities that must be set against perceptions of the world (*EC* 97; *VI* 83). He writes that "our task is clear: we must make that world even more unintelligible, even more enigmatic" (*VI* 83). Thinkers, writers, theorists—or those who might otherwise be called rhetors—must, in Baudrillard's opinion, marshal the mystery of the world against the perceived meaning of the world. To be sure, this task is a task for an aphorist, too. After all, Baudrillard claims that "behind all [his] theoretical and analytical formulations, there are always traces of the aphorism" (*BL* 166).

CHAPTER 8

Appearing as Illusionist: Baudrillard, Aristotle, and Rhetoric

In 1990 Arthur C. Danto wrote a review of Baudrillard for the *New Republic.* Toward the end of the review, Danto offers a synopsis of Baudrillard's work and remarks, "My sense is that Baudrillard is less a writer than a performer of some kind, a sporadically brilliant illusionist whose feats of analysis are capable of making salient features of social reality that might never come to consciousness without him" (48). The sense that Danto shares with *New Republic* readers is germane to the present study for two reasons. First, his review suggests that Baudrillard is more of a performer than a writer. This suggestion reinforces Baudrillard's appearance as an aphorist, which, as the previous chapter details, stresses the performative dimension of his rhetorical theory—namely, that his writing enacts symbolic exchange by challenging meaning-making; or, that his writing does what it says "*by* saying or *in* saying" what it says, as J. L. Austin might put it (12; emphasis original). Second, Danto calls Baudrillard a "sporadically brilliant illusionist," which is the focus of this chapter. Baudrillard's appearance as an illusionist is significant, for among treatments of Baudrillard, illusionist is a recurrent appearance (cf. Senese 40) that speaks to his classification as a Sophist.

Baudrillard's appearance as an illusionist is, to be sure, a provocative one, for the moniker of illusionist harkens back to the discussion of appearance-making found in Plato's *Sophist* dialogue. Indeed, the question taken up by the *Sophist*—that is, the question of the nature and art of the Sophist—proves to be a question centrally concerned with illusion. Recall that commentators view the *Sophist* as exemplifying Plato's method of division (*diaresis*), wherein interlocutors resolve one question by dividing and subdividing that question into smaller component parts. As Plato's interlocutors, Theaetetus and the Eleatic visitor, parse these smaller points, they draw distinctions between an image and an apparition, as well as between being and nonbeing. Whereas an image is defined as an appearance that preserves the likeness and truth of an original, an apparition is not concerned with the truth of an original (Notomi 154). Thus an image can be understood as "being like" an original or otherwise classified as a "true appearance," while an apparition can be understood as "not being like" an original or otherwise classified as a false appearance (Notomi 154). The division between the image and the apparition can, as John A. Palmer notes in *Plato's Reception of Parmenides*, be understood as a division between "representation and illusion," in which illusions are false appearances (123). Eventually, Theaetetus and the Eleatic visitor determine that the Sophist with whom they are familiar—presumably, the Sophist of the fourth century B.C.E.—makes use of illusions to persuade audiences. The interlocutors describe the Sophist as partaking in the "semblance-making" type of art—a rhetorical art that is further described as "a shadow play of words," "a word juggling," and a "conjuring in words" (Cornford 1016, 1017; White 293; Ambuel 247). Sophists are, in short, illusionists: they use illusion to forge false appearances, which are perceived and judged by audiences to be true. Thus, the *Sophist* dialogue suggests that illusions are among the primary means used by Sophists to effect the formulation of judgments based on perception—judgments that are otherwise called *phantasia*—in their audiences.

Since the *Sophist* dialogue largely defines illusion in opposition to truth, illusionists or Sophists are subsequently associated with untruthfulness and deception. Just as illusions advance false appearances, so too do illusionists assume unsavory personae as conjurers, shadow players, and word jugglers. To be sure, the personae of conjurer and word juggler are ones that Baudrillard often invokes for himself. At points in his writing, he positions himself as conjurer and a juggler. For instance, he describes playing the whole game of appearance and disappearance as "knowing how to conjure up concepts, effects, and knowing how to resolve them" (*BL* 45).[1] Further, he distances his work from ideological critique—which he disparages for never taking "into account writing, the act of writing, the poetic, ironic, allusive force of language, of *juggling* with meaning" (*PC* 104; emphasis added).[2] That Baudrillard does play the game of appearance and disappearance, as well as embrace the act of writing, makes him a conjurer of words and a juggler of meaning. Despite his propensity to label himself with terms that echo descriptions in Plato's *Sophist*, Baudrillard is not well classified as the type of illusionist the *Sophist* describes. The definition of an illusionist on which Theaetetus and the Eleatic visitor agree fundamentally depends on acts of deception and the propagation of false appearances. As chapter 4 of the present study demonstrates, Baudrillard patently rejects any conception of the truth, and his theorization of the art of appearance moves drastically away from processes of representation in order to dislocate references to truth. On account of Baudrillard's rejection of the true and, consequently, the false, he does not appear to be the kind of illusionist described in Plato's dialogue.

A more provocative and more traditionally rhetorical consideration of Baudrillard's appearance as an illusionist occurs, however, if his work is considered alongside Aristotle's description of illusion in his *Rhetoric*. In order to consider Baudrillard's appearance as an illusionist in relationship to Aristotle's *Rhetoric*, the following section outlines Aristotle's treatment of illusion-making in the single most seminal text to rhetorical theory. As Alan G. Gross and Arthur E. Walzer note, all rhetorical theory subsequent to *Rhetoric* "is but a series of responses to issues raised by that central work" ("Preface" ix). Examining the issue of illusion-making in Aristotle's *Rhetoric* therefore illustrates a way to respond to Baudrillard's appearance as an illusionist, and subsequent sections in this chapter will take up that response.

Aristotle's *Rhetoric* and the Language of Appearance

Treatments of illusion are woven through Aristotle's *Rhetoric*, and these treatments are usually marked in translation with what Allan Silverman calls "the language of appearance" (138). Words such as *apparent*, *resembles*, *appears*, and *seems* imply that the *Rhetoric* is a text concerned with illusion. One translation of the *Rhetoric*, by W. Rhys Roberts, deploys the very word *illusion* during its explication of what Aristotle categorizes as the first of nine "spurious," "fallacious," or "apparent" enthymeme types (Roberts; Kennedy 184). This particular section of the *Rhetoric* explains that a rhetor's use of "wording" or "verbal style" can make any statement appear to be a reasoned conclusion. Roberts's translation reads, "One variety of this [apparent enthymeme] is when—as in dialectic, without having gone through any reasoning process, we make a final statement as if it were the conclusion of such a process, 'Therefore so-and-so is not true,' 'Therefore also so-and-so must be true'—so too in rhetoric a compact and antithetical utterance passes for an enthymeme, such language being the proper province of enthymeme, so that it is seemingly the form of wording here that causes the *illusion* mentioned" (1401a; emphasis added). As this translation makes clear, an illusion is, for Aristotle, an effect of an apparent enthymeme that has been used by a rhetor on an audience. Thus, Aristotle's *Rhetoric* implies that the first step in illusion-making occurs when an illusionist rhetor invents an apparent enthymeme.

The apparent enthymeme, as William Grimaldi notes, is rarely discussed by rhetorical studies scholars in treatments of Aristotle's *Rhetoric* (102). But scholars who do examine apparent enthymemes suggest that they differentiate themselves from enthymemes according to logic—specifically in the rhetor's ability to invent, arrange, and deliver a logically valid argument to an audience. When the distinction between the enthymeme and the apparent enthymeme is viewed as a logical distinction, the role of the audience is a uniform role—one that entails testing and validating the undergirding of both logically sound enthymemes and logically corrupt apparent enthymemes. While this distinction is perhaps the most conventional among rhetorical studies scholars, it is undermined by Aristotle's discussion of arguments from nonnecessary signs as a type of apparent enthymeme and his inclusion of weaker types of sign inferences as enthymemes (Allen 26–29).

Scholarship on Aristotle's *Rhetoric* does, however, suggest a second way in which the distinction between the enthymeme and the apparent enthymeme might be understood. This second kind of distinction is a perceptual distinction that positions the rhetor's enthymeme as dependent on the audience's perception. This perspective is perhaps most strongly implied by Thomas Farrell when he defines a kind of rhetorical validation of the enthymeme as centrally involving the participation of the audience: "The enthymeme brings aspects of our experienced world, the array of our appearances, to the fore," Farrell writes, explaining that "the enthymeme, for better or for worse, offers a provisional interpretive frame, a caption, that lends temporary stability to an otherwise unstable and ambiguous complex of appearances" (100). Farrell's discussion of enthymeme, here, is derived from the work of Lloyd F. Bitzer as well as from the work of Arthur B. Miller and John D. Bee. While Bitzer establishes "that enthymemes occur only when speaker and audience jointly produce them" ("Aristotle's" 408), Miller and Bee explain that that the enthymeme's ability to serve as rhetorical proof depends on the audience's "knowledge of the facts of the case" and the involvement of the argument "with the judgment of the hearers, including implicitly the feelings and emotions" (212–13). Importantly, this line of thought suggests that enthymemes work by making the evidence or facts of a claim appear to an audience in a way that invites the audience to judgment, regardless of whether or not the audience believes the claim. The emphasis is, therefore, on the audience's perception, belief, and judgment. In short, the distinction between enthymemes and apparent enthymemes in Aristotle's *Rhetoric* is a distinction that depends on Aristotle's discussion of *phantasia*.

Importantly, Aristotle's understanding of *phantasia* differs from Plato's in that Aristotle preserves distinctions between perception, belief, and judgment. Whereas Plato considers the perception of appearance to be a kind of judgment, Aristotle sees *phantasia* as somewhere in between the perception of appearance and the rendering of judgment (Lycos 497). On the one hand, Plato's notion of *phantasia* combines perception and opinion, arriving at a formulation wherein "'appearing' is judging" and *phantasia* and *doxa* are simultaneous, coextensive, or combined (Lycos 507; Modrak 232). On the other hand, Aristotle's notion of *phantasia* differentiates between *phantasia* and *doxa*, separating perception from opinion or judgment. According to Deborah K. W. Modrak, Aristotle's work on *phantasia* in *De Anima* and *De Insomniis* directly counters Plato's notion of *phantasia*, in that Aristotle demonstrates "that *phantasia* is not *doxa* (opinion)" (Modrak 232; emphasis original). Scholars concerned with the role that *phantasia* play in Aristotle's rhetorical theory and, more specifically, the place of *phantasia* in Aristotle's *Rhetoric* concur: Aristotle's understanding of *phantasia* separates perception from judgment. Debra Hawhee, for one, acknowledges that Aristotle's concept of "*phantasia* hovers around the categories of sensation, opinion, knowledge, and intelligence," for "these are interconnected means by which judgments get made" ("Looking" 142; emphasis original). Nonetheless, Hawhee clarifies Aristotle's position: "*Phantasia* is not the same thing as judgment" (142; emphasis original). José M. González's "The Meaning and Function of *Phantasia* in Aristotle's *Rhetoric* III.1" advances a similar argument—namely, that Aristotle's interest in *phantasia* is in "the mediating role phantasia plays between sense perception (αἴσθησις) and judgment (ὑπόληψις)" (118). The same point is put differently by Ned O'Gorman, who understands Aristotle as suggesting that "opinion makes judgments about the world of appearances" only "[t]hrough phantasia" (25). Thus, for Aristotle, perception must come before opinion and judgment, and an individual can judge only after that individual has been appeared to in a certain way (Lycos 507).

In the *Rhetoric* Aristotle invokes this sense of *phantasia* no fewer than nine times (cf. Hawhee; Gonzáles). In the first book of the *Rhetoric*, he uses the word *phantasia* at 1370a28, 1370b33, 1371a9, and 1371a19. In the second book, *phantasia* occurs at 1378b10, 1382a21, 1383a17, and 1384a22. And, finally, in the third book, *phantasia* is used in 1404a, when Aristotle implores rhetors to pay attention to delivery:

> But since the whole business of rhetoric is with opinion, one should pay attention to delivery, not because it is right but because it is necessary,

> since true justice seeks nothing more in a speech than neither to offend nor to entertain; for to contend by means of the facts themselves is just, with the result that everything except demonstration is incidental; but, nevertheless, [delivery] has great power, as has been said, because of the corruption of the audience. The subject of expression, however, has some small necessary place in all teaching; for to speak in one way rather than another does make some difference in regard to clarity, though not a great difference; but all these things are forms of *outward show* and intended to affect the audience. As a result, nobody teaches geometry this way. (Kennedy 195–96; emphasis added)

In this passage Kennedy translates the Greek *phantasia* as "outward show" (196). Other translations of this passage use "mere outward show" (Freese 349; cf. O'Gorman 23). But, as González convincingly argues, there is good reason to consider *phantasia* as more than outward show, since this passage stresses the importance of delivery in the communication of all evidence, facts, and types of proof. The point of this particular passage and its use of *phantasia* is, as González notes, "that even an orator with the purest of intentions must have recourse to oral delivery, because no *polis* can boast of citizens who will embrace the bare facts of an issue without having to overcome the potential obstacles of misunderstanding and prejudice" (104). The appearance of fact to an audience is, therefore, of more rhetorical importance than the fact itself. *Phantasia*—the mediations of a perceived appearance and a rendered judgment—thus serve an essential role by clarifying and steering the logical dimension of claims. To be sure, the suggestion, here, is that the distinction between the enthymeme and the apparent enthymeme is one of perception tied to delivery: Perhaps the apparent enthymeme distinguishes itself from the enthymeme in that an apparent enthymeme is the enthymeme that has appeared to, or been delivered to, an audience. According to Aristotle's understanding of *phantasia*, once the enthymeme has been made to appear to an audience, it is capable of being judged by that audience. Thus, an apparent enthymeme invites judgment in accordance with the audience's perceptions of the evidence, or facts, it contains.

By distinguishing enthymemes from apparent enthymemes using perception rather than logic, the making of illusion becomes a process that more fully involves the audience. Indeed, the logical distinction connects the making of illusion to the deceptive work of the rhetor who crafts a logically invalid enthymeme to cause the audience to fall under an illusion. Illusion is, in other words, something to which the illusionist's audience can be subjected. However, the perceptual distinction entertains the possibility that the audience's involvement in enthymematic reasoning might bring about an illusion. Having been appeared to through the perceived facts of an apparent enthymeme, an audience might render a judgment that brings about illusion. Thus, Aristotle's *Rhetoric* suggests that the audience might very well participate in illusion-making, and it is with this point in mind that Baudrillard's appearance as an illusionist can be more adequately assessed.

Making Fact Appear

Since Aristotle's notion of illusion-making in the *Rhetoric* involves the appearance of facts as invented, arranged, and delivered by the rhetor and as perceived, believed, and judged by the audience, an initial way to assess Baudrillard's appearance as an illusionist is to consider his position on facts. Indeed, as the following discussion demonstrates, Baudrillard's position on facts shares some surprising similarities with Aristotle's position on facts in rhetorical contexts, in that Baudrillard connects facts to artistic processes of meaning-making and indicates that the communication of facts is always susceptible to illusion. Putting similarities aside, however, Baudrillard goes much farther than Aristotle by endorsing a return to a radical form of illusion.

Like Aristotle in his *Rhetoric*, Baudrillard understands the meaning of any fact to be a product of the art of appearance. In the third book of the *Rhetoric*, Aristotle suggests that the meaning of a fact must be made to appear and that this appearance matters. Recall that Aristotle views *phantasia* as affecting the clarity of the facts and that he implores rhetors to "pay attention to delivery" (1404a). Similarly, Baudrillard understands the meaning of facts to be a product of the art of appearance. According to Baudrillard, "you have to produce facts" (*RC* 31; cf. *BL* 63).[3] By emphasizing the art of appearance's role in the production of facts, he reinforces Aristotle's notion that the meaning of facts in rhetorical contexts must be made by the communication between rhetor and audience—that is, the invention, arrangement, delivery, perception, belief, and judgment that accompany an apparent enthymeme. Put differently, facts appear and, sometimes, appear to have meaning.

Baudrillard views the production of facts as symptomatic of a bloated economy of communication, where meaning and value are inflated beyond belief. He suggests that facts are subject to processes of simulation, which produce simulacra. According to Baudrillard, contemporary communication has ushered in the "most factitious" phase of the modern era (*CM* 150).[4] In this phase a profusion and confusion of fact allows for all facts—"the merest fact" and "even the most contradictory" fact—to appear factual (*SS* 16, 17).[5] Baudrillard's comments on this factitious phase imply that contemporary audiences see meaning and value as inherent to fact. In other words, facts are meaningful as facts, and audiences will preemptively value and validate anything made to appear factual. In a discussion of sociological discourse, Baudrillard recognizes a widespread "conformity to facts" (*RC* 31; cf. *BL* 63).[6] He further views this conformity as a kind of discursive "tautology," explaining that this conformity to, or compliance with, facts merely seeks to "verify itself" (*RC* 31; cf. *BL* 63).[7] Here, the verification to which Baudrillard refers might best be understood as what Farrell describes as rhetorical validation or a kind of rhetorical soundness (98–100). Baudrillard's point seems to be that an audience validates an argument from fact because the audience values the appearance of fact, not necessarily because the audience values the evidence that is presented as fact. He stresses this point when he observes that "[f]acts do not have to be true," explaining that the analysis of the fact remains the same regardless of "[w]hether the world is a particular way or not, whether it has or has not fallen prey to simulation" (*CM3* 119).[8] In the contemporary communicative economy, the value of fact has become so widely recognized that, when the audience perceives a statement of fact as such, its belief in that fact necessarily follows, as does its affirmative judgment of the claim supported by the fact.

In effect, Baudrillard sees contemporary communication as jumbling the three phases of perception, belief, and judgment that Aristotle's notion of *phantasia* preserves. As Baudrillard notes, the simulation characteristic of contemporary communication no longer charts a path for facts that leads from perception to belief and from belief to judgment. Instead, "facts no longer have a specific trajectory, they are born at the intersection of models, a single fact can be engendered by all the models at once" (*SS* 16–17).[9] Simulation, he explains, "no longer has anything to do with a logic of facts," and in accordance with the process of simulation, "the search for proof, indeed the objectivity of the facts does not put an end to this vertigo of interpretation" (16).[10] In the end, facts are used to make meaning and advance any interpretation in such a way that the meaning is self-validating.

Not only does Baudrillard observe a dizzying proliferation of fact as indicative of excessive meaning-making and unchecked use of symbols; he also understands facts as perpetually susceptible to illusion. Likewise, Aristotle's discussion of apparent enthymemes and *phantasia* in the *Rhetoric* suggests that facts are susceptible to illusion, insomuch as a mistaken audience can turn fact into illusion through perception, belief, and judgment. If Aristotelian *phantasia*—that is, perception of an appearance occurring separately from, if not before, either belief or judgment—constitute the faculty with which a judgment is made, then an audience is certainly capable of corrupting itself by perceiving, believing, and judging a fact as an illusion. Indeed, O'Gorman's "Aristotle's *Phantasia* in the *Rhetoric: Lexis*, Appearance, and the Epideictic Function of Discourse" testifies to the susceptibility of facts to illusion. According to O'Gorman, Aristotle understands *phantasia* as "not entirely reliable or accurate" and appearances as "inherently instable and unreliable" (22). In an Aristotelian rhetorical context, then, an audience's reliance on the unreliable *phantasia* to connect perception, belief, and judgment implies that the facts presented by a given rhetor are susceptible to being turned into an illusion by that rhetor's audience. Thus, Aristotle's *Rhetoric* allows for a certain degree of reversibility between fact and illusion—that is, an exchange between a rhetor and an audience in which a fact might be transformed into an illusion.

The limited degree of reversibility between fact and illusion that can be observed in Aristotle's *Rhetoric* is amplified to an extreme degree in Baudrillard's own work. Keeping with his notion of a reversibility between appearance and disappearance, Baudrillard argues that a reversibility always exists between fact and illusion. Just as in the relationship between the art of appearance and the art of disappearance, where the art of appearance proliferates to the point of overwhelming the art of disappearance, so too does the simulation of fact and reality begin to overwhelm illusion and threaten reversibility. Whereas Aristotle's notion of the reversibility between fact and illusion in rhetorical contexts was limited to mistaken communicative exchanges between humans, Baudrillard's notion of reversibility is more expansive and targets the fundamental relationship between humans and the world. He contends that the belief humans place in facts has inflated to such a degree that they "no longer believe in this illusion of the world, but in its reality" (*AA* 18). In a manner consistent with appearance's attempt to exterminate disappearance, reality-as-fact has begun to exterminate illusion-as-fact (*VI* 70).

To respond to the threat of this extermination and to sustain the reversibility between fact and illusion and, more generally, the exchange between appearance and disappearance, Baudrillard sides with the weaker hypothesis and champions illusion. Illusion, he argues, "is indestructible" (*PC* 19)[11] and also "is the general rule of the universe" (*VI* 72). By championing the universe's fundamental illusoriness, Baudrillard emphasizes the permanent distance that separates the human from the universe, a distance that makes full perception, true representation, and complete knowledge impossible (*VI* 75; *PC* 56; *LP* 41–42). Baudrillard follows Nietzsche in referring to the illusion that separates humans from the world as a "vital illusion" (*IE* 93–95; cf. *VI* 80)[12] or, at other places, a "radical illusion" (*PC* 17).[13] According to Baudrillard, humans have attempted to put "the illusion of the world to death" and "leave an absolutely real world in its stead," thereby closing the distance between themselves and the world (17).[14] This process of "disillusionment" is, Baudrillard declares, "what is properly meant by simulation" (*PC* 17; cf. *AA* 18).[15] To work against that which escapes perception, representation, and knowledge, humans invent reality as a simulacrum, constructing the illusion of reality in response to the radical illusion of the world (*PC* 102).

Baudrillard's work rhetorically performs the reversibility of fact and illusion by turning the illusion of the world into fact and by turning the purported fact of reality into illusion. On the one hand, he contends that the fundamental illusoriness of the world is a "physical fact" (*PC* 53).[16] His argument, here, transforms illusion into fact. For support he invokes cosmology, noting "that the light of the stars needs a very long time to reach us; sometimes we perceive it after the star itself has disappeared" (*VI* 71). On the other hand, he rails against human attempts to position reality as fact. "Reality," he writes, is "a substitutive illusion" (*LP* 43),[17] and the disavowal of illusion in favor of the fact of reality "is the last and the worst of illusions" (*AA* 18). Here, Baudrillard transforms the fact of reality into illusion, and this rhetorical performance of the reversibility between fact and illusion is characteristic of his work. As Paul Patton observes, Baudrillard's writings "occasionally force facts to fit their own rhetorical oppositions" (*GW* 6). In this case, Baudrillard forces fact to fit into or, perhaps more accurately, turn into illusion. Concomitantly, he forces illusion to turn into fact, calling upon humans to "remake illusion" and to "rediscover illusion" (*FS* 75).[18] To be sure, he anticipates a "dramatic changeover" from fact to illusion, and he summons humans to seemingly follow his own performance and to "defy any accomplished fact" (*LP* 46).[19] He accepts the title of "weaver of illusions" when the title is bestowed on him (*P* 71).[20] He argues that the world, which he calls the "inexhaustible producer of illusion," stands against the human, whom he labels "the producer of meaning" (*PC* 18).[21] While humans "continue to manufacture meaning," the world produces "the illusion of meaning" assisted by "the involuntary complicity of the [human] subject" (18).[22] Indeed, the agonistic challenge between fact and illusion is one that Baudrillard locates in language use. He claims that there is "a secret reversion, a showing-through of the illusion of the world in the very techniques we use to transform it" (*P* 71).[23] Chief among these techniques, according to Baudrillard, is language: "language, our essential and most primitive technology, is the place where the definitive ambivalence of the world rebounds on us" (71).[24] Thus, the ambivalence of language highlights our alterity to the world: when facts disappear, humans are reminded that not everything can be fully perceived, truly represented, and completely known.

Fact and Illusion in *America*

Ultimately, then, Baudrillard appears very much to be an illusionist. He admits that rhetors and audiences, alike, might turn fact into illusion or illusion into fact, and he posits that the fundamental reversibility between facts and illusions is a relationship like that between humans and the world. To illustrate the provocativeness of Baudrillard's appearance as an illusionist, this chapter closes with an analysis of one of his most controversial texts—*America.* Originally published in 1986 and comprising six essays that chronicle Baudrillard's visit to and journey through the United States, *America* presents his unbridled commentary on a range of issues, figures, and cities that constitute the country. For instance, in the essay "Utopia Achieved," Baudrillard engages Alexis de Tocqueville's *Democracy in America*, revisiting and updating de Tocqueville's observations about America. In another essay titled "The End of US Power?" Baudrillard displays his penchant for issuing indictments of power that cut across media, economics, and politics, as he analyzes the Reagan-era United States vis-à-vis President Reagan. Across all six of these essays, Baudrillard contrasts his observations of the United States and its citizens with his own experiences in Paris, France, and Europe. The contrast is striking and, at times, biting. Ultimately, the text and its reception confirm Baudrillard's appearance as a rhetor who posits the hypothesis that the world is fundamentally illusory and who tests the effectiveness of this hypothesis through language use.

In his interviews and in his writings, Baudrillard frequently mentions the way in which he advances an argument—that is, a "hypothesis" (*CA* 201)[25]—only to have readers mistakenly receive that argument "as an irrefutable fact" (201).[26] While these receptions might very well exasperate or even amuse Baudrillard, they nonetheless indicate that even his work is susceptible to the turning of illusion into fact. In such cases it might be said that both Baudrillard and his audience introduce illusion into the exchange. As the illusionist rhetor, Baudrillard is advancing an illusory hypothesis; and, although his writing might not be outwardly deceptive, it certainly does not attempt to mitigate misunderstanding through clarity of delivery. As the audience, readers mistake the illusionist's rhetoric for fact and thereby introduce illusion into the exchange. The problem with such a turning, troping, or reversing of Baudrillard's work is that, when one of his hypotheses is assumed "irrefutable" as a "fact," the hypothesis is rendered ineffective in promoting symbolic exchange. Recall, as chapter 6 details, that Baudrillard, following Popper's notion of falsifiability, premises the success of his hypotheses as inviting a strong challenge or refutation.

To address the problem of turning Baudrillard's illusionist work into irrefutable fact, a number of Baudrillard studies scholars have attempted to guide the reception of his writing by outlining approaches by which audiences can read it. Mike Gane, for one, offers such a guide in *Baudrillard: Critical and Fatal Theory* by outlining the structure of and providing the context for reading Baudrillard's works (6–14). Bryan S. Turner offers a similar guide to Baudrillard's *America.* Turner argues that readers of *America* ride or "cruise" with Baudrillard, as if they are driving through major cities—from New York to Los Angeles, Minneapolis to Salt Lake City—and considering the country's character in a way akin to fast-paced tourism (152). By offering what amount to guides for the reception of Baudrillard's work, Gane and Turner reinforce the impression that the rhetor is solely responsible for making illusion appear in a text. This impression corresponds with the thought that enthymemes and apparent enthymemes are differentiated on logical grounds.

The case of *America,* however, reveals that any attempt at guiding the reception of Baudrillard, as if he is illogically deceiving his readers, proves a rhetorically mistaken approach. According to Turner, *America* "is self-consciously designed as a text with an audience in mind" (152). But if Turner's suggestion is to be believed, then the audience that Baudrillard invoked when he crafted the text was not the same audience that actually read the text. Actual readers—and particularly American readers—did not receive *America* favorably. "When Americans read *America*" Baudrillard recalls, "they reacted very badly" (*F* 23).[27] Gane elaborates, noting that although the book was "widely reviewed," the reviews were "generally negative" (*Baudrillard* 178). Two such reviews—one from James Marcus of the *New York Times* and one from Alex Raksin of the *Los Angeles Times*—capture the criticisms that readers in 1989 leveled at *America* upon its translation into English and distribution in the United States. Marcus's review, for example, contends that "Baudrillard will leave most American readers rubbing their eyes with disbelief: his astral America has jumped the rails from hermetic to solipsistic to nonsensical." Likewise, Raksin's review observes that "Baudrillard, calling our country 'the last remaining primitive society,' is sure to rile American readers just as he has already offended a host of American publishers who turned down this book." Acknowledging that "[i]t is not difficult to take issue with Baudrillard's main points," Raksin further reads Baudrillard's *America* as offering "evidence" of Americans' detachment.

Both Marcus and Raksin object to *America* on the grounds of its logic, evidence, and its author's overall approach to argumentation, which, according to both reviewers, are not shared by American readers. In *America* Baudrillard articulates claims such as these:

> "Deep down, the US, with its space, its technological refinement, its bluff good conscience, even in those spaces which it opens up for simulation, is the *only remaining primitive society*" (7; emphasis original)[28]
> "Only tribes, gangs, mafia families, secret societies, and perverse communities can survive [in New York], not couples." (18)[29]
> "America is a giant hologram" (29)[30]
> "[N]o vision of America makes sense without this reversal of our [European] values: it is Disneyland that is authentic here! The cinema and TV are America's reality!" (104)[31]
> "Indeed, that is what has changed so profoundly in the atmosphere of America: the Reagan effect has sapped the nation's energy." (117)[32]
> "This country is without hope." (121, 123)[33]
> "What is arresting here is the absence of all these things—both the absence of architecture in the cities, which are nothing but long tracking shots of signals, and the dizzying absence of emotion and character in the faces and bodies." (125)[34]

On account of such claims, their illogic, and their lack of supporting evidence, Marcus and Raksin take issue with Baudrillard's *America*. Neither reviewer validates the claims that Baudrillard makes because the logic of these claims seems patently spurious or fallacious.

However, if *America* is approached in a way that foregrounds perception and not logic, the reviewers' issues with the book seem to be, quite literally, a point of fact that implicates the audience in bringing about illusion. Both Marcus and Raksin reviewed *America* as a nonfiction work—that is, as a kind of travelogue—but *America* is often listed among Baudrillard's theory fictions, which are aphoristic works with an undeniably literary quality. The inability of readers to categorize *America* according to the established generic categories of fiction or nonfiction seems to reflect Baudrillard's overall approach to argumentation in the text itself: The text instigates the reversibility between fact and illusion. It seeks to defy fact, making this purpose clear in what is arguably the most revealing passage of the entire book:

> Americans believe in facts, but not in facticity. They do not know that facts are factitious, as their name suggests. It is in this belief in facts, in the total credibility of what is done or seen, in this pragmatic evidence of things and an accompanying contempt for what may be called appearances or the play of appearances—a face does not deceive, behaviour does not deceive, a scientific process does not deceive, nothing deceives, nothing is ambivalent (and at bottom this is true: nothing deceives, there are no lies, *there is only simulation*, which is precisely the facticity of facts)—that the Americans are a true utopian society, in their religion of the *fait accompli*, in the naivety of their deductions, in their ignorance of the evil genius of things. You have to be utopian to think that in a human order, of whatever nature, things can be as plain and straightforward as that. All other societies contain within them some heresy or other, some dissidence, some kind of suspicion of reality, the superstitious belief in a force of evil and the possible control of that force by magic, a belief in the power of appearances. Here, there is no dissidence, no suspicion. The emperor has no clothes; the facts are there before us. (85; emphasis original)[35]

As this passage reveals, Baudrillard finds a complicity with and conformity to facts in Americans. Americans, according to Baudrillard, believe in facts with an almost religious fervor. He suggests that, in America, facts are beyond reproach, objection, or refutation. Americans, in other words, do not question their perception of apparent facts, their belief in perceived facts, or their judgment of claims based on perceived facts.

Baudrillard and, for that matter, Aristotle both advance rhetorical theories that distinguish between an audience's perception, belief, and judgment. In doing so, both theorists elaborate on the ways in which fact and illusion work rhetorically. Baudrillard's rhetorical theory, in particular, engages perception through symbolic exchange, in which the appearance of perception is challenged by the disappearance of perception. Baudrillard suggests that the faith Americans place in facts resists symbolic exchange, largely because perceptions go unchallenged. However, he holds that human perception needs to be challenged when considering fact and illusion, for perceptions of fact are invented, while illusions are discovered (*PC* 56–59; *LP* 39–40)

It is only fitting then that Baudrillard crafts *America* as an ambivalent text—a text that is capable of defying fact and, at the same time, its audience's factitious expectations. On the one hand, he attempts to nullify the value of fact. As the above passage makes clear, Baudrillard understands facts to be illusions—complicated, involved, and perhaps even deceptive—and he takes Americans to task for believing otherwise. On the other hand, he baits a trap that would turn the illusion of his writing into a fact—namely, that Americans believe in facts. Peppering the text of *America* with vignettes and cruising quickly through examples that audience members might presume to be facts, Baudrillard tempts American readers to interpret his illusory writing as an irrefutable fact. From the text's reception, it appears that many readers took the bait and fell into the trap, providing Baudrillard with evidence that Americans believe in arguments from facts. The turnings, trappings, and tropings of *America*, no doubt, attest to Baudrillard's appearance as a master illusionist.

CHAPTER 9

Appearing as Ignoramus: Baudrillard, Susan Sontag, Ferdinand de Saussure, and Rhetoric

On more than one occasion, Susan Sontag remarked on what she perceived as Baudrillard's ignorance. This appearance of Baudrillard is one that harkens back to the definition of the Sophist articulated by Plato, and it is an appearance that was produced by Sontag in the midst of a fifteen-year intellectual volley, during which Baudrillard commented on Sontag's work and she on his.

Baudrillard's comments about Sontag varied, ranging from complimentary to caustic and invoking Sontag's work connected to photography as well as to Sarajevo. His 1990 *The Transparency of Evil* borrows Sontag's concepts (32), and his 1992 *The Intelligence of Evil or the Lucidity Pact* compliments her stories as "good" (78).[1] Furthermore, his 1997 interviews with Philippe Petit reveal his amenability to Sontag's writings about photography (*P* 97). And, in a series of 2001 interviews, Baudrillard admits to reading Sontag "with great interest" (*F* 98).[2] However, in a 1993 essay for the Paris newspaper *Libération*, Baudrillard challenges Sontag's travel to Sarajevo, condemning it as "fashionably emblematic of what has now become a widespread situation, in which harmless, powerless intellectuals trade their woes with the wretched, each supporting the other in a kind of perverse contract" (*SC* 47).[3] Here, Baudrillard invokes Sontag to make a point about reference—namely, that "[t]o refer to misfortune, if only to combat it, is to give it a base for objective reproduction in perpetuity" (48).[4] His argument is that the efforts of Sontag and others produce misfortune as an appearance, and he notes that producing misfortune is not the same as combatting it. When intellectuals produce misfortune, misfortune becomes a meaningful, value-laden, and significant appearance that, according to processes of simulation, is predisposed to proliferate.

Even though Baudrillard deploys Sontag's work to make a point about meaning-making, reference, and signification, Sontag understandably took issue with his comments, and, in response, she criticized Baudrillard's work. In 1997, for instance, Sontag was tasked with completing a questionnaire on the role of the intellectual. She describes this task in an essay published in *Where the Stress Falls*, explaining that the questionnaire brought her to the following conclusion: "Intellectuals responsibly taking sides, and putting themselves on the line for what they believe in (as opposed to signing petitions), are a good deal less common than intellectuals taking public positions either in conscious bad faith or in shameless ignorance of what they are pronouncing on" (296). Sontag lists Baudrillard among the latter, "shamelessly ignorant" type of intellectual (296). In a 2000 interview with Evans Chan, Sontag was asked for her reaction to a statement issued by Baudrillard that concerned her work in Sarajevo. In her response Sontag did not mince words: "Baudrillard is a political idiot" and, perhaps, "a moral idiot, too" (Chan, par. 29). When pressed further for her views about Baudrillard, she declared "I think he's ignorant" (par. 32).

By perceiving him as ignorant, Sontag outlines an appearance of Baudrillard that has bearing on his classification as a Sophist. Indeed, Sontag's remarks harken back to Plato's discussion of the nature and art of the Sophist in the *Sophist* dialogue. Just as Sontag focuses on ignorance with respect to Baudrillard's rhetoric, Theaetetus and the Eleatic visitor also focus on ignorance in defining the Sophist. As they zero in on a definition in the closing lines of the dialogue, Plato's interlocutors distinguish between two types of imitators, both of whom use mimicry to make themselves appear knowledgeable to their audience (267e–268c). Both types do not possess any knowledge of what they attempt to imitate; indeed both lack knowledge. However, the first kind of imitator remains ignorant of this lack, while the second kind of imitator is aware of it. Plato's interlocutors refer to the, first, ignorant type of imitator as "simple-minded" or "sincere" (Cornford 1016), explaining that this "simple-minded type" is one "who imagines that what he believes is knowledge" (1016). This imitator ignorantly, but sincerely, proceeds under the false opinion of knowing about what he or she speaks. Plato's interlocutors refer to the second type of imitator as ironic. The second type is aware of not possessing knowledge on that which he or she speaks; nonetheless the speaker issues claims by which the audience will perceive him or her to be knowledgeable. This ironic kind of imitator is taken up in the next chapter of the present study, but suffice it to note that Plato's interlocutors agree that the Sophist is the kind of speaker who deploys "ironic imitation" (Ambuel 246; cf. Rosen 313; Notomi 287–88). In other words, the Sophist proves to be an ironic imitator, not a simpleminded or ignorant imitator.

Understood through the discussion of ignorance in Plato's *Sophist*, Sontag's comments do not suggest that Baudrillard is a Sophist. Sontag does not give any indication that she views him as knowingly ignorant or, put differently, as an ironic imitator. Instead, her remarks suggest that Baudrillard's ignorance positions him as what Plato's interlocutors call the "simple-minded type" of speaker (Cornford 1016). This suggestion is, of course, provocative when viewed from a rhetorical studies perspective. The remainder of this chapter focuses on Baudrillard's appearance as ignorant—that is, as idiotic, simpleminded, or what might otherwise be termed stupid—by arguing, first, that the disagreement between Baudrillard and Sontag emerges from a point of theoretical disagreement about signification and, second, that Baudrillard might have actually embraced stupidity as a means by which overproduced and overvalued intelligence could be challenged.

Against or Beyond Signification

That Baudrillard would appear ignorant to Sontag is perhaps all the more perplexing because of striking similarities in their work. Indeed, an uncanny resemblance exists between them in terms of their interests and writings. Both Baudrillard and Sontag were drawn to the same topics—topics that include Antonin Artaud, Roland Barthes, photography, the attacks of September 11, 2001, and the Abu Ghraib travesty. On the subject of Artaud, both Baudrillard and Sontag penned essays (Baudrillard *CA* 217–38; Sontag "Artaud"), and, on Barthes, both were disciples. As for photography, Baudrillard—a practicing photographer—published a number of essays and interviews on photography (*AA*), not to mention collections of his own photographs (Bonnal; *PH*), while Sontag's 1977 *On Photography* is one of her most popular titles. Each thinker also produced inflammatory pieces on the attacks of September 11, 2001. Baudrillard, for his part, defied his audience's genre expectations and crafted an intentionally unacceptable piece (Gogan, "Rhetoric" 173). Sontag, for her part, "offered emotional affiliations that demeaned most of the public" (Condit, "How" 47–50). Given their mutual interest in photography and their perspectives on 9/11, it is not surprising that Baudrillard and Sontag were further drawn to analyze the Abu Ghraib incident. Of note, also, is the fact that both relinquished positions in the academy to concentrate more on their writing—writing that eventually trended toward nonacademic genres, including fiction, poetry, and the aphorism.

However, in the context of the present study, the most significant commonality between Baudrillard and Sontag proves to be their shared disdain for interpretation. In a 1993 interview with Nicholas Zurbrugg, Baudrillard distances himself from any kind of interpretive process in which he might be viewed as partaking. During an otherwise verbose statement on his approach to writing theory and taking photographs, Baudrillard curtly states, "I don't interpret anything" (*AA* 34). Interpretation, as he understands it, is symptomatic of simulation. As he explains in "The Precession of Simulacra," interpretation is a kind of "violence" that, through its production of meaning, ultimately brings about a sense of "vertigo" (*SS* 42 n. 7; 16).[5] Likewise, as its title suggests, Sontag's 1964 essay "Against Interpretation" argues that critics should forgo the process of interpretation—that is, a hermeneutics of art—and return to the sensory experience of art—that is, "an erotics" of art (14). "Interpretation," according to Sontag, "takes the sensory experience of the work of art for granted," and she would like to recover that sensory experience (13). The departure of both Baudrillard and Sontag away from hermeneutics is predicated on both thinkers viewing interpretation as a productive process in a world besieged by overproduction.

The positions that Baudrillard and Sontag take contra interpretation can be understood as departures from the theory of signification advanced by Ferdinand de Saussure. Saussure's theory of signification is a systematic, scientific approach to understanding language as it is shaped by society and constructed through usage. But his is also a theory of meaning-making. The theory of signification defines a sign (*signe*) as the unification of a "sound pattern," called the signifier (*signifiant*), with a "concept," called the signified (*signifé*) (Harris 58). Saussure's theory informs a great many fields, including rhetorical studies. As Bradford Vivian recognizes, Saussure's understanding of language relies "on assumptions about language, speech, and the pragmatic functions of discourse equally valued in rhetorical studies, whether in its classical or modern incarnations" (72). According to Vivian, Saussure reinforces traditional conceptions of rhetoric, in that both Saussure and those traditional conceptions "value the place and time of the oratorical performance as the ideal manifestation of rhetorical activity" (72). Here, rhetorical activity must be understood as a productive, meaning-making activity, one that both Sontag and Baudrillard feel is overdone in contemporary society.

By standing against interpretation, Sontag repudiates Saussure's theory of signification. As Jay Prosser acknowledges in "Metaphors Kill: 'Against Interpretation' and the Illness Books," Sontag's "Against Interpretation" was boldly "anticonventional" for the way in which the essay stood apart from the critical moment (191). Prosser explains that, at the time of the essay's publication, the study and criticism of art had turned "to the signifier" and "resulted in explanations of signification" (191). Sontag's disavowal of the hermeneutic enterprise was concomitantly a disavowal of Saussure's theory of signification and the assumption that a work of art, like a sign, says something or means something ("Against" 4). Sontag associates signification with the "excess" and "overproduction" that marks contemporary culture (13). From Sontag's perspective this proliferation of meaning dulls "our sensory experience" (13). She advocates for an abandonment of meaning-making with the hope of recovering sensory experience: "We must," Sontag writes, "learn to see more, to hear more, to feel more," and the purpose of art criticism "should be to show how it is what it is, even that it is what it is, rather than to show what it means" (14). Thus, as she advocates turning away from meaning-making and back toward sensory experience, her use of the word *recover* suggests that a critic must locate some sensory space that stands alone—that is, a perception based in the reality of the senses, which stands apart from illusory perceptions based in thought or in discourse. Perception—as in a visceral, sensory, and real perception—is, for Sontag, the antidote to meaning-making. She seems to encourage a rewinding of interpretation that brings humans back to a process of perception that is pre-signification and pre-Saussure. As such, Sontag suggests that sensory perceptions are real: they occur prior to language, so an individual can resort to sensory experience as untainted by meaning. In sum, Sontag argues against interpretation and for an almost prelinguistic notion of sensory experience.

Herein resides the theoretical conflict between Baudrillard and Sontag that, arguably, feeds the animosity between the two thinkers and that results in Baudrillard's appearance as ignorant. Baudrillard, of course, holds the position that sensory perception, like any other kind of perception, is complicit in making perceptions appear meaningful and value laden. Moreover, given his endorsement of illusion as detailed in the previous chapter, it is doubtful that Baudrillard would suggest that humans could access the kind of prelinguistic perception for which Sontag advocates. Rather than supporting a recovery of or a return to a position before signification, Baudrillard argues that signification needs to be challenged. He describes this challenge as one in which signification is turned against itself and Saussure is turned against himself (*SED* 2). In particular, he declares that the "Saussure of the *Anagrams* must be set against Saussurian [*sic*] linguistics" and that Saussure must further be turned "against even his own restricted hypotheses concerning the anagram" (2).[6] The turning to which Baudrillard refers, here, is the turning of one body of Saussure's work (on signification) against another body of his work (on anagrams). In 1906, one year before Saussure began studying signification, he embarked on research into anagrams that was focused on the study of sounds in ancient poems (Starobinski vii). This research has been referred to as Saussure's "crazy obsession" or, alternatively, his "almost obsessive interest" (Culler 124; Wunderli 174). And, although Saussure pursued this research for three years, he ultimately "abandoned" it in 1909 (*SED* 195).[7]

Baudrillard executes the challenge about which he writes by turning the disappearance of the anagram against the appearance of the sign. He observes that "the code of signification never ceases to monitor and systematically control meaning" (*CPS* 150).[8] Like Sontag, he understands the goal of signification to be the production of meaning. For Baudrillard, the effect of signification is "*the limitless production of signifying material*"—or the establishment of an unlimited discursive freedom in which the speaking subject is free to "use and abuse words" (*SED* 201; emphasis original).[9] Put differently, speakers, writers, and composers enjoy the "'freedom' of discourse,'" wherein all are "free to endlessly use and endlessly draw upon phonemic material" (201).[10] Signification, in other words, aligns with Baudrillard's hypothesis of appearance. While his earliest works were heavily influenced by signification (Ritzer 22 n. 6), his work gradually began pushing back against the code of signification and challenging the internal logic of the sign: the logic that posits equivalence between the signifier and the signified. As part of that challenge, Baudrillard takes up Saussure's work on anagrams as a platform from which he can develop his hypothesis of disappearance—a hypothesis that advances Saussure's work on anagrams to "subversive consequence" (*SED* 195, 198).[11]

First, working from a group of Saussure's hypotheses concerning sound cancellations in anagrams, Baudrillard posits a theory of symbolic exchange that views disappearance as doubling, countering, and canceling the meaningful and valuable signs produced by appearance. According to Baudrillard, disappearance strives to ensure that "*nothing remains*" of an appearance by "following a rigorous procedure" whereby the disappearance initiates "the *cyclical cancellation of terms, two by two*" (*SED* 198–99; emphasis original).[12] The canceling that disappearance facilitates takes direct aim at Saussurean signification. Baudrillard describes the disappearance of the meaning of the sign as the "*extermination of the term*" or "the extermination of the code" that is signification (*SED* 200; emphasis original, 210).[13]

Second, Baudrillard draws on Saussure's hypotheses concerning fragmentation to associate a kind of decomposition—what he calls "an explosion, a dispersion, a dismembering where this name is annihilated" (*SED* 199)[14]

—with disappearance. For him, disappearance tears words apart, shredding the value attached to them and fragmenting their meaning. Thus, Saussure's second group of hypotheses encourages Baudrillard to write by making ample use of the fragmentary form or the aphorism genre, both of which are detailed in chapter 7 of the present study.

Accordingly, Baudrillard's appearance as ignorant can be traced back to the fact that his work on symbolic exchange is indebted to Saussure's work on anagrams. While Saussure's work was, for decades, dismissed as obsessive or mad, Baudrillard's work was dismissed by Sontag as ignorant. Although crazy and ignorant are appearances that are not exactly synonymous, these appearances were used in a similar fashion—namely, to deride the work of a thinker. Baudrillard was undoubtedly aware that he was building his rhetorical theory on a theory that had not been received well. As such, his choice was deliberate—not ignorant or idiotic. What is more, Baudrillard's deliberate choice to build his rhetorical theory on Saussure's work with anagrams can, as Victor J. Vitanza suggests, be understood as an attempt to embrace a radical kind of rhetorical invention ("From Heuristics" 199–202). Indeed, Baudrillard's turning of, and on, signification charted a new course for rhetorical invention and also demonstrated the way in which personal disagreements can be invented from theoretical disagreements. To be sure, the rift between Baudrillard and Sontag can be understood as a theoretical disagreement that unfortunately became personal. Baudrillard did not think it was possible for Sontag, or anyone else for that matter, to use sensory perception and experience as an escape from signification, and his comments about Sontag's work were initially a theoretical challenge to signification—that is, an inventive turning designed to exceed signification through disappearance. That Baudrillard's rhetorical theory led to a personal disagreement between two similar thinkers is lamentable. Instead of Sontag accepting his challenge, she dismissed it (Coulter "Passings"). Baudrillard, in turn, eventually dismissed Sontag: in his 2005 *Cool Memories V*, Baudrillard invokes Sontag as emblematic of the kind of American intellectual who uses notions of reality to naively dismiss the thought of Continental and, more specifically, French intellectuals (81–82).

Against or Beyond Intelligence

As this chapter has argued, Baudrillard's appearance as ignorant, idiotic, or simpleminded finds little support in his own writing. The appearance of ignorance is perhaps best understood as one resulting from an unfortunate interpersonal disagreement that was, at root, indicative of a theoretical rift. As a conclusion to the present chapter, however, this section supposes that the appearance of Baudrillard as ignorant has merit. As this section explains, there is evidence in Baudrillard's writing that he might have actually been somewhat amenable to his appearance as ignorant or simpleminded. At points throughout his work, he discusses stupidity, and these discussions suggest that stupidity might provide an individual who is barraged by unrelenting signification, overproduction of appearances, and perpetual meaning-making with the means to initiate and sustain symbolic exchange. Just as disappearance counters appearance, so too does stupidity challenge intelligence.

Baudrillard explains that stupidity is necessary for intelligence. For intelligence to have any significance or meaning, it must exclude stupidity from the meaning-making equation. The sign of intelligence pairs the signifier *intelligence* with a signified that excludes stupidity. Intelligence is that which is not stupidity, and, therefore, "stupidity remains the sanctuary of the referent, the indestructible refuge of meaning" (*CM* 10).[15] Put differently, because intelligence is defined vis-à-vis stupidity, stupidity ensures that intelligence maintains meaning and value. "Intelligence," Baudrillard claims, "speculates on stupidity" (10).[16] Thus, the appearance of intelligence bets on its value in contradistinction to stupidity; intelligence can appear as anything so long as it does not appear as stupidity. In such a way, the appearance of intelligence—even illusory or artificial intelligence—becomes hegemonic (*LP* 178). When intelligence becomes hegemonic, everything can be produced as intelligent and, consequently, it dominates stupidity.

However, Baudrillard cautions that, when intelligence reigns hegemonically, stupidity "gains the upper hand" (*CM* 10).[17] Drawing a comparison between "the game of 'scissors, stone, paper'" and the game between intelligence and stupidity, Baudrillard argues that the games' "cycles always bring the superior powers back down to an inferior position" (10).[18] Here, he identifies a turning or troping, in which intelligence turns into stupidity—what he terms an "ecstasy of stupidity in the presence of intelligence" (*CM4* 59).[19] Baudrillard's point is that, when intelligence is produced as artificial intelligence, intelligence "sees itself as purged of all stupidity; it prefers to overlook the eternal duel between intelligence and stupidity—it is in this sense that it is stupid" (*LP* 179).[20] Overlooking the duel between intelligence-as-appearance and stupidity-as-disappearance does not dismantle the theory of symbolic exchange. Indeed, Baudrillard's rhetorical theory would lock intelligence and stupidity in a sustained agonistic relationship. For his part, he issues a warning to those who would unconditionally elevate the perception of intelligence as appearing full of meaning and value. “Condemning stupidity,” he writes, “is an immediately reversible act” (*CM4* 58).[21] Calling this reversibility a “boomerang-effect,” he explains that pointing up stupidity will result in stupidity “showing up intelligence as arrogant” (58).[22]

According to the reversible relationship that characterizes Baudrillard’s rhetorical theory, stupidity can quickly turn into intelligence. Baudrillard argues that, under the “tyranny” of intelligence, stupidity regains “a degree of nobility” (*LP* 178).[23] “When intelligence becomes hegemonic,” he contends that “stupidity” or “any other hypothesis than intelligence becomes preferable” (178–79).[24] Here, he positions stupidity as “a sort of higher intelligence, on the verge of a radical thought” (179).[25] Thus, for Baudrillard, “[w]hen the hypothesis of intelligence ceases to be sovereign and becomes dominant, then it is the hypothesis of stupidity that becomes sovereign” (179).[26] Confronted by hegemonic intelligence, stupidity functions as the means to “hold intelligence in check” (*CM* 10).[27] The metamorphosis of stupidity into intelligence effects a state that Baudrillard describes as an “ecstasy of intelligence in the presence of stupidity” (*CM4* 59).[28] Here, the reversibility of symbolic exchange rules, and the intelligence of stupidity challenges the stupidity of intelligence (*CC* 61–62).

Evidently, there is reason to believe that Baudrillard might have been somewhat amenable to his appearance as ignorant. If the appearance of ignorance is understood as analogous to stupidity, then ignorance can be understood as gaining the upper hand over the hegemony of overproduced intelligence. At one place in his writing, in fact, Baudrillard appears to identify himself with ignorance-as-stupidity:

> They say that stupidity is a crime, but it seems to me that explanation is the real crime. I understand very well when things are explained to me, but deep down, I am at one with those who will never understand. A brute slumbers within me who sneers at such understanding and doesn’t give a damn for intelligence. With those who understand, I make a contract of intelligence, but with the others, at the very same instant, I secretly make a pact of stupidity. The intellectual or the person who claims the title (there are no others) is the one who has broken that pact of stupidity, and feels release from it. In doing so, he plumbs the very depths of stupidity. (*CM* 201)[29]

This passage is provocative, for in it Baudrillard admits to upholding what he describes as a pact of stupidity at the same time he is bound by what he calls a contract of intelligence. The implication here is that there is always an element of his work that challenges the sign of intelligence. Viewed within the context of this chapter, Baudrillard's admission might well suggest that he maintained a theoretical pact with Saussure and his work on the anagram. What is more is that the admission opens up the possibility of the same kind of pact with Sontag. Although Baudrillard and Sontag were outwardly at odds over a contract of intelligence, the two thinkers might have been allied in ignorance: they understood that they would no longer understand each other.

CHAPTER 10

Appearing as Ironist: Baudrillard, Kenneth Burke, and Rhetoric

Baudrillard appears as "a master ironist" to Roger Scruton in *An Intelligent Person's Guide to Modern Culture* (159). Although Scruton's characterization of Baudrillard is hardly complimentary, the appearance of Baudrillard as an ironist aptly captures the sentiment of many Baudrillard studies scholars who recognize the ironic nature of his work. Anne-Marie Willis recognizes irony in Baudrillard's photography (*AA* 140). Victoria Grace, among others, finds irony in Baudrillard's writing ("Editorial"). And, Andrew Wernick sees Baudrillard as swimming in, mirroring, and exaggerating a particular "kind of irony" (70). Indeed, as this chapter will discuss, Baudrillard both appears as an ironist and makes his work appear as ironic: irony is foregrounded in his rhetorical theory, and, because of this emphasis on irony, he may well appear to be a Sophist—for irony is one of the defining characteristics of Sophists as outlined by Plato in the *Sophist* dialogue.

Irony, according to Plato's interlocutors, is a distinguishing mark of a Sophist, in that irony protects the Sophist against charges of ignorance. In the closing section of the *Sophist* dialogue (268a6–8), Theaetetus and the Eleatic visitor agree that the Sophist is the kind of speaker who deploys "ironic imitation" (Ambuel 246; cf. Rosen 313; Notomi 287–88) and label the Sophist as such. Among commentators on the *Sophist*, Noburu Notomi outlines the significance of this label most directly, noting that the alignment of the Sophist with the ironical imitator suggests that "[c]oncealment is the main feature of irony" (291) and that "[t]he ironical sophist may be 'within us,' if we do not admit our own ignorance" (292). Here, once again, the nature and the art of the Sophist boils down to the art of appearance. Irony, in Notomi's reading of the *Sophist*, depends on the audience's perception of a false appearance. The Sophist uses imitation knowingly to communicate the appearance of knowledge, even though the Sophist does not possess that knowledge. Notomi declares that the Sophist "boldly claims to know what he does not know" (292). Accordingly, the Sophist conceals ignorance and is perceived to be knowledgeable. This act of concealment further distinguishes the Sophist from Socrates, as Socrates admits his ignorance and is perceived to be ironic. Thus, while irony is an appearance for Socrates, irony is "an essential feature of the sophist" (Notomi 292).

Initially, then, classifying Baudrillard as a Sophist depends on whether his irony is a mere appearance of his rhetoric or whether it is an essential feature of his rhetoric. More particularly, Baudrillard's classification as a Sophist depends on whether he admits his lack of knowledge and reveals his ignorance or whether he claims knowledge and conceals ignorance. But as the preceding two chapters illustrate, Baudrillard claims no knowledge beyond that of symbolic exchange, and, even then, he would more likely classify symbolic exchange as a rule or belief rather than a kind of knowledge. Indeed, symbolic exchange is the fundamental rule that governs his theorization, and Baudrillard asserts that the only belief he holds is in symbolic exchange—that is, the form of reversibility (*CA* 59). Furthermore, Baudrillard endorses a kind of nonsensical escape from meaning that shares an affinity with ignorance. Recall, here, that he picks up on Saussure's abandoned theorems that were called crazy. Thus, an assessment of Baudrillard as a Sophist based on claims to knowledge and his concealment of ignorance leads quite quickly to the conclusion that his positions with respect to knowledge and ignorance are not indicative of the ironic imitator described by Plato's interlocutors. Labeling Baudrillard as an ironist should not, therefore, be construed as classifying him as a Sophist.

Instead, labeling Baudrillard as an ironist highlights his view that irony is a quality of being. He states that the "instant things become man-made products, artefacts, signs, commodities, they perform an artificial and ironic function by their very existence" (*UB* 134). Whereas Notomi's reading of the *Sophist* suggests that irony is an essential feature of human being, irony, for Baudrillard, is an essential feature of all being, not just human being. In fact, he writes that "irony has passed into things" (*UB* 134), and the significance of this assertion is one that not only decenters humans from the function of irony but one that also impacts language use. When the irony of things becomes clear, no humans are needed to "project irony into a natural world" (134). This transparency of irony begins to "emphasize the absence of the other, of the interlocutor" (136). Thus, what Baudrillard describes as a "superior power of irony" is a power through which irony divests itself of human perception (136). According to Baudrillard, irony works independently of human perception—that is, no human is needed to make something appear as ironic; irony just *is*.

More to the point, the kind of irony that Baudrillard deploys in his own writing and in conjunction with his rhetorical theory is deployed in order to challenge the production of perceptual appearances. In other words, he views irony as aligned with the art of disappearance and its characteristic alterity and ambivalence. He refers to this kind of irony as *objective irony*. "Objective irony," he explains, "is precisely the irony whereby one is able to turn the system, to make it work against itself, to play against itself" (*BL* 138). Baudrillard describes objective irony as enabling a position that is outside the subject and outside a dialectic (*FS* 98, 220; *BL* 138). Indeed, objective irony constitutes a perspective of alterity that allows Baudrillard to create "'ironic' distance" that dissolves dialectical processes of negation (*BL* 138). He views irony as what enables language to get beyond ecstatic information or the metastatic production of meaning (*FS* 98). As a strategy belonging to the art of disappearance, objective irony couples the perspective of alterity with ambivalence. "Irony," as Patrick Brantlinger points out, "permits Baudrillard ambivalence" (197). Baudrillard goes so far as to rename ambivalent or fatal strategies as "ironic strategies" (*FS* 97),[1] explaining that ironic strategies promote "movement within the text" by challenging meaning (*BL* 138). To be sure, the strategies that Baudrillard associates with irony provoke metamorphosis or a transformation, as irony "plays from one form to another" (*FS* 108).[2] The "ironic effect within the text"—or what could otherwise be described as metamorphosis via alterity and ambivalence—goads the analyst or the subject to disappear (*BL* 138). The "necessity of irony" (*FS* 108)[3] that Baudrillard identifies is, thus, the same need for the art of disappearance: without irony, symbolic exchange would not occur.

Baudrillard associates irony with the tropological movement and exchange that is essential to his rhetorical theory. Rhetorical studies scholars, of course, ought to recognize that his positioning of irony as a trope invites comparison with Kenneth Burke—another rhetorical theorist who positions irony as a master trope and who also exerts a profound influence on modern rhetorical theory. In an appendix to *A Grammar of Motives*, Burke lists irony as the last of what he terms four "master tropes." Irony, for Burke as for Baudrillard, is associated with "a strategic moment of reversal," or a turning "that involves matters of form in art" (517, 516). But whereas Baudrillard finds irony in all *things*, Burke locates irony in *humans*. Irony weds the human and the idea, a point that Burke makes clear when he states that "one might speak of 'Socratic irony' as 'dramatic,' and of 'dramatic irony' as 'Socratic'" (512). The human and the idea are, for Burke, interchangeable to such a degree that to speak of the idea of irony is to speak of the idea of human irony. Indeed, Burke argues that irony carries out a "dual function" that unites disparate human characters in a "duality of rôle" (516). Burke seems to anticipate Notomi's assertion that "[t]he ironical sophist may be 'within us'" (292), when he contends that "[t]rue irony, humble irony, is based upon a sense of fundamental kinship with the enemy, as one *needs* him, is *indebted* to him, is not merely outside him as an observer but contains him *within*, being consubstantial with him" (Burke, *A Grammar* 514; emphasis original). For Burke, irony transforms a human dialectic by nesting opposed or antithetical characters within one another. This kind of kinship, debt, and internal agonism reflects Baudrillard's understanding of irony as he associates it with the art of disappearance, since disappearance emerges from within the art of appearance, pays a symbolic debt to appearance, and is symbolic kin with appearance. The striking similarities between Baudrillard's and Burke's notions of irony continue, as Burke writes that "true irony" involves "an 'internal fatality'" (*A Grammar* 517). Thus, Baudrillard and Burke both link irony to a fatality and a duality that emerges from the movement associated with turning, reversing, and troping.

Baudrillard's appearance as ironist thus enables a reading of him against Burke. Although Baudrillard is often read alongside other theorists (e.g., Genosko *McLuhan*; McQueen) and Burke has increasingly been read alongside contemporary theorists (e.g., Brock; Rickert; Wess), these two rhetorical theorists are, with rare exception (cf. Condit, "Kenneth" 232–37; Kärreman 106), seldom read alongside each another. However, such a reading proves especially helpful to developing an understanding of the lesser-known theorist, Baudrillard. As their respective discussions of irony demonstrate, Baudrillard and Burke articulate their theories of rhetoric using a common set of terms: *irony*, *art*, *form*, *duality*, *fatal*, and *reversal*, to name just a few. That both theorists deploy a common set of terms is notable, for, as Burke argues in *Language as Symbolic Action*, the terms used by an individual to interpret the world direct "attention into some channels rather than others" (45). Thus, both Baudrillard and Burke can be understood as interpreting the world through a common set of terms; however, their use of these terms is not commensurate, and, despite the commonality, Baudrillard and Burke direct their theoretical attention into markedly different channels. Their discussions of irony, for one, reveal that, while Burke's notion of irony focuses on humans and works within a dialectic, Baudrillard's notion of irony examines all existence and attempts to work outside dialectic.

Taking this provocation further, the remainder of this chapter examines some additional terms—*identification*, *motivation*, *symbolic*, *poetic*, *rhetoric*, and *ambiguity*—deployed by both Baudrillard and Burke in order to, first, elaborate the subtleties of Baudrillard's rhetorical theory with references to Burke's "master theory that functions virtually hegemonically in the study of rhetoric" (Foss and Griffin 231); and, second, contrast Baudrillard's rhetorical theory with Burke's, a theory that has been repeatedly classified as a sophistical or neosophistical rhetoric theory (cf. McComiskey; Ballif).

Identification

A discussion of irony in Baudrillard and Burke necessarily leads to a consideration of their individual theories of identification. When explaining the fundamental duality captured in the trope of irony, Burke advances what he calls "an over-all ironic formula," where "what goes forth as A returns as non-A" (*A Grammar* 517). This formula is one that he refers to often in his work, such as when he discusses identification and rhetoric (*A Grammar* xix; *A Rhetoric* 20). Finding non-A, or B for that matter, in A is not only the formula for irony but also the formula for identification—the central concept in Burke's rhetorical theory. His theory of rhetoric involves both identification and persuasion. "Rhetoric," according to Burke, "is the art of persuasion" (*A Rhetoric* 46). However, Burke's conception of persuasion necessitates identification, for "a speaker persuades an audience by the use of stylistic identifications" (46). The "stylistic identifications" to which he refers are appeals made to facilitate shared substance between a rhetor and an audience. Burke's theory of rhetoric mandates that rhetors deploy "the appeal of *identification*" (62; emphasis original) to forge a sense of common being with their audience, because humans are neither purely identified with one another, nor are they resolutely divided from one another (22). Burke holds that two people (person A and person B) are never identical, but "insofar as their interests are joined"—or insofar as they are "persuaded" to believe that their interests are joined—"A is identified with B" (20). In other words, identification is a process by which A and non-A are joined. As Burke's formula suggests, irony constitutes one way that a rhetor might join A and non-A. For him, identification and division always occur together, and, as such, they provide "the characteristic invitation to rhetoric" (25). According to Burke's theory, the rhetor's task is to persuade an audience to identify with the rhetor or the rhetor's cause, and one way that a rhetor might masterfully accomplish this task is through using the trope of irony.

Baudrillard, like Burke, acknowledges that identification and division occur in tandem. Put differently, Baudrillard argues that the probability "of a total identification" occurring between two things "is equal to zero" (*VI* 71). Especially with regard to relationships between two humans, he notes that "there is always a hiatus, a distortion, a rift that precludes any reduction of the same to the same" (71). Notably, appeals to shared substance (qua Burke) or presence (qua Perelman and Olbrechts-Tyteca; cf. Gross and Dearin 135–36) cannot, in Baudrillard's opinion, minimize the division between two things, humans and language included. By acknowledging a fundamental division between things, Baudrillard drives a wedge between language use and human psychology. The division between language use and psychology enables him to challenge the communicative enterprise of appearance-making. Communication, as Baudrillard understands it, transfers human psychology onto language use via the "*positive economy of the metaphor*" (*SED* 235; emphasis original).[4] The metaphorical tropings, here, emphasize content over form, meaning over movement. When psychology is transferred onto language use, communication results, and perceptions of apparent meaning and apparent value abound. Psychologized language use is communication, and communication perpetuates the perception that language use "always warrants an interpretation" (234).[5] The interpretation that Baudrillard references, here, is psychoanalysis, replete with its "analytic reason" (234).[6]

Motivation + Symbolic + Poetic

Tracing the trope of irony in both Baudrillard and Burke leads to a discussion of identification, which, in turn, leads to a discussion of how the two theorists address motivation. For Burke, the study of irony, identification, and, more generally, rhetoric grows out of an interest in motivation. Two of his most widely read texts among rhetorical studies scholars—*A Grammar of Motives* and *A Rhetoric of Motives*—make up a major portion of what Burke describes as his "*Motivorum* project" (*Counter-Statement* 218). The goal of this unfinished project was, as Ross Wolin notes, to investigate relationships among humans by studying "the various ways of accounting for human motivation," with language use being chief among these ways (144–45). As he foregrounds ways to account for human motivation, Burke positions the symbolic and the rhetorical as two roughly equivalent categories of appeals. The equivalence of the symbolic and the rhetorical can be seen in his plans for the "*Motivorum* project" (*Counter-Statement* 218): he planned to discuss rhetorical and symbolic approaches each in its own book-length treatment, *A Rhetoric of Motives* and *A Symbolic of Motives*, respectively (218). Burke's writing further reveals that the distinction between a symbolic and a rhetorical approach to motives resides in what can essentially be described as the audience targeted by the appeal. Whereas symbolic appeals target human motivation psychologically and individually, rhetorical appeals target human motivation consubstantially and socially (Duncan 165). Thus, the symbolic and the rhetorical are, for Burke, two categories of appeals distinctive for the audiences at which they are aimed.

Burke unpacks the symbolic appeal and the way it targets human motivation psychologically and individually through a discussion of poetic language. Yoking the term *symbolic* to the term *poetic*, Burke explains that *symbolic* connotes the "poetic" (*Counter-Statement* 218) or, more generally, the "modes of expression and appeal in the fine arts" (*A Grammar* xvii). Thus, his treatment of the symbolic focuses on the way that language use associated with the fine arts motivates humans. According to Burke, these expressive appeals associated with the fine arts work internally on a psychological or psychoanalytic level (*A Grammar* xvii). As William Rueckert notes, Burke's early approach to studying "the symbolic function" of the poetic focuses on the creator and the creative process in an attempt to learn more about the relationship between "poetry, the human psyche, and human relations generally" (126). Thus, Burke approaches the poetic from the perspective of the individual artist, which is why, as Hugh Dalziel Duncan observes, "Burke places the individual under the head of the Symbolic" (165). To comprehend the symbolic, Burke's readers and his critics seek meaning. Rueckert explains the process thus: "At best, poetry as symbolic action is a kind of private code, and the critic of symbolic action a kind of cryptologist whose main object is to break the code so that he can understand and make public the vital secrets being transmitted" (71). This symbolic code cracking focuses on technique, content, as well as psychology, or on what Rueckert describes as the "vital function for poet and reader" (65).

Whereas Burke's work on motivation reads the symbolic as an appeal through poetic language that targets individual human psychology, Baudrillard lambasts the concept of motivation for its complicity with a psychological interpretation of language use. Baudrillard argues that a psychological interpretation of language produces concepts that support the idea of communication: concepts including motivation, intent, drive, desire, and force. As he explains, these concepts are produced when interpretation couples the appearance of language with psychology—"the fate of language and the fate of pulsion, the figure and the force" (*SED* 234).[7] The result of this coupling is what he describes as "profound motivation" (234),[8] and motivation is not a concept that Baudrillard endorses. He calls motivation "a hollow and somewhat supernatural concept" (*CPS* 153),[9] a "nebulous" concept remarkable for its "emptiness" (154).[10] Nonetheless, he recognizes that, "[f]or the psychologist," motivation constitutes "the key idea," in that it theorizes "a kind of pre-existent, ill-defined necessity" (*CS* 69).[11] The concept of motivation derives its importance from its conceptual amorphousness and pliability. According to Baudrillard, the conceptual stretch of motivation bridges a gap between language and psychology (*CPS* 154). He holds, in fact, that motivation proves "the only relation thinkable" that could possibly bridge this gap (153).[12] Thus, he understands motivation as carrying out an important function in communication by binding words, things, and people. As the central concept in psychologized language, motivation—a vague, but consequential compulsion—produces meaning. Motivation makes meaning appear and adds value to language on a psychological level. Since the psychological interpretation of language works to produce meaning, decipher reasoning, and to locate motivation from "behind" language (*SED* 234),[13] Baudrillard remains adamant that it does not promote symbolic exchange. On this point he is unequivocally clear: "*The symbolic must never be confused with the psychological*" (*MP* 102; emphasis original).[14] In fact, he explains that "distinctions, which are characteristic of psychology"—those that typically involve motivation—"are excluded by the symbolic relation" (103).[15] For Baudrillard, psychology autonomizes specific positions, including those of the subject and the object, the conscious and the unconscious, and, by extension, the message sender and the message receiver (102). These psychological distinctions direct communication in a linear, productive fashion and render symbolic exchange impossible.

Far from performing any meaningful function or working in any productive economy, poetic language constitutes the paradigmatic example of the art of disappearance for Baudrillard. That the poetic is paradigmatic of the disappearance is fitting for Baudrillard, as he derives the tenets of disappearance from Saussure's study of anagrams in ancient poems. But rather than following Burke and focusing on the poetic as a category of appeal, Baudrillard directs his attention to the effects of the poetic, chastising overly narrow views of poetic language for ignoring "the poetic 'effect'" or "the enjoyment [*jouissance*] proper to texts" (*SED* 197; emphasis original).[16] According to Baudrillard, the effect of the poetic is an enjoyment attained when the message (which is characteristic of communication) is lost, as are the other conventional components of the message sender and the message receiver (216). By radically destroying the components of meaning-making (i.e., the rhetorical signposts of encoder, decoder, and code), the poetic brings about an enjoyment akin to that of a joke or a dream. Baudrillard asserts, however, that the effects of a poem, joke, or dream cannot be understood in terms of psychology or as "*the labour of the unconscious*" (223; emphasis original).[17] He writes, "The poetic and the psychoanalytic do not mix" (223).[18] In contradistinction to Burke's association of the terms *symbolic* and *poetic* with appeals to psychology, Baudrillard dissociates the psychological from the symbolic and invokes the poetic as an example of the art of disappearance. For him, the effects of poetic language use become a means to symbolic exchange: the poetic contributes to the symbolic movement that constitutes his rhetorical theory.

Rhetoric + Ambiguity

Discussing the theorizations of irony advanced by both Baudrillard and Burke necessarily leads to a treatment of the term *rhetoric*. Burke famously invokes his formula for irony to connect the terms *rhetoric* and *ambiguity*; Baudrillard, likewise, connects the same two terms. While both Baudrillard and Burke couple the terms *rhetoric* and *ambiguity*, they do so to make drastically different points. Burke holds that any substance or thing possesses ambiguity and that this "ambiguity of substance" proves "a major resource of rhetoric" (*A Grammar* 51). For Burke, any act of definition or classification draws distinctions between what something is and what it is not. Thus, when humans use language, they are drawing innumerable distinctions, which according to Burke, "arise out of a great central moltenness, where all is merged" (xix). The moltenness to which he refers is the ambiguity of substance, and he suggests that any distinction can be drawn out of the ambiguity of substance. Burke writes,

> Let one of these crusted distinctions return to its source, and in its alchemic center it may be remade, again becoming molten liquid, and may enter into new combinations, whereat it may be again thrown forth as a new crust, a different distinction. So that A may become non-A. But not merely a leap from one state to the other. Rather, we must take A back into the ground of its existence, the logical substance that is its causal ancestor, and on to a point where it is consubstantial with non-A; then we may return, this time emerging with non-A instead. (xix)

As the above passage implies, the affordances granted the rhetor by ambiguity are such that a given thing—idea, cause, argument, identity, or substance—may be melted by a rhetor to a point at which that thing can be forged into its opposite. Burke refers to this malleability as the "paradox of substance" (37), but it may also be understood as formulaic irony wherein a dialectic is contained from within. And although this paradox or irony enables an individual to identify with a collective motive (38), paradox or irony also allows a rhetor to claim that a particular thing is substantially true or in principle true, "[e]ven in cases where the nature of the case does not justify the usage grammatically" (52). Thus, Burke's point is that ambiguity provides rhetors with unlimited resources for invention but that ambiguity also allows rhetoric to circumvent difference, division, and, in the most extreme cases, the truth. Irony, in all of its paradoxical ambiguity, serves as a master resource to the rhetor.

Baudrillard, for his part, decries what he refers to as a "*rhetoric of ambiguity*" that is incipient in certain studies of language, studies that are similar to Burke's *Motivorum* project (*SED* 216; emphasis original).[19] In his reference to a "rhetoric of ambiguity," Baudrillard deploys the term *rhetoric* as he does in many of his earlier studies—that is, to connote the manifestation of an ideology. By deriding the rhetoric of ambiguity, Baudrillard attacks the ideology of ambiguity—namely, as it is deployed to characterize poetic language (215). In particular, he disputes claims made by William Empson and Roman Jakobson that "[a]mbiguity is what characterizes the poetic and distinguishes it from the discursive" (215).[20] These arguments, according to Baudrillard, view ambiguity as a scramble of communicative discourse: ambiguity "merely produces floating values, renders identities diffuse, and makes the rules of the referential game more complex, without abolishing anything" (216).[21] The problem with ambiguity, as Baudrillard sees it here, is that ambiguity is understood as using the same terms, supporting the same concepts, and functioning according to the same economy as communication or the art of appearance. Ambiguity, in other words, connotes a kind of confused form of communication. Rather than challenging communication's goal of producing meaning, ambiguity ultimately produces a kind of jumbled meaning, but meaning nonetheless. Of course, Baudrillard sees the kinds of language use that he associates with the art of disappearance as mounting a strong challenge to the ambiguity of communication he associates with the art of appearance. Baudrillard's rhetorical theory depends on a perpetual movement between ambiguity and ambivalence.

In the end, then, a consideration of Baudrillard's appearance as an ironist has provoked an alternative way to define his rhetorical theory. In a passage from *A Rhetoric of Motives* widely cited by rhetorical studies scholars, Burke observes that "the characteristic invitation to rhetoric" emerges when you "put identification and division ambiguously together, so that you cannot know for certain just where one ends and the other begins" (25). A Baudrillardian revision to Burke's observation would position exchange as "the characteristic invitation to rhetoric," and such exchange would occur when the ambiguity of appearance is put together with the ambivalence of disappearance so that the two arts are locked in an agonistic challenge.

CONCLUSION

CHAPTER 11

Rhetoric, Invention, and Symbolic Exchange

Baudrillard, as this study has demonstrated, advances a novel rhetorical theory positing that perception is rhetorical and necessarily involves invention. The focus on perception in Baudrillard's theory reflects a focal point in classical rhetoric—namely, Plato's *Sophist* dialogue and the concept of *phantasia*. Above all else, though, Baudrillard's rhetorical theory embraces a radically expansive notion of rhetorical invention that facilitates symbolic exchange. Part one of this study explained the logistics of Baudrillard's rhetorical theory, whereby rhetorical invention functions as the fulcrum on which the art of appearance and the art of disappearance pivot. Invention, as part one argued, engages Baudrillard's twin arts in a sustained challenge, enabling the production of perceptions as well as the destruction of perceptions. Invention further makes possible the thought and discourse that produce and, also, seduce perceptual appearances, and such appearances were evaluated in part two of this study. Indeed, the chapters that composed part two of this study each assessed an appearance of Baudrillard that corresponds with one of the defining characteristics of the Sophist, as outlined in the *Sophist* dialogue. Part two, in other words, engaged the art of appearance and the art of disappearance so as to challenge perceptions of Baudrillard and his theory. Both parts of this cross-disciplinary study underscored that, for Baudrillard, symbolic exchange is the goal of rhetoric, and exchange is dependent on rhetorical invention. Invention, thus, sits at the center of Baudrillard's rhetorical theory as well as at the center of this study, and it is by interceding in an ongoing discussion about the place of invention in rhetoric that this study concludes.

Invention, admittedly, can be difficult for rhetorical studies scholars to perceive. For example, Janice M. Lauer observes, "Of all the five canons—or major parts—of classical rhetoric, invention is the only one that directly addresses the content of communication as well as the process of creation, thus dealing with one of the most visible parts of published rhetorical performance, the content, and one of the most often invisible—the process by which a writer produced that content" (1–2). As Lauer's statement suggests, rhetorical invention proceeds with varying degrees of visibility, or appearance, meaning that rhetorical studies scholars can perceive invention, in some cases, as readily transparent and, in other cases, as perplexingly opaque. The more opaque instances of rhetorical invention seemingly require more scholarly interpretation. In cases of concealed or invisible invention, rhetorical studies scholars must perceive invention where it is neither obvious nor explicit. Further, rhetorical invention proceeds with varying degrees of intentionality and systemization. Victor J. Vitanza, for instance, notes that invention might be carried out in accordance with algorithmic procedures, heuristic procedures, or aleatory procedures—with each procedure opening the process of invention to varying levels of chance or accident (185). Again, such a wide range of possible invention procedures opens up an equally wide range of scholarly interpretations of rhetoric and rhetors, meaning that rhetorical studies scholars must necessarily perceive and interpret these procedures as they study invention. To be sure, while rhetorical invention is crucial to language use, invention is not a readily apparent part of rhetoric—in order to get at those invisible or accidental processes that undergird the rhetorical product, some perception and some interpretation are required of scholars.

The relationship between rhetorical invention and rhetorical interpretation receives a considerable amount of attention in rhetorical studies scholarship. Rather than survey the scholarship that treats the relationship between rhetorical invention and rhetorical interpretation, this conclusion considers the relationship between them by focusing on one specific treatment, Dilip Parameshwar Gaonkar's "The Idea of Rhetoric in the Rhetoric of Science." In his essay Gaonkar argues that contemporary rhetorical studies has "reversed" its priorities. According to Gaonkar, rhetoric's priority in the classical era was the rhetor and his or her invention of discourse—that is, studying rhetoric aided the rhetor in the invention of more rhetoric (27). But Gaonkar argues that, with the revival of rhetoric in the late twentieth century, rhetoric's priority has become the interpretation of texts as rhetorical (27). As he sees it, the study of rhetoric is now executed in the service of interpreting rhetoric as everywhere (26). He worries that interpretation has usurped invention in rhetorical studies, and he enumerates several specific concerns about rhetorical studies that emerge from the privileging of interpretation over invention. The paragraphs that follow address two of Gaonkar's specific concerns—with reference to Baudrillard, of course—before revisiting his larger worry about the relationship between invention and interpretation in rhetoric as it relates to the present study.

By no small degree, this study of Baudrillard responds forcefully and in a unique way to Gaonkar's first concern about the study of individual writers as rhetorical theorists. Gaonkar expresses this concern when he writes,

> [I]t is not uncommon to find that those who are celebrated as masters of "implicit rhetorical analysis" react indifferently, if not with hostility, to such interpretations of their work. To the best of my knowledge, none of these masters (and the list is formidable: Kuhn, Feyerabend, Gadamer, Habermas; Toulmin is the possible exception) so far has either conceded that what they have been doing all along is a form of rhetorical reading, or gone on to incorporate rhetorical vocabulary in their subsequent work. (74)

The implication here is that, by interpreting certain texts as rhetoric, rhetorical studies scholars transform the writers of those texts into master rhetorical theorists. Thus, Gaonkar takes issue with the sentiment, perhaps best captured by Alan G. Gross and William M. Keith, that "there are many 'rhetorical' theorists (e.g., Thomas Kuhn, Stephen Toulmin) who only use the word occasionally and have no grounding in the 'tradition'—but we can see their work is *actually* rhetorical anyway, provided we can (re-)describe it properly" ("Introduction" 7; emphasis original). Gaonkar's remarks position such a sentiment as misguided, and his remarks further intimate that most thinkers would not embrace the moniker of rhetorical theorist. Gaonkar, in other words, speculates that these implicit masters of rhetoric neither concede that their past work is rhetoric nor do they craft future work that explicitly positions itself as rhetoric.

Gaonkar's position has been repudiated on many grounds by a number of rhetorical studies scholars (cf. Gross and Keith, *Rhetorical*; Schiappa, "Second"), with some rhetorical studies scholars fully embracing the notion that the study of rhetoric can be called redescription (Schiappa, Gross, McKerrow, and Scott). Nonetheless, the present study responds to Gaonkar's first concern about interpretive redescription in two ways. First, this study quite clearly demonstrates that Baudrillard recognizes and concedes that his work and his theory are rhetorical. He describes the symbolic exchanges and the oppositional reversals that are key to his thought as possessing "something rhetorical about them" (*CA* 233),[1] and he directly refers to his theory of simulation as rhetoric (*PC* 102). More to the point, he admits his awareness of the rhetorical nature of his writing (*HD* 186) and uses the term rhetoric (*rhétorique*) over forty times in his oeuvre. These instances establish that he was well aware, for example, of Barthes's work on rhetoric (cf. *SO* 62, 66; Barthes, *Fashion*) and of rhetoric's regular affiliation with style (*CPS* 40–41) and deception (*FS* 115). Baudrillard was, in other words, familiar with the rhetorical tradition. Second, this study presents a compelling case that Baudrillard aligns his work with a line of inquiry in rhetoric—albeit an often overlooked one—that connects Plato's *Sophist* dialogue with the work of a number of contemporary thinkers. Importantly, this line of inquiry shifts the focus of the study of rhetoric from questions about labeling, naming, and describing to questions about perceiving. In this line of inquiry, it is perception, not description, that should be central to the study of rhetoric, so Gaonkar's concern over naming becomes a secondary one. Regardless of what rhetorical studies scholars call Baudrillard or even what Baudrillard calls himself, if he is perceived to be practicing or theorizing rhetoric, then inquiry into his practice or theory is well justified. Such focus on perception—rather than description or even redescription—further warrants the rhetorical study of additional thinkers who appear to be theorists of rhetoric.

This study of Baudrillard also resolves Gaonkar's second concern: what he terms the *placebo effect* of rhetoric. Gaonkar worries that, if rhetoric's priorities have shifted so drastically from invention to interpretation, then rhetoric's function might have shifted just as drastically. At the conclusion of his essay, Gaonkar outlines rhetoric's function using the three drug metaphors—rhetoric as mixer, sweetener, and placebo. As a mixer, rhetoric functions to dilute the potency of a drug, but it does not conceal the original drug. According to Gaonkar, rhetoric as a mixer is "not something worth studying," ostensibly since reference to the original persists (77). As a sweetener, rhetoric functions to "camouflage" or "obscure" the original drug. Gaonkar suggests that rhetoric, when it functions as a sweetener, is worth studying since concealment creates "room for ethical mischief and ideological distortion" by obscuring reference to the original (77). Finally, as a placebo, rhetoric does not function as an additive to the drug but rather functions in place of the drug itself. Gaonkar is highly skeptical of this third kind of function—that is, rhetoric's metaphorical functioning as a placebo—especially when it comes to the case of the rhetoric of science. In the final paragraph of his essay, Gaonkar writes, "No one doubts that rhetoric functions as the mixer, sometimes as the sweetener, but can one argue that science is a simulacrum (in Baudrillard's sense), a rhetorical construction without reference?" (77). Here, then, with mention of Baudrillard, Gaonkar casts doubt on rhetoric's ability to function without respect to reality, as is indicated in his follow-up statement: "Without some mediating reality, reference becomes a sort of placebo, a fiction created by rhetoric" (77).

By outlining Baudrillard's conception of the simulacrum, this study surveys the basis on which one might very well perceive anything, including Gaonkar's example of science, as operating as a rhetorical construction without reference. Such a construction (e.g., science) would monopolize value (e.g., the cultural meanings of truth and worth) and drive production (e.g., the need for more science) in an unchecked, irreferential, and nonlinear way. But, more to the point, this study follows Baudrillard in his theorization of perception as rhetoric. Such theorization, which was broached in Plato's use of the term *phantasia*, speaks more directly to Gaonkar's concern about rhetoric functioning independently of reality. Reference, indeed, can become a placebo; but, rather than term it a "fiction created by rhetoric," as Gaonkar does, it might be more etymologically precise to call it a "fantasy"—that is, a *phantasia* or perceptual appearance invented through rhetoric.

By emphasizing the connection between perception and rhetoric, this study reinforces the argument that matter must be perceived (and concomitantly constructed rhetorically) for that matter to have any meaning (as "science" or anything else). As such, this study speaks to the burgeoning work on materialist and new materialist rhetorics within rhetorical studies scholarship. Here, again, the study confronts a perception of Baudrillard as a theorist who ignores the relationship between language and materiality. This perception, which would require its own book-length treatment to address, is voiced most pointedly by Celeste Condit, who asks rhetorical studies scholars, "Why has Baudrillard been more popular among us than Burke?" ("Materiality," 334). The point behind Condit's question is not one about Baudrillard or even Burke, per se, but rather about the tendency of rhetorical studies scholars to privilege language over materiality and to "privilege the linguistic over the real" (331). Here, Condit's characterization of Baudrillard echoes Dana Cloud's characterization of him as a thinker whose rejection of "the economic and political realms as sites of struggle" and whose endorsement "of a politics of textuality" marks out an extreme theoretical position (143). When viewed only in terms of one component part of his rhetorical theory (i.e., the art of appearance or the production of simulacra), the descriptions of Baudrillard offered by Condit and Cloud are accurate, and they concur with Gaonkar's invocation of Baudrillard in the closing lines of his essay.

However, Baudrillard's larger rhetorical theory, with its embrace of the art of disappearance, does make space for the material world to push back on the appearances produced by discursive constructions. By interrogating the relationship between perception and rhetoric, Baudrillard's rhetorical theory might well be seen as compatible with work on materialist rhetorics, including work by Michael Calvin McGee, who argues, as a principle of material rhetoric, that "because rhetorics are forms, I can perceive them in any arena of experience where I am able to see the paradigm of relationships" (24); Ronald Walter Greene, who argues that "rhetorical materialism, then, should attend to how the rhetorical does some of the communicative work of immaterial labor and how the rhetorical subject becomes dispersed into a host of productive apparatuses" (60–61); and even Graham Harman, an object-oriented theorist, who notes that the work of "the maltreated Baudrillard" possesses relevance to the study of the object (242).

More generally, the present study of Baudrillard pushes back on Gaonkar's worry over the relationship between invention and interpretation. This study of Baudrillard's appearance as a rhetorical theorist, with its examination of the appearance and disappearance of perception, suggests that the relationship between invention and interpretation is, in fact, a necessary relationship in rhetoric. As Baudrillard emphasizes, there is strategy behind the game of exchange, which constructs perceptions through the art of appearance and which destructs perceptions through the art of disappearance. Symbolic exchange holds appearance accountable through disappearance and, likewise, holds disappearance accountable through appearance. The invention and interpretation of thought, discourse, and perception sustain the movement in and about language that Baudrillard so vociferously endorses. On account of the metamorphic troping, the agonistic challenging, and the hypothetical testing that undergirds his rhetorical theory, Baudrillard's theory seems to be a kind of rhetorical theory that holds language responsible or answerable. Indeed, symbolic exchange might well exemplify the kind of rhetorical theory that meets the standard of accountability articulated by William M. Keith in his response to Gaonkar. Documenting the confounding relationship between invention and interpretation and its effect on rhetorical studies, Keith states, "Scholars of rhetoric find themselves in the uncomfortable position of claiming to see rhetoric where others don't, and then claiming that the rhetoric is there precisely because it doesn't appear to be!" (233). According to Keith, the "invisibility of rhetoric is exactly accounted for by rhetoric's focus on strategy," and rhetorical study "is too important not [to] be accountable" (233, 244). As this study has demonstrated, it is by coupling the readily more visible art of appearance with the decidedly more invisible art of disappearance that the strategy in Baudrillard's rhetorical theory is able to be perceived: Baudrillard views interpretive theory and cultural practice as united in an effort to initiate and sustain symbolic exchange. For Baudrillard, theory, writing, and the world are all about rhetoric, invention, and symbolic exchange.

APPENDIX

NOTES

WORKS CITED

INDEX

Appendix: Jean Baudrillard and Rhetoric; A Critical Review of the Literature

This book perceives Jean Baudrillard as a rhetorical theorist, and such a perception is based on Baudrillard's radical understanding of rhetoric and, more precisely, rhetorical invention as the means to symbolic exchange. This book also positions Baudrillard as a rhetorical theorist who sports a wide range of appearances, including those of aphorist, illusionist, ignoramus, and ironist. Given the many appearances of Baudrillard and the sheer quantity of his work, it is not surprising that he has been read widely across disciplines and that his work has been applied to countless concepts, artifacts, and phenomena. However, as a result of the wide audience that Baudrillard draws and the wide applicability that his writing enjoys, characterizations of him are often partial and explanations of his ideas are often inaccurate. His work can leave the most fastidious scholars frustrated and the most careful readers confused. This appendix provides an overview of the scholarship most relevant to Baudrillard and rhetoric.

English translations of his work experienced a confused publication history that contributes significantly to imprecise scholarship on Baudrillard. Seminal early texts, such as *Symbolic Exchange and Death*, were not translated until decades after their original French-language publication. Because these early works lay the foundation upon which an understanding of Baudrillard's later works can be built, English-language audiences read and often misguidedly interpreted his later texts without the crucial scaffolding provided by the earlier works. Gane speculates that, with the translations of certain texts into English, "many of the misunderstandings that have surrounded the writings of Baudrillard [. . .] will find they have no textual basis" ("Introduction" xiii). As a starting point, then, scholars working in English should consult the chronological bibliography that appears in *The Baudrillard Dictionary*, edited by Richard G. Smith. Full references for each of Baudrillard's forty-four books to appear in English—either as a full, freestanding translation or as a work originally published in English—are listed according to original publication date. Where applicable, each reference makes a clear distinction between the date of original publication and the date of the English-language version. Additionally, this bibliography cites the three books by Baudrillard that are not available in English translation, as well as the French-language versions of German-language texts for which Baudrillard served as translator. References for a good number of Baudrillard's essays and a thorough list of secondary sources on Baudrillard are also included in this bibliography.

Scholars interested in the publication history of Baudrillard's works that are listed in Smith's bibliography might supplement this history with histories of Baudrillard's texts and his life. Short histories of Baudrillard's life and works have been written by Gerry Coulter, Mike Gane, Gary Genosko, Sylvère Lotringer, William Pawlett, and Richard G. Smith. Interviews of Baudrillard are collected in Gane's *Baudrillard Live* as well as Smith and Clarke's *Jean Baudrillard: From Hyperreality to Disappearance*. Other interviews are included in *Forget Foucault*, *Radical Alterity*, *Art and Artefact*, *Utopia Deferred*, *The Uncollected Baudrillard*, and Paul Hegarty's *Jean Baudrillard: Live Theory*. Published, long-form dialogues include *Exiles from Dialogue*, *Fragments*, *Paroxysm*, and *Radical Alterity*. Those readers of the present study who have followed many of the citations will note that the published interviews and dialogues are often more lucid than Baudrillard's published books. Rhetorically, these interviews compel Baudrillard to produce himself as speaking subject, while his writings—as he well notes—permit him to play the seductive object.

Scholars who have oriented themselves to Baudrillard's history and biography but who maintain a keen interest in one or more of his concepts will find a number of additional resources valuable. Two texts, Baudrillard's 2000 *Passwords* and Smith's *The Baudrillard Dictionary*, survey Baudrillard's major concepts. *Passwords* details twelve, and *The Baudrillard Dictionary* treats many dozen. Neither text intends to function as a glossary—that is, neither aims to isolate and propagate one extended definition of each concept over and above other definitions of those same concepts. Rather, *Passwords* provides "accessible and enjoyable entry points into Baudrillard's thought" (*PW* cover copy), and the *Baudrillard Dictionary* invites its reader "to appreciate how Baudrillard's words convey a decentered world of radical uncertainty" (Smith, "Introduction" 4). One of the limits to the entries in *Passwords* and *The Baudrillard Dictionary* is brevity. Due to their short length, the entries cannot comprehensively identify every place in Baudrillard's work where a particular concept appears. To address this deficiency, scholars should access *The Baudrillard Index*. Compiled by Gerry Coulter, who was the founding editor of the *International Journal of Baudrillard Studies*, this 475-page document indexes forty-one of Baudrillard's forty-four books in

English. The meticulous entries of this index span an exhaustive list of the concepts, topics, and thinkers referenced or discussed in Baudrillard's books between 1968 and 2006. Scrupulous cross-indexing reveals the interconnections among Baudrillard's references and discussions. The index helps scholars navigate the conceptual and topical breadth of Baudrillard's oeuvre, and it is available, free of charge, through the website of the *International Journal of Baudrillard Studies.*

Within rhetorical studies, references to Baudrillard are widespread, but sustained treatments of Baudrillard are less common. The present study builds upon three pieces of scholarship, each of which significantly contributes to an understanding of Jean Baudrillard as a rhetorical theorist. Because these pieces were published in a one-year period between 2001 and 2002, little conversation exists among them. In fact, each takes a distinctive approach to Baudrillard's rhetorical theory in service of a larger project.

In 2001 Sonja K. Foss, Karen A. Foss, and Robert Trapp included a profile of Jean Baudrillard as the tenth chapter to the third edition of their *Contemporary Perspective on Rhetoric*, a text that provides an overview of "thinkers who have exerted a profound influence on contemporary rhetorical theory," as the publisher Waveland announces on the cover. Baudrillard had not been included in the earlier two editions of the text, suggesting that his prominence in rhetorical studies grew substantially throughout the last decade of the twentieth century. Foss, Foss, and Trapp open their profile of Baudrillard with a brief biography and a chronology of his work. The coauthors explain that Baudrillard's writing can be understood as falling into four periods: (1) a period of relatively close alignment with "traditional sociology," between 1966 and 1973; (2) a period of rupture from "the empirical, academic, and sociological emphases of his earlier writings," between 1976 and 1983; (3) a period of "experimentation with various genres and forms," between 1987 and 1990; and (4) a period that overlaps with its predecessor in which Baudrillard "returns to more conventionally structured books" (308–11). After explaining Baudrillard's work according to this chronology, the profile investigates topics found within his work that Foss, Foss, and Trapp consider to be applicable to contemporary rhetorical studies, including his notion of simulation, his writings on mass media, his critique of commodity culture, his emphasis on the object, and his strategies for response. The authors conclude the profile with a brief commentary, noting the consistency of Baudrillard's work over decades and its distinctive challenges to certain kinds of logic, agency, style, and technology.

The broad sketch of Baudrillard offered by Foss, Foss, and Trapp proves ambitious and effective in arguing for his prominent place among rhetorical theorists. The authors should be commended for their firm and unequivocal statement that "[a]lthough Baudrillard dislikes the current connotations of the word *communication*, the centrality of the notions of sign and symbolic exchange in his work places him squarely in the field of rhetoric" (3rd ed., 300; emphasis original; cf. 30th anniv. ed., 303). In addition to supporting the perception of Baudrillard as a rhetorical theorist, this statement correctly identifies the concept of symbolic exchange as central to a rhetorical understanding of Baudrillard. At times, the profile stresses the importance of symbolic exchange, noting that his rhetorical theory depends on "challenge" and the playing of a "counter-game" (30th anniv. ed., 303, 311). Here, the profile makes a point that is extended in the discussion of symbolic exchange in chapter 6 of the present study. At other times, however, the centrality of symbolic exchange to Baudrillard's theory seems forgotten, as Foss, Foss, and Trapp attempt to emphasize the applicability of his theory. In other words, the profile sacrifices the larger point of Baudrillard's rhetorical theory for the particulars of application. For example, the authors present his theoretical and rhetorical challenge *of* reality as a response *to* reality (3rd ed., 325). As such, the profile seems to depart from Baudrillard's rhetorical theory and enter into Lloyd F. Bitzer's theory of the rhetorical situation, a theory that positions rhetoric as a fitting response to a realistic situation. As for the reality of the situation, Foss, Foss, and Trapp read Baudrillard as if he were arguing that simulacra are characteristics of reality. In fact, the authors go so far as to reference, paradoxically, "today's reality of simulation" (3rd ed., 325). The paradox, as chapter 4 of the present study argues, is that Baudrillard's theory does not claim that simulation is reality but rather that simulacra substitute and are taken for reality. As for the fitting rhetorical response to such a reality, Foss, Foss, and Trapp read Baudrillard as having outlined "possibilities of resistance" (30th anniv. ed., 328). In the third edition of their text, the authors rename these strategies "rhetorical strategies" and even refer to one of them as an "example of response" to simulacra (321, 325). The issue with framing Baudrillard's rhetorical strategies as responses, and resistant ones at that, is that he challenges perceptions of reality and also does not invest himself in response-as-resistance, or critique.

Two additional historiographical points about Foss, Foss, and Trapp's profile also deserve mention. First, the profile relies heavily on two collections of Baudrillard's work, the 1983 collection *Simulations* and the 1990 collection *Revenge of the Crystal*. Both of these texts contain essays extracted from French-language collections or excerpts taken from full French-language works. Reading Baudrillard's rhetorical theory from these collections results in a woefully decontextualized interpretation of his writing. All of the passages contained in both collections are now available in English translations, and scholars working on Baudrillard and rhetoric should consult those translations instead of consulting either of these collections. Second, the periodization offered in the profile's opening pages is not the periodization that is typically offered by Baudrillard studies scholars. Indeed, the most accepted periodization of Baudrillard's work has been advanced by Gane (*Baudrillard: Critical* 4–6; *Jean* 12–23). Although Foss, Foss, and Trapp's profile refers to Gane's work, the profile departs from Gane's periodization and does not provide any rationale for the departure, not one grounded in rhetorical theory or one that would facilitate a better understanding of Baudrillard's rhetorical theory.

Also in 2001, Michelle Ballif published *Seduction, Sophistry, and the Woman with the Rhetorical Figure*, a book that provides a rhetorical reading of three individuals—Gorgias of Leontini, Friedrich Nietzsche, and Jean Baudrillard—against whom the charge of misogyny has been leveled. Ballif's goal is to examine the way in which these individuals represent the sign *Woman*. While Ballif's study does not, therefore, concentrate solely on Jean Baudrillard, his rhetorical theory factors prominently in Ballif's approach to the study. The word *seduction* in the title of Ballif's book suggests as much, for it invokes Baudrillard's 1979 book of the same name. Ballif, when introducing the study, explicitly articulates an interest in seduction as rhetoric and also signals the study's debt to Baudrillard's rhetorical theory, stating, "there are few rhetoric and composition scholars who have engaged the radical question posed by Baudrillard: We have all been produced, but can we be seduced?" (10).

Drawing on Baudrillard's rhetorical theory, *Seduction, Sophistry, and the Woman with the Rhetorical Figure* examines the unique rhetorical capacities of Gorgias, Nietzsche, and Baudrillard to battle dualisms in Western thought that involve the representation of *Woman*. Accordingly, Baudrillard's rhetorical theory provides for the salvage of what little is left of these thinkers' reputations. Ballif notes that there is an irony in using Baudrillard's rhetorical theory as the basis for a recovery or liberatory reading of these three thinkers. As Ballif explains, "[a]lthough Baudrillard would never claim to offer a revolutionary program or agenda for liberation—for such claims are fraught with the totalizing impulses of modernism—he has, however, suggested that within the realm of seduction (vis-à-vis the realm of production), we may find ways to resist the dialectical violence of truth and subjectivity" (20). This acknowledgment reveals that Ballif is not only very familiar with Baudrillard's work but also that she is quite careful in her application of it. Historiographically, Ballif's text is thorough in its use of Baudrillard to anchor the larger project.

The thoroughness with which Ballif approaches the book's larger aims is also apparent in the specific treatment of Baudrillard offered in the book's fourth chapter, "*Après l'orgie*: Baudrillard and the Seduction of Truth." After situating this chapter among other readings that characterize Baudrillard as a misogynist in the book's introduction, Ballif argues, in this chapter, that the signifiers *Woman* and *the feminine* comprise a series "rhetorical tropings" that occur throughout Baudrillard's work (145). As she explains in one instance, "[*the feminine*] is not a known term; it is not a gender; it is a challenge, a challenge to the comfortable binaries which sustain truth, a challenge to our social, gender coding" (145). Here, Ballif works against the notion that one can "know" what the "true" meaning of *the feminine* is and thus provides Baudrillard with some shelter from claims of misogyny. Throughout her reading of Baudrillard, Ballif arrives at a number of key insights about his rhetorical theory. These insights—broadly covering points related to his radical challenge to production (140), disavowal of truth (145), understanding of language (147), and abandonment of the revolutionary subject (151)—receive further elaboration in the present study.

In 2002 Bruce McComiskey published *Gorgias and the New Sophistic Rhetoric*, a book that not only invokes the prototypical Sophist, Gorgias, but seeks to unpack his rhetorical theory. As McComiskey explains, the study endeavors to offer historical readings of Gorgias and also to appropriate him so as "to interpret what Gorgias might have said about twenty-first-century rhetoricians" (12). Since McComiskey's book is focused on the rhetorical theory of an individual other than Baudrillard, his treatment of Baudrillard is understandably abbreviated. In the fourth chapter of McComiskey's book, Baudrillard is listed, along with Kenneth Burke, Jean-François Lyotard, and Jacques Derrida, as one of four postmodern sophistics. In this chapter McComiskey argues "that contemporary postmodern critical theory is sophistic in terms of it epistemic foundations and characteristic rhetorical strategies" (77). According to McComiskey, Baudrillard, Burke, Lyotard, and Derrida carry on Gorgian rhetoric in that they all hold that reality is rhetorical and that the structure and style of language affects this rhetorical reality (88). McComiskey supports his argument and his categorization of each individual as a postmodern sophistic by presenting a multipage overview of each thinker. Baudrillard is profiled third, and McComiskey notes that Baudrillard rejects psychoanalytic interpretation as well as originary reference (84). As such, his treatment emphasizes some salient points about Baudrillard's rhetorical theory. The treatment, though, is short and so limits its robustness.

In terms of its historiography, McComiskey's text is provocative for three reasons. First, his classification of Baudrillard as a postmodern sophistic is a classification that is open to debate. The present study of Baudrillard outlines arguments, in chapter 1, against labeling Baudrillard a postmodern and, in chapters 3 and 7 through 10, against labeling Baudrillard a Sophist. Certainly, as both McComiskey and Ballif demonstrate, the apparent connections between Baudrillard's rhetoric and the approaches to argumentation often attributed to the Sophists can be quite convincing, and even I have used these connections to make a point about Baudrillard's unconventional rhetorical theory (Gogan, "Exchange"). Second, McComiskey's overview of Baudrillard draws from a limited number of Baudrillard's primary texts—namely, his 1979 *Seduction* and the 1983 collection *Simulations*. This limited sampling of his writings can be attributed to the fact that McComiskey is not interested in Baudrillard qua Baudrillard, but rather he is interested in Baudrillard as a thinker who invokes Gorgian rhetoric. Like the profile that Foss, Foss, and Trapp offer, McComiskey relies on the collection *Simulations* as opposed to the English-language translation of *Simulacra and Simulations*. This choice results in a decontextualized and slightly inaccurate reading of Baudrillard's theory of simulation. Third, and relatedly, McComiskey's limited sampling of Baudrillard's primary texts leads to some overstated conclusions about his relationship to rhetoric. In particular, he contends that Baudrillard "enters the debate over representation through Freud's works, most clearly articulating in *Seduction* his discontentment with theories of psychoanalytic interpretation" (83). While critical consensus might support the second part of McComiskey's claim (that *Seduction* most clearly articulates Baudrillard's "discontentment with theories of psychoanalytic interpretation"), the first part of his claim (that Baudrillard entered "the debate over representation through Freud's works") is a bit too restrictive. Early in his work Baudrillard was significantly influenced by Marxism, structuralism, philosophy, and sociology. One could argue that all of these influences address representation, as McComiskey defines it.

Notes

Acknowledgments

1. "un mode de défi" (30)
2. "les relations intéressantes entre les gens" (30)

Chapter 1. Cross-Disciplinary Perceptions of Baudrillard and Rhetoric

1. "qu'elle exigeait de passer au travers de ces disciplines, qu'elle imposait une transversalité" (15)

Chapter 2. Biographical Sketch: Jean Baudrillard, Rhetor

1. "le jury n'étant pas du tout d'accord" (9); "Nietzsche [. . .] m'ait fait une faveur en me barrant le chemin du concours" (9)
2. "Quel a été votre rapport aux « enragés » de Nanterre?" (34); "Nous étions au cœur des « événements »" (34); "Nous participions aux AG" (34); "nous sommes allés sur les barricades" (34–35)
3. "Il faut aussi que l'opinion publique se persuade que les problèmes de l'Université ne seront pas réglés seulement par une répression visant les éléments les plus conscients du milieu étudiant" (Duteuil 129)
4. "Ce qu'il ne voit pas, c'est que le pouvoir n'est jamais là, que son institution n'est jamais, comme celle de l'espace perspectif et « réel » de la Renaissance, qu'une simulation de perspective" (56); "En effet toute l'analyse du pouvoir est à reprendre." (57)
5. "réfraction interne" (118)
6. "un pari stupide" (17)
7. "propre" (40); "Blanchissement" (51); "lessivés, blanchis" (51)
8. "Puisque cette guerre était gagnée d'avance" (63)
9. "A l'endroit voulu (le Golfe), il n'y a rien eu, la non-guerre. A l'endroit voulu (la télé, l'information), il n'y a rien eu, pas d'images, que du remplissage." (94)
10. "Dans nos têtes à tous, il ne s'est pas passé grand-chose non plus, et ça aussi, c'est dans l'ordre. Le fait qu'il n'y ait rien à tel endroit voulu étant harmonieusement compensé par le fait qu'il n'y ait rien non plus ailleurs. Ainsi l'ordre mondial unifie tous les ordres partiels." (94)
11. "Pas d'images de champ de bataille" (35)
12. "La guerre, sauf justement dans le Nouvel Ordre Mondial, naît d'un rapport antagonique" (64)
13. "Elle ne fonctionne bien qu'à armes égales." (75)

14. "duperie" (72); "hyperréalité'" (72); "truquage" (72)
15. "Les Twin Towers valaient la peine d'être détruit" (transcript 16; audio 10:44–10:46)

Part I. Appearance, Disappearance, and Jean Baudrillard's Rhetoric of Symbolic Exchange

1. "L'échange ne doit jamais avoir de cesse" (27)

Chapter 3. Rhetoric, Sophistry, and Appearance-Making

1. "notre phantasme le plus profond, et le phantasme de notre science" (39); "Phantasme d'immortalité" (39)
2. "Normalement celles-ci sont destinées à se diviser un certain nombre de fois, puis à mourir. Si lors de ces divisions, une perturbation intervient (altération du gène anti-tumeur ou de la fonction apoptose), alors a cellule devient cancéreuse : *elle oublie de mourir*, elle oublie comment mourir. Elle va se cloner elle-même en milliards de copies identiques, formant une tumeur. Habituellement le sujet en meurt, et les cellules cancéreuses meurent avec lui. Mais dans le cas d'Henrietta Lacks, des cellules tumorales prélevées de son vivant furent cultivées en laboratoire et continuèrent de proliférer sans fin. Parce qu'elles offraient un specimen particulièrement virulent et remarquable, elles furent expédiées dans toutes les parties du monde, et jusque dans l'espace, à bord de *Discoverer 17*. C'est ainsi que le corps disséminé d'Henrietta Lacks, cloné au niveau moléculaire, poursuit sa ronde immortelle, bien des années après sa mort." (40)

Chapter 4. Baudrillard's Art of Appearance: The Construction of Perceptual Appearance

1. "Mais ce qui est avant tout gênant dans ce film, c'est que le problème nouveau posé par la simulation y est confondu avec celui, très classique, de l'illusion, qu'on trouvait déjà chez Platon" (57)
2. "nous sommes des simulacres (pas au sens classique d'« apparence »)" (218)
3. "l'emportent sur l'histoire" (87)
4. "un gigantesque jeu opérationnel de questions/réponses" (108)
5. "question/réponse" (89); "la nouvel configuration opérationnelle" (89)
6. "la réponse est induite par la question" (97)
7. "la réponse est incluse dans la question" (114)
8. "le cycle [. . .] de question/réponse" (96); "unïlatéralité de la question, qui n'est justement plus une interrogation, mais l'imposition immédiate d'un sens où le cycle s'accomplit tout d'un coup" (97)
9. "La circularité question/réponse trouve des prolongements dans tous les domaines" (103)

10. "L'irruption du schéma binaire question/réponse est d'une portée incalculable: elle désarticule tout discours, elle court-circuite tout ce qui fut, en un âge d'or désormais révolu, dialectique d'un signifiant et d'un signifié, d'un représentant et d'un représenté" (99)
11. "seule la boite noire du code, la molécule émettrice de signaux dont nous sommes irradiés, traversés de questions/réponses comme de radiations signalétiques, testés sans discontinuer par notre propre programme inscrit dans les cellules" (90)
12. "Fini le théâtre de la représentation" (90)
13. "Telle est la simulation, en ce qu'elle s'oppose à la représentation" (16)
14. "Celle-ci part du principe d'équivalence du signe et du réel" (16); "La simulation part à l'inverse de l'*utopie* du principe d'équivalence" (16)
15. "qu'elle finit par recouvrir très exactement le territoire" (9)
16. "fable" (10)
17. "« vrai »" (12); "« faux »" (12); "« réel »"; (12); "« imaginaire »" (12)
18. "la simulation s'ouvre donc par une liquidation de tous les référentiels" (11)
19. "celle d'une indistinction" (67)
20. "La simulation se caractérise par une *précession du modèle*" (31–32)
21. "Agencement circulaire" (121); "processus [. . .] irréversible" (60)
22. "Inutile de se demander quel est le terme premier, il n'y en a pas, c'est un processus circulaire—celui de la simulation" (122)
23. "Le territoire ne précède plus la carte" (10)
24. "la carte qui précède le territoire" (10)
25. "celles de court-circuiter à l'avance toute possibilité de communication" (122)
26. "L'interview non directif" (121)
27. "contenu fantôme" (121)
28. "circuit intégré" (121)
29. "un circuit ininterrompu dont ni la référence ni la circonférence ne sont nulle part" (16)
30. "la logique des simulacres" (56); "puissante" (85); "inexorable" (85); "c'est la précession des modèles" (85)
31. "les modèles sont là d'abord" (32)
32. "circulation pure" (12)
33. "orbite" (12)
34. "orbitale" (32)
35. "Le rôle des messages n'est plus d'information" (98)
36. "l'information est orbitale" (36); "Ça circule, ça tourne, ça accomplit ses révolutions, parfois parfaitement inutiles (mais justement on ne peut plus poser la question de l'utilité), et ça grossit à chaque spirale ou à chaque révolution." (36)
37. "Tant de messages et de signaux sont produits et diffusés qu'ils n'auront plus jamais le temps d'être lus." (39)
38. "Inutile de se demander si c'est la perte de la communication qui entraîne cette surenchère dans le simulacre, ou si c'est le simulacre qui est là d'abord" (121)
39. "nous sommes entraînés dans un mouvement orbital qui risque de devenir perpétuel" (38)

40. "l'univers des hommes s'est circonscrit en une vaste machine orbitale" (36)
41. "mais tout [. . .] s'infléchit subtilement pour se mettre sur orbite" (36)
42. "*Le désert du réel lui-même*" (10)
43. "*irréférence*" (12)
44. "Il ne s'agit plus d'imitation" (11)
45. "Il s'agit d'une substitution au réel des signes du réel, c'est-à-dire d'une operation de dissuasion de tout processus réel par son double opératoire, machine signalétique métastable, programmatique, impeccable, qui offre tous les signes du réel et en court-circuite toutes les péripéties" (11)
46. "les spectateurs eussent été trop angoissés à la longue de ne savoir lequel était « vrai »" (79); "L'illusionniste se vit alors obligé de mécaniser ses propres gestes et, par un comble de l'art, de détraquer légèrement sa propre apparence pour rendre son sens" (79)
47. "L'illustration d'une société dont l'appareil technique serait si perfectionné qu'il apparaîtrait comme un appareil gestuel « de synthèse » supérieur à l'appareil gestuel traditionnel" (80); "rien n'interdit de penser que la *technè*, selon ses progrès incessants, ne doive aboutir à une *mimèsis* et substituer à un monde naturel un monde fabriqué intelligible" (80)
48. "s'est substituée à tout autre valeur" (76)
49. "l'éternelle substitution d'éléments homogènes" (26)
50. "sinon que dans la réalité moderne on ne se réveille pas aux applaudissements d'un public heureux d'avoir été si bien trompé" (79–80)
51. "il s'agit de cacher que le réel n'est plus le réel, et donc de sauver le principe de réalité" (26)
52. "le simulacre n'est pas ce qui cache la vérité, mais ce qui cache l'absence de vérité" (25)
53. "c'est la simulation qui est efficace, jamais le réel" (86)
54. "Si le simulacre est si bien simulé qu'il devient un ordonnateur efficace de la réalité,—n'est-ce pas l'homme alors qui, en regard du simulacre, se fait abstraction" (80)
55. "simulacres de simulation" (177); "visée de contrôle total" (177)
56. "le partage collectif des simulacres" (71); "La seule souveraineté est dans la maîtrise des apparences, la seule complicité est dans le partage collectif de l'illusion et du secret" (71)
57. "la manipulation tous azimuts de ces modèles" (179)
58. "hyperréel" (10); "la génération par les modèles d'un réel sans origine ni réalité" (10)
59. "Plus réel que le réel" (122); "plus « achevée »" (52)
60. "la carte qui précède le territoire" (10); "qui engendre le territoire" (10)

Chapter 5. Baudrillard's Art of Disappearance: The Destruction of Perceptual Appearance

1. "l'absence de réalité profonde" (17); "sans rapport à quelque réalité que ce soit" (17)

2. "Il ne s'agit plus d'une représentation fausse de la réalité (l'idéologie), il s'agit de cacher que le réel n'est plus le réel, et donc de sauver le principe de réalité" (26)
3. "Hallucination du réel" (182)
4. "Production affolée de réel" (17)
5. "Cette puissance-là, celle des choses en mal d'apparition" (172)
6. "tout disparaît par excès de réalité" (12); "l'idée (mais aussi le phantasme, l'utopie, le rêve, le désir) s'évanouissent dans leur réalisation même" (12)
7. "*lorsque la carte couvre tout le territoire, quelque chose comme le principe de réalité disparaît*" (181)
8. "ne saurait se défaire du langage" (77)
9. "La métaphore n'est encore que *transfert d'un champ à l'autre* de la valeur" (317–18)
10. "Danger de la métaphore" (317); "Danger de *remplir* cet espace" (317); "phantasmes additionnels" (317)
11. "pure répétition" (128)
12. "production du sens en trop" (46)
13. "répétition immuable" (125); "redondance exacerbée" (126)
14. "positivité dévorante" (111)
15. "Partout on cherche à produire du sens, à faire signifier le monde, à le rendre visible" (56)
16. "Mais notre péril n'est pas de manquer de sens, bien au contraire, nous en regorgeons, et nous en périssons" (56)
17. "déterritorialisation" (45)
18. "métastases envahissent tout le réseau" (71)
19. "dans la pure promiscuité à lui-même" (15)
20. "La métamorphose fait passer de la forme à la forme sans qu'intervienne la valeur" (45)
21. "On ne peut pas en extraire un sens, ni idéologique, ni esthétique" (45)
22. "passer d'une espèce à l'autre, d'une forme à l'autre, est une façon de *disparaître*" (42)
23. "tout ce qui a été produit doive être détruit, que tout ce qui apparaît doive disparaître" (62)
24. "cette métamorphose des effets" (75)
25. "Le défi" (51); "est ce à quoi on ne peut pas ne pas répondre" (51)
26. "une perspective de l'altérité accidentelle" (135)
27. "Tout ce qui est accident, panne, lapsus, dérapage, folie" (135); "est un peu notre altérité" (135)
28. "une autre, plus positive [perspective]" (135)
29. "joue sur [. . .] une manipulation de signes" (136)
30. "Ce serait la qualité de ce qui joue avec la facticité" (136)
31. "laisse faire les signes là où les autres croient manipuler des substances ou des êtres" (136)
32. "bien jouer dans un système opérationnel, mais qui, subrepticément, joue si bien qu'il le transforme en système de signes et d'illusion en quelque sorte" (136)
33. "Il faut maintenir l'autre dans son étrangeté." (154)

34. "d'étrangeté et d'incompréhensibilité" (153); "des cultures, des mœurs, des visages, des languages" (152)
35. "obéit à la loi de la communication et de l'échange" (145–46); "sa règle, son arbitraire, sa logique implacable" (145)
36. "inéluctable" (146); "irréductible" (146); "indestructible" (146)
37. "elles sont et restent éternellement intraductibles les unes dans les autres" (146)
38. "pourquoi elles sont toutes aussi « belles », c'est parce qu'elles sont étrangères les unes aux autres" (146)
39. "est *autre* que" (132)
40. "incompréhensibilité" (144)
41. "comme de la relation aux autres" (155)
42. "fascination par l'absence" (92); "faut que [. . .] cela voyage" (92); "absence qui est toujours mobile" (92)
43. "Ce qu'on cherche dans le voyage [. . .] une prise en charge par le voyage lui-même, donc par l'absence" (155)
44. "de se « balader » dans ce qui est autre, ce qui est étranger, d'en palper un peu 'étrangeté'" (81)
45. "voyage comme metamorphose" (155)
46. "au-delà de la fin, au-delà du sujet, au-delà de toute signification" (16); "les prémices d'un art de la disparition" (16); "qui ne peut surgir que de la disparition de toutes les valeurs ajoutées" (16)
47. "la possibilité [. . .] d'un art" (16)
48. "stratégie" (16); "jeu" (16)
49. "L'ambivalence n'est pas la négation dialectique de la valeur" (263)
50. "*disparition peut être elle aussi une stratégie*" (121)
51. "autre stratégie" (16)
52. "manipulation" (63); "ne peut jamais être ni tenir lieu de stratégie" (63)
53. "viser à côté, au défaut de l'apparence" (60)
54. "des stratégies pour échapper à la facticité" (137)
55. "Le terme de fatal n'a rien de fataliste ni d'apocalyptique" (75); "porte les choses vers un point de non-retour, dans une spirale qui n'est plus celle de leur production, mais celle de leur disparition" (75–76)
56. "le relais de l'information" (46)
57. "sa stratégie fatale" (167); "enveloppe le sujet" (167)
58. "métamorphose des effets" (75)
59. "passer [. . .] d'une forme à l'autre, est une façon de *disparaître, et non de mourir*" (42)
60. "L'obligation qu'il crée est du même ordre que celle du défi" (181)
61. "on ne peut pas ne pas répondre à un défi" (86)
62. "la sphère du jeu" (181)
63. "on ne lâche pas le jeu" (181); "l'impossibilité de nier le jeu" (181)
64. "nous révèle au contraire la passion de la règle, le vertige de la règle" (181)
65. "crée en même temps un pacte symbolique, une contrainte d'observance sans restriction et l'obligation d'aller au bout du jeu comme d'aller au bout du défi" (181)

66. "que tout peut être mis en jeu" (185)
67. "n'est pas de l'ordre du phantasme, et sa récurrence n'est pas la répétition du phantasme" (202)
68. "L'ambivalence est définitive" (43)
69. "d'un jeu [. . .] de la valeur" (209)
70. "« nullité »" (51)
71. "le terme nullité est ambivalent" (44); "un domaine du discours qui ne peut plus être clarifié véritablement" (51)
72. "il faut aussi jouer" (51)
73. "grand jeu" (34)
74. "qui permet le jeu d'une règle" (140)
75. "*EST* la règle fondamentale" (59)
76. "C'est un art de la disparition" (58)
77. "exprime cette règle fondamentale qui veut *que tout ce qui a été produit doit être séduit*" (192)
78. "être initié à la disparition après avoir été initie a l'existence" (192)
79. "La séduction n'est pas ce qui *s'oppose* à la production" (52)
80. "le corps est le premier objet pris à ce jeu" (42)
81. "c'est sur ces rapports de séduction, de jeu, que se fonde l'équilibre symbolique du monde" (53); "ils jouent continuellement à se séduire" (52)
82. "faisant fondre les circuits polaires du sens" (52)
83. "une théorie séduisante du langage" (52)
84. "Car séduire les choses, c'est les replacer sur leur cycle d'apparition et de disparition, de métamorphoses incessantes" (237)
85. "métamorphose est au fond de toute séduction" (42)

Chapter 6. Symbolic Exchange and Rhetorical Invention

1. "L'échange ne doit jamais avoir de cesse" (27)
2. "une disposition réciproque" (108); "enchaînement duel et parallèle" (108); "des signes, des événements, des affects, des passions" (110)
3. "retournement" (75)
4. "un effet réversible" (47)
5. "réversibilité générale" (117)
6. "Le principe de réversibilité [. . .] s'exprime dans l'obligation que tout ce qui a été produit doive être détruit, que tout ce qui apparaît doive disparaître." (62)
7. "stratégie souple et antagoniste" (77)
8. "force antagoniste" (165)
9. "La forme duelle, l'*agôn*, est une forme symbolique" (137)
10. "duel qui est au cœur du langage" (131)
11. "ce qu'on a découvert, on ne peut plus jamais l'inventer" (141)
12. "nous avons inventé la réalité, qui reste à découvrir" (141)
13. "il faut reprendre la tentative artistique comme [. . .] d'inventer" (31)
14. "invention des stratagèmes" (65)

15. "c'est d'inventer l'autre" (168)
16. "art de la disparition" (10); "c'est que l'espèce humaine est sans doute la seule à avoir inventé un mode spécifique de disparition" (9–10)
17. "C'est quand une chose commence à disparaître que le concept apparaît" (11)
18. "si on regarde de près, on voit que le monde réel commence, à l'époque moderne, avec la décision de le transformer, et ceci à travers la science, la connaissance analytique du monde et la mise en œuvre technologique—c'est-à-dire, selon Hannah Arendt, avec l'invention d'un point d'Archimède hors du monde" (10)
19. "paradoxalement, le monde réel commence de disparaître dans le temps même où il commence d'exister" (10)
20. "Parlons donc du monde d'où l'homme a disparu" (9)
21. "Le moment où une chose est nommée, où la représentation et le concept s'en emparent, est le moment où elle commence de perdre de son énergie—quitte à devenir une vérité ou à s'imposer comme idéologie" (11)
22. "En se représentant les choses, en les nommant, en les conceptualisant, l'homme les fait exister et en même temps les précipite vers leur perte" (11)
23. "C'est l'hypothèse la plus intéressante" (120)
24. "le réel est ce qui résiste, ce sur quoi butent toutes les hypothèses" (145)
25. "Contrairement à ce qui en est dit" (145)
26. "rien ne distingue l'hypothèse de l'assertion" (87)
27. "Rien n'interdit alors cette hypothèse paradoxale" (113)
28. "faisons un seul instant l'hypothèse qu'il y ait un parti pris fatal et énigmatique de l'ordre des choses" (272)
29. "l'hypothèse d'une stratégie fatale ne peut être que fatale elle aussi" (271)
30. "hypothèse passionnante" (79–80); "faire jouer dans l'autre sens" (79)
31. "caractère immuable" (227); "Si vous connaissez le signe de l'apparition, l'hypothèse de la fatalité, [. . .] cette hypothèse permet de prédire cet événement, parce que c'est l'événement d'un signe sûr" (227)
32. "l'hypothèse de l'iceberg" (120); "n'est que la partie émergée" (120); "la partie immergée" (120)
33. "Il n'y a pas de solution de continuité entre eux, seulement une ligne de flottaison" (120); "ils sont faits secrètement d'une même substance, d'une même masse qui d'ailleurs à l'occasion bascule" (120)
34. "la continuité réversible des hypothèses" (33)
35. "toujours" (30); "les hypothèses « réversibles »" (30)
36. "Les oppositions de ce genre ont encore quelque chose de rhétorique" (35)
37. "Artaud entendait recréer la réalité, ou entendait retrouver un niveau de réalité" (34); "jouer des jeux [. . .] morbides" (20); "la fin de la réalité" (34); "L'irruption d'une vision du monde" (34)
38. "L'idéal théorique serait de mettre en place des propositions telles qu'elles puissent être démenties par la réalité" (143)
39. "Ainsi vous avancez l'idée de simulacre, sans cependant vraiment y croire, et en espérant même que le réel la réfute (gage de scientificité selon Popper)" (145)
40. "L'idée du simulacre était une arme conceptuelle contre la réalité" (23)

41. "l'a absorbée et se pare désormais de toute la rhétorique de la simulation" (23)
42. "la rhétorique de la simulation" (146)
43. "vous êtes désarmés devant la lamentable confirmation de vos dires par une réalité sans scrupules" (145)
44. "Le simulacre est devenu réalité" (23–24)
45. "c'est un tour pendable" (145)
46. "la continuité du rien" (146)
47. "la continuité du Rien" (24)
48. "solution imaginaire à l'absence de problèmes" (35); "perfection du jeu" (31)
49. "rhétorique" (146)

Chapter 7. Appearing as Aphorist: Baudrillard, Writing, and Theory

1. "*entre la manière du peintre qui consiste à ajouter de la matière et celle du sculpteur qui au contraire consiste à en retirer*" (41)
2. "*par ajouts successifs*" (41); "*jusqu'au fragmentaire*" (41)
3. "L'image est belle" (42); "deux formes d'écriture, celle qui agglomère et construit des ensembles et celle qui, au contraire, disperse, attentive aux détails" (42)
4. "c'est un sacrilège contre la forme canonique qu'est l'exposé avec son argumentation" (42)
5. "J'ai été très fervent de Nietzsche" (9); "Si je le retrouve maintenant, c'est sans doute parce que je reviens à la forme aphoristique" (11)
6. "une sorte de journal" (84); "une livre à double entrée, où il y aurait d'un côté la partie plus théorique, et de l'autre, le journal" (84)
7. "Le côté énigmatique est au moins aussi essentiel que la forme brève" (51)
8. "défie l'interprétation" (51)
9. "L'énigme du sens est le secret de l'écriture, et cela se traduit dans sa concision et sa forme aphoristique" (23)
10. "« *Aphorizein* » (d'où vient « aphorisme »), c'est prendre une distance telle qu'un horizon de la pensée se dessine sans qu'elle se referme jamais sur elle-même." (46)
11. "Notre perception la plus ordinaire obéit à une sorte de protocole esthétique selon lequel il doit toujours y avoir quelque chose à voir et quelqu'un pour le voir. Dans d'autres cultures, seules quelques rares choses sont données à voir. Le reste est suprasensible et échappe aussi bien à l'esthétique qu'à la culture. C'est quand cette règle est abolie que le monde est livré à un protocole universel de la sensibilité, où l'apparence même des choses est convertie en une valeur culturelle." (111)
12. "C'est une tentative de fragmentation" (49)
13. "les choses apparaissent, il faut les saisir quand elles apparaissent en ne leur laissant presque pas le temps de prendre du sens et en les menant directement à leur disparition" (49)
14. "l'écriture est une activité à part entière" (64)
15. "l'écriture n'est jamais une interaction" (62)

16. "Mon travail, c'est d'essayer de faire apparaître ou disparaître les choses" (57)
17. "d'écrire. Je le fais pour moi" (57)
18. "un défi" (66)
19. "En fait, écrire c'est le seul acte politique que je peux faire" (56)
20. "jouer tout le jeu" (66); "les faire apparaître autant que disparaître" (66)
21. "elle est l'invention d'un autre monde, antagoniste" (62)
22. "L'écriture a une action plus offensive" (62)
23. "peut aller à l'extrême de sa logique" (187)
24. "autodestruction" (84); "pour arracher les choses à leur condition" (84)
25. "Le statut de la théorie ne saurait être que celui d'un défi au réel" (84)
26. "L'objet de la théorie est de faire un constat du système qui suit sa logique interne jusqu'à sa fin, sans rien y ajouter, et en même temps l'invertit totalement, révélant son non-sens caché, ce Rien qui le hante, cette absence au cœur du système, cette ombre qui le double" (186–87)
27. "il cherche à préserver l'énigme de l'objet par l'énigme du discours" (83)

Chapter 8. Appearing as Illusionist: Baudrillard, Aristotle, and Rhetoric

1. "arriver à faire surgir des concepts, des effets, et arriver à les résoudre" (66)
2. "ne tient jamais compte de l'écriture, de l'acte d'écriture, de la force poétique, ironique, allusive, du langage, du jeu avec le sens" (148)
3. "va nous produire de l'évidence" (32)
4. "la phase [. . .] la plus factice" (187)
5. "le moindre fait" (32); "les plus contradictoires" (32)
6. "L'espèce d'évidence, de conformité" (32)
7. "tautologie" (32); "elle va se vérifier tout le temps" (32)
8. "Les faits n'ont pas à être vrais" (136); "Que le monde soit tel ou tel, qu'il soit tombé ou non sous le coup de la simulation" (136)
9. "faits n'ont plus de trajectoire propre, ils naissent à l'intersection des modèles, un seul fait peut être engendré par tous les modèles à la fois" (32)
10. "n'a plus rien à voir avec une logique des faits" (31), "la recherche de la preuve, voire l'objectivité des faits n'arrête pas ce vertige de l'interprétation" (31)
11. "l'illusion est indestructible" (36)
12. "Nietzsche a magnifiquement parlé de l'illusion vitale" (135)
13. "illusion radicale" (33)
14. "de mise à mort de l'illusion du monde au profit d'un monde absolument réel" (33)
15. "Cette gigantesque entreprise de désillusion" (33); "c'est cela qui est proprement la simulation" (33)
16. "fait physique" (80)
17. "La réalité elle aussi est [. . .] une illusion substitutive" (35)
18. "refaire illusion" (72); "retrouver l'illusion" (72)
19. "basculement" (37); "il faut défier la réalité comme n'importe quel fait accompli" (37)

20. "fabricant d'illusion" (132)
21. "Face au sujet, irréductible producteur de sens, il y a le monde, inépuisable producteur d'illusion" (34)
22. "continuons à fabriquer du sens" (34); "l'illusion du sens" (35); "la complicité involontaire du sujet" (35)
23. "une réversion secrète, une transparence de l'illusion du monde à travers les techniques mêmes dont nous usons pour le transformer" (131)
24. "Notre langage même, notre technique essentielle et la plus primitive, est le lieu où l'ambivalence définitive du monde rejaillit sur nous" (131)
25. "l'hypothèse" (57)
26. "un état de fait" (57)
27. "Lorsque les Américains ont lu *Amérique*, ils ont très mal réagi" (42)
28. "Au fond les États-Unis, avec leur espace, leur raffinement technologique, leur bonne conscience brutale, y compris dans les espaces qu'ils ouvrent à la simulation, sont *la seule société primitive actuelle.*" (21)
29. "Seuls, les tribus, les gangs, les mafias, les sociétés initiatiques ou perverses, certaines complicités peuvent survivre, mais pas les couples." (41)
30. "L'Amérique est un gigantesque hologramme." (59)
31. "[N]ulle vision de l'Amérique ne se justifie en dehors de ce renversement : Disneyland, ça, c'est authentique! Le cinéma, la télé, ça, c'est le réel!" (208–09)
32. "C'est même cela qui a change profondément dans l'air du temps américain : l'effet Reagan a pompé l'air de la nation." (234)
33. "Ce pays est sans espoir." (238, 240)
34. "Ce qui est saisissant, c'est l'absence de tout cela, aussi bien celle de l'architecture dans les villes qui ne sont plus que de longs travellings signalétiques, que l'absence vertigineuse d'affect et de caractère dans les visages et dans les corps." (243)
35. "Les Américains croient aux faits, mais pas à la facticité. Ils ne savent pas que le fait est factice, comme son nom l'indique. C'est dans cette croyance au fait, dans la crédibilité totale de ce qui se fait et de ce qui se voit, au mépris de ce qu'on peut appeler l'apparence, ou le jeu des apparences c'est dans cette évidence pragmatique des choses : un visage ne trompe pas, un comportement ne trompe pas, un processus scientifique ne trompe pas, rien ne trompe, rien n'est ambivalent (et c'est vrai au fond : rien ne trompe, il n'y a pas de mensonge, *il n'y a que de la simulation*, qui est justement la facticité du fait), c'est en ce sens que les Américains sont une véritable société utopique, dans leur religion du fait accompli, dans la naïveté de leurs déductions, dans leur méconnaissance du malin génie des choses. Il faut être utopique pour penser que dans un ordre humain, quel qu'il soit, les choses puissent être aussi naïves. Toutes les autres sociétés sont marquées par une quelconque hérésie, par une quelconque dissidence, par une quelconque méfiance vis-à-vis de la réalité, par la superstition d'une volonté maligne et l'abduction de cette volonté à force de magie, par la croyance en la puissance des apparences. Ici, pas de dissidence, pas de suspicion, le roi est nu, les faits sont là." (168–69)

Chapter 9. Appearing as Ignoramus: Baudrillard, Susan Sontag, Ferdinand de Saussure, and Rhetoric

1. "une belle histoire" (66)
2. "Susan Sontag, en effet, que j'ai lue avec beaucoup d'intérêt" (151)
3. "l'illustration mondaine d'une situation désormais générale, où les intellectuels inoffensifs et impuissants échangent leur misère avec celle des misérables, chacun supportant l'autre dans une sorte de contrat pervers" (59)
4. "Se référer au malheur, même si c'est pour le combattre, c'est lui donner une base de reproduction objective indéfinie" (60)
5. "violence" (53 n. 7); "vertige" (31)
6. "Il faut dresser le Saussure des *Anagrammes* contre celui de la linguistique, et même contre sa propre hypothèse restreinte sur les Anagrammes" (8)
7. "de l'hypothèse abandonnée de Saussure" (285)
8. "le code de la signification y joue toujours comme système de contrôle du sens" (181)
9. "*de la production sans limites du matériel signifiant*" (292); "usons et abusons de mots" (293)
10. "« liberté » du discours" (293); "Chacun est libre d'user sans fin, de puiser sans fin dans le matériel phonique" (293)
11. "Saussure lui-même n'a jamais formulé cette conséquence subversive" (289)
12. "selon un processus rigoureux, *qu'il ne reste rien*" (289); "*annulation cyclique des termes deux à deux*" (290)
13. "*extermination du terme*" (291); "l'extermination du code" (305)
14. "d'un éclatement, d'une dispersion, d'un démembrement où ce nom est anéanti" (290)
15. "la bêtise demeure le sanctuaire du réfèrent, le refuge indestructible du sens" (19)
16. "L'intelligence spécule sur la bêtise" (20)
17. "prend le pas"(20)
18. "Comme dans le jeu du ciseau, de la feuille et du papier, les cycles ramènent toujours les puissances supérieures en position inférieure" (20)
19. "Extase de la bêtise devant l'intelligence" (79)
20. "se veut purgée de toute bêtise, elle fait l'impasse sur ce duel éternel entre l'intelligence et la bêtise—c'est en cela qu'elle est bête" (153)
21. "Sa dénonciation est immédiatement réversible" (78)
22. "par effet [. . .] de boomerang" (78); "sans renvoyer l'intelligence à son arrogance" (78)
23. "tyrannie" (153); "retrouver une noblesse" (153)
24. "Quand l'intelligence devient hégémonique" (153); "bêtise" (153); "toute autre hypothèse que l'intelligence devient préférable" (153)
25. "Une bêtise qui serait une sorte d'intelligence supérieure, à la limite d'une pensée radicale" (153)
26. "Quand l'hypothèse de l'intelligence, cessant d'être souveraine, devient dominante, alors c'est celle de la bêtise qui devient souveraine" (153)

27. "la bêtise fait échec à l'intelligence" (20)
28. "extase de l'intelligence devant la bêtise" (79)
29. "On dit que la bêtise est une offense, mais c'est plutôt l'explication qui en est une. J'entends fort bien ce qu'on m'explique, mais au fond de moi je suis complice de ceux qui ne comprendront jamais. Une brute sommeille en moi qui ricane de cet entendement et se moque éperdument de l'intelligence. Avec ceux qui comprennent, je passe un contrat d'intelligence, mais avec les autres, au même moment, je scelle en secret un pacte de bêtise. L'intellectuel, ou celui qui se prétend tel (il n'y en a pas d'autres), est celui qui a rompu ce pacte de bêtise, et s'en croit libéré. Il touche par là même le fond de la stupidité." (250–51)

Chapter 10. Appearing as Ironist: Baudrillard, Kenneth Burke, and Rhetoric

1. "les stratégies ironiques" (99)
2. "joue d'une forme à l'autre" (114)
3. "nécessite de l'ironie" (115)
4. "*économie positive de la métaphore*" (339)
5. "il est justiciable d'avance de l'interprétation" (338)
6. "raison analytique" (338)
7. "du destin de langage et du destin de pulsion, de la figure et de la force" (338)
8. "Motivation profonde" (338)
9. "Concept vide et magique" (186)
10. "vides" (186); "vide" (187)
11. "Pour le psychologue, c'est la « motivation »" (94); "d'une sorte de nécessité pré-existante, mal définie" (94)
12. "la seule relation pensable" (186)
13. "derrière" (337)
14. "*Jamais le symbolique ne doit se confondre avec le psychologique*" (86)
15. "distinctions, qui ont pour elles l'évidence de la psychologie" (86); "la relation symbolique les exclut" (86)
16. "de l'« effet » poétique" (287); "de la jouissance propre aux textes" (288)
17. "*travail de l'inconscient*" (322)
18. "Le poétique et le psychanalytique ne se confondent pas" (323)
19. "*rhétorique de l'ambiguïté*" (313)
20. "Car ce qui caractérise le poétique, et le distingue du discursif, c'est l'ambiguïté" (312)
21. "simplement elle fait flotter ces valeurs, elle rend diffuses les identités, elle complexifie la règle du jeu référentiel, sans l'abolir" (312)

Chapter 11. Rhetoric, Invention, and Symbolic Exchange

1. "Les oppositions de ce genre ont encore quelque chose de rhétorique." (35)

Works Cited

Agnew, Lois Peters. *Thomas De Quincey: British Rhetoric's Romantic Turn.* Carbondale: Southern Illinois UP, 2012. Print. Rhetoric in the Modern Era.

Allen, James. *Inferences from Signs: Ancient Debates about the Nature of Evidence.* New York: Oxford UP, 2001. Print.

Ambuel, David. *Image and Paradigm in Plato's* Sophist. Las Vegas: Parmenides, 2007. Print.

Arendt, Hannah. *The Human Condition.* 2nd ed. 1958. Chicago: U of Chicago P, 1998. Print.

Aristotle. *The Art of Rhetoric.* Trans. John Henry Freese. New York: G. P. Putnam's Sons, 1926. Print.

———. *On Rhetoric: A Theory of Civic Discourse.* Trans. George A. Kennedy. 2nd ed. New York: Oxford UP, 2007. Print.

———. *Rhetoric.* Trans. W. Rhys Roberts. Ed. Lee Honeycutt. Iowa State University, 27 Sept. 2011, rhetoric.eserver.org. Web. 9 Jan. 2012.

Armitage, John. "Beaubourg." Smith, *The Baudrillard* 24–26.

———. Rev. of *Why Hasn't Everything Already Disappeared?*, by Jean Baudrillard. *Times Higher Education* 7 Jan. 2010, n. pag. Web. 2 Feb. 2010.

Arrington, Phillip K. "Tropes of the Composing Process." *College English* 48.4 (1986): 325–38. PDF file.

Audouard, Xavier. "Le Simulacre." *Cahiers pour l'analyse* 3 (1966): 57–72. PDF file.

Austin, J. L. *How to Do Things with Words.* New York: Oxford UP, 1962. Print.

Ballif, Michelle. *Seduction, Sophistry, and the Woman with the Rhetorical Figure.* Carbondale: Southern Illinois UP, 2001. Print. Rhetorical Philosophy and Theory.

Barthes, Roland. *The Fashion System.* 1967. Trans. Matthew Ward and Richard Howard. New York: Hill and Wang, 1983. Print.

Baudrillard, Jean. *The Agony of Power.* Trans. Ames Hodges. Los Angeles: Semiotext(e), 2010. Print.

———. *America.* 1986. Trans. Chris Turner. New York: Verso, 1988. Print. Trans. of *Amérique.* Paris: Grasset, 1986.

———. *Arte and Artefact.* Ed. Nicholas Zurbrugg. Thousand Oaks: Sage, 1997. Print.

———. *Baudrillard Live: Selected Interviews.* Ed. Mike Gane. New York: Routledge, 1993. Print.

———. "Baudrillard's Seductions: Interview with Patrice Bollon." Trans. Mike Gane and G. Salemohamed. Baudrillard, *Baudrillard Live* 36–40. Trans. of "Les Séductions de Baudrillard." *Magazine Litteraire* Mar. 1983: 80–85. PDF file.

———. *Carnival and Cannibal, or the Play of Global Antagonism.* Trans. Chris Turner. London: Seagull, 2010. Print. Trans. of *Carnaval et cannibal, suivi de Le mal ventriloque.* Paris: L'Herne, 2008.

———. "La Commedia dell'Arte." Interview by Catherine Francblin. Trans. Ames Hodges. Baudrillard, *The Conspiracy* 65–74. Trans. of "Jean Baudrillard: La commedia dell'arte." *Art Press* 216 (1996): 43–48. PDF file.

———. *The Conspiracy of Art: Manifestos, Interviews, Essays*. Ed. Sylvère Lotringer. Trans. Ames Hodges. New York: Semiotext(e), 2005. Print.

———. *The Consumer Society: Myths and Structures*. Trans. George Ritzer. London: Sage, 1998. Print. Trans. of *La Société de consommation: Ses mythes, ses structures*. Paris: Denoël, 1970.

———. *Cool Memories*. Trans. Chris Turner. New York: Verso, 1990. Print. Trans. of *Cool memories, 1980–1985*. Paris: Galilée, 1987.

———. *Cool Memories II, 1987–1990*. Trans. Chris Turner. Durham: Duke UP, 1996. Print. Trans. of *Cool memories II, 1987–1990*. Paris: Galilée, 1990.

———. *Cool Memories IV, 1995–2000*. Trans. Chris Turner. New York: Verso, 2003. Print. Trans. of *Cool memories IV, 1995–2000*. Paris: Galilée, 2000.

———. *Cool Memories V, 2000–2004*. Trans. Chris Turner. Malden: Polity, 2006. Print. Trans. of *Cool memories V, 2000–2004*. Paris: Galilée, 2005.

———. *The Divine Left: A Chronicle of the Years 1977–1984*. Trans. David L. Sweet. Los Angeles: Semiotext(e), 2014. Print. Trans. of *La Gauche divine: Chronique des années 1977–1984*. Paris: Grasset, 1985.

———. *The Ecstasy of Communication*. Ed. Sylvère Lotringer. Trans. Bernard Schutze and Caroline Schutze. New York: Semiotext(e), 2008. Print. Trans. of *L'Autre par lui-même: Habilitation*. Paris: Galilée, 1987.

———. *Fatal Strategies*. Trans. Philippe Beitchman and W. G. J. Niesluchowski. Los Angeles: Semiotext(e), 2008. Print. Trans. of *Les Stratégies fatales*. Paris: Grasset, 1983.

———. *For a Critique of the Political Economy of the Sign*. Trans. Charles Levin. St. Louis: Telos, 1981. Print. Trans. of *Pour une critique de l'économie politique du signe*. Paris: Gallimard, 1972.

———. "Forget Artaud." Interview by Sylvère Lotringer. 1996. Trans. Ames Hodges. Baudrillard, *The Conspiracy* 217–39. Trans. of *Oublier Artaud*. Trans. Sylvère Lotringer. Paris: Sens & Tonka, 2005.

———. *Forget Foucault*. Trans. Nicole Dufresne. Los Angeles: Semiotext(e), 2007. Print. Trans. of *Oublier Foucault*. Paris: Galilée, 1977.

———. *Fragments: Conversations with François L'Yvonnet*. Trans. Chris Turner. New York: Routledge, 2004. Print. Trans. of *D'un Fragment l'autre: Entretiens avec François L'Yvonnet*. Paris: Albin Michel, 2001.

———. *Fragments: Cool Memories III, 1990–1995*. Trans. Emily Agar. New York: Verso, 2007. Print. Trans. of *Fragments: Cool memories III, 1990–1995*. Paris: Galilée, 1995.

———. *The Gulf War Did Not Take Place*. Trans. Paul Patton. Bloomington: Indiana UP, 1995. Print. Trans. of *La Guerre du golfe n'a pas eu lieu*. Paris: Galilée, 1991.

———. *The Illusion of the End*. Trans. Chris Turner. Stanford: Stanford UP, 1994. Print. Trans. of *L'Illusion de la fin, ou la grève des événements*. Paris: Galilée, 1992.

———. *Impossible Exchange*. Trans. Chris Turner. New York: Verso, 2001. Print. Trans. of *L'Échange impossible*. Paris: Galilée, 1999.

———. *In the Shadow of the Silent Majorities or the End of the Social.* 1978. Trans. Paul Foss, John Johnson, Paul Patton, and Andrew Berardini. Los Angeles: Semiotext(e), 2007. Print. Trans. of *Á l'ombre des majoritiés silencieuses ou la fin du social.* Paris: Sens & Tonka, 1997.

———. *The Intelligence of Evil or the Lucidity Pact.* Trans. Chris Turner. New York: Berg, 2005. Print. Trans. of *Le Pacte de lucidité ou l'intelligence du mal.* Paris: Galilée, 2004.

———. *Jean Baudrillard: From Hyperreality to Disappearance, Uncollected Interviews.* Ed. Richard G. Smith and David B. Clarke. Edinburgh: Edinburgh UP, 2015. Print.

———. "*The Matrix* Revisited." Interview by Aude Lancelin. Trans. Ames Hodges. Baudrillard, *The Conspiracy* 201–04. Trans. of "Baudrillard decodé « Matrix »." *Le nouvel observateur* 19–25 June 2003: 56–58.

———. *The Mirror of Production.* Trans. Mark Poster. St. Louis: Telos, 1975. Print. Trans. of *Le Miroir de la production ou l'illusion critique du matérialism historique.* Paris: Casterman, 1973.

———. "On *Utopie,* an Interview with Jean Baudrillard." Interview by Jean-Louis Voileau. Trans. Stuart Kendall. Baudrillard *Utopia* 13–30. Trans. of *Á propos d'*Utopie. Paris: Sens & Tonka, 2005. Print.

———. *Paroxysm: Interviews with Philippe Petit.* Trans. Chris Turner. New York: Verso, 1998. Print. Trans. of *Le Paroxyste indifférent: Entretiens avec Philippe Petit.* Paris: Grasset, 1997.

———. *Passwords.* Trans. Chris Turner. New York: Verso, 2003. Print. Trans. of *Mots de passe.* Paris: Pauvert, 2000.

———. "Pataphysics." Trans. Ames Hodges. Baudrillard *The Conspiracy* 213–16. Trans. of *Pataphysique.* Paris: Sens & Tonka, 2002.

———. *The Perfect Crime.* Trans. Chris Turner. New York: Verso, 2008. Print. Trans. of *Le crime parfait.* Paris: Galilée, 1995.

———. *Photographies, 1985–1998.* New York: Distributed Art, 1999. Print.

———. "Please Follow Me." Afterword. *Suite Vénitienne.* By Calle. Trans. Dany Barash and Danny Hatfield. Seattle: Bay, 1988. 76–86. Print.

———. "Radical Thought." Trans. Ames Hodges. Baudrillard, *The Conspiracy* 162–80. Trans. of *La Pensée radicale.* Paris: Sens & Tonka, 1994.

———. "Requiem for the Twin Towers." Trans. Chris Turner. Baudrillard, *The Spirit* 35–48. Trans. of "Requiem pour les Twin Towers." *Power Inferno.* Paris: Galilée, 2002. 9–25. Print. Transcription of "Jean Baudrillard à propos des Twin Towers." *Radio libre.* France Culture. Manhattan, New York, 23 Feb. 2002. Radio.

———. "The Revenge of the Crystal." Interview by Guy Bellavance. Trans. Mike Gane and Monique Arnaud. Baudrillard, *Baudrillard Live* 50–66. Trans. of "Le cristal se venge: Une entrevue avec Jean Baudrillard." *Parachute* 31 (1983): 26–33. PDF file.

———. *Revenge of the Crystal: Selected Writings on the Modern Object and Its Destiny, 1968–1983.* Trans. Paul Foss and Julian Pefanis. London: Pluto, 1990. Print.

———. *Screened Out.* Trans. Chris Turner. New York: Verso, 2002. Print. Trans. of *Écran total.* Paris: Galilée, 1997.

———. *Seduction*. Trans. Brian Singer. New York: St. Martin's, 1990. Print. Trans. of *De la séduction*. Paris: Galilée, 1979.

———. *Simulacra and Simulation*. Trans. Sheila Faria Glaser. Ann Arbor: U of Michigan P, 1994. Print. Trans. of *Simulacres et simulation*. Paris: Galilée, 1981.

———. *The Spirit of Terrorism and Other Essays*. 2002. New ed. Trans. Chris Turner. New York: Verso, 2003. Print.

———. *Symbolic Exchange and Death*. Trans. Iain Hamilton Grant. Thousand Oaks: Sage, 1993. Print. Trans. of *L'Échange symbolique et la mort*. Paris: Gallimard, 1976.

———. *The System of Objects*. Trans. James Benedict. New York: Verso, 2005. Print. Trans. of *Le système des objets*. Paris: Gallimard, 1968.

———. *Telemorphosis*. Trans. Drew S. Burk. Minneapolis: Univocal, 2011. Print. Trans. of *Télémorphose*. Paris: Sens & Tonka, 2001.

———. *The Transparency of Evil: Essays on Extreme Phenomena*. Trans. James Benedict. New York: Verso, 1993. Print. Trans. of *La Transparence du mal: Essai sur les phénomènes extrêmes*. Paris: Galilée, 1990.

———. *The Uncollected Baudrillard*. Ed. Gary Genosko. Thousand Oaks: Sage, 2001. Print.

———. *Utopia Deferred: Writings from* Utopie *(1967–1978)*. Trans. Stuart Kendall. New York: Semiotext(e), 2006. Print.

———. "The Vanishing Point of Communication." 1992. Clarke, Doel, Merrin, and Smith 15–23.

———. *The Vital Illusion*. 1999. Ed. Julia Witwer. New York: Columbia UP, 2000. Print.

———. *Why Hasn't Everything Already Disappeared?* Trans. Chris Turner. London: Seagull, 2009. Print. Trans. of *Pourquoi tout n'a-t-il pas déjà disparu?* Paris: L'Herne, 2007.

Baudrillard, Jean, and Marc Guillaume. *Radical Alterity*. Trans. Ames Hodges. Los Angeles: Semiotext(e), 2008. Print. Trans. of *Figures de l'altérité*. Paris: Descartes & Cie, 1994.

Baudrillard, Jean, and Enrique Valiente Noailles. *Exiles from Dialogue*. Trans. Chris Turner. Malden: Polity, 2007. Print. Trans. of *Les Exilés du dialogue*. Paris: Galilée, 2005.

Baudrillard, Jean, and Jean Nouvel. *The Singular Objects of Architecture*. Trans. Robert Bononno. Minneapolis: U of Minnesota P, 2002. Print. Trans. of *Les Objets singuliers: Architecture et philosophie*. Paris: Calmann-Lévy, 2000.

Bauman, Zygmunt. "The Sweet Scent of Decomposition." Rojek and Turner 22–46.

Beier, J. Marshall. "Criticial Interventions: Subjects, Objects, and Security." *Contemporary Security Studies*. 4th ed. Ed. Alan Collins. New York: Oxford UP, 2016. Print. 108–21.

Best, Steven, and Douglas Kellner. *Postmodern Theory: Critical Interrogations*. New York: Guilford, 1991. Print.

Biesecker, Barbara A., and John Louis Lucaites, eds. *Rhetoric, Materiality, and Politics*. New York: Peter Lang, 2009. Print.

Bishop, Ryan, ed. *Baudrillard Now: Current Perspectives in Baudrillard Studies*. Malden: Polity, 2009. Print.

Bishop, Ryan, and John Phillips. "Baudrillard and the Evil Genuis." Bishop 28–46.

Bitzer, Lloyd F. "Aristotle's Enthymeme Revisited." *Quarterly Journal of Speech* 45.4 (1959): 399–408. PDF file.

———. "The Rhetorical Situation." *Philosophy and Rhetoric* 1 (1968): 1–14. PDF file.

Bluck, Richard S. *Plato's* Sophist. Ed. Gordon C. Neal. Manchester: Manchester UP, 1975. Print.

Bogard, William. "Baudrillard, Time, and the End." Kellner, *Baudrillard* 313–33.

Bonnal, Marite. *Passage.* Paris: Galilée, 1986. Print.

Brantlinger, Patrick. *Who Killed Shakespeare? What's Happened to English Since the Radical Sixties.* New York: Routledge, 2001. Print.

Brillant, Bernard. *Les clercs de 68.* Paris: P U de Frances, 2003. Print.

Brock, Bernard L., ed. *Kenneth Burke and Contemporary European Thought: Rhetoric in Transition.* Tuscaloosa: U of Alabama P, 1995. Print.

Brummett, Barry. *A Rhetoric of Style.* Carbondale: Southern Illinois UP, 2008. Print.

———. *The World and How We Describe It: Rhetorics of Reality, Representation, Simulation.* Westport: Praeger: 2003. Print.

Burke, Kenneth. *Counter-Statement.* 1931. Berkeley: U of California P, 1968. Print.

———. *A Grammar of Motives.* 1945. Berkeley: U of California P, 1969. Print.

———. *Language as Symbolic Action: Essays on Life, Literature, and Method.* Berkeley: U of California P, 1966. Print.

———. *A Rhetoric of Motives.* 1950. Berkeley: U of California P, 1969. Print.

Butler, Rex. "Foucault + Dead Power." Smith, *The Baudrillard* 78–80.

Calle, Sophie. *Suite Vénitienne.* Trans. Dany Barash and Danny Hatfield. Seattle: Bay, 1988. Print. Trans. of *Suite vénitienne.* Paris: de l'Étoile, 1983.

Chan, Evans. "Against Postmodernism, etcetera—A Conversation with Susan Sontag." *Postmodern Culture* 12.1 (2001): n. pag. Web.

Cholodenko, Alan. "Photography." Smith, *The Baudrillard* 155–57.

Cholodenko, Alan, and Edward Colless. "Envoi." Baudrillard, *Revenge* 9–10.

Clarke, David B. "Commentaries on Jean Baudrillard's 'On Disappearance.'" Clarke, Doel, Merrin, and Smith 32–35.

Clarke, David B., Marcus A. Doel, William Merrin, and Richard G. Smith. "Introduction: The Evil Genius of Jean Baudrillard." Clarke, Doel, Merrin, and Smith 1–14.

———, eds. *Jean Baudrillard: Fatal Theories.* New York: Routledge, 2009. Print.

Cloud, Dana L. "The Materiality of Discourse as Oxymoron: A Challenge to Critical Rhetoric." *Western Journal of Communication* 58.3 (1994): 141–63. PDF file.

Condit, Celeste M. "How Should Our Rhetoric Make Us Feel?" *Purpose, Practice, and Pedagogy in Rhetorical Criticism.* Ed. Jim A Kuypers. New York: Lexington Books, 2014. 39–52. PDF file.

———. "Kenneth Burke and Linguistic Reflexivity: Reflections on the Scene of the Philosophy of Communication in the Twentieth Century." Brock 207–62.

———. "The Materiality of Coding: Rhetoric, Genetics, and the Matter of Life." *Rhetorical Bodies.* Ed. Jack Selzer and Sharon Crowley. Madison: U of Wisconsin P, 1999. 326–56. Print.

Consigny, Scott. "Rhetoric and Its Situations." *Philosophy and Rhetoric* 7.3 (1974): 175–86. PDF file.

Cooper, John M. "Introduction." *Plato: Complete Works.* Ed. John M. Cooper with D. S. Hutchinson. Cambridge: Hackett, 1997. vii–xxvi. Print.

Cornford, Francis Macdonald, trans. Plato, *Sophist* 958–1017.

Coulter, Gerry. "The Baudrillard Index—An Obscene Project." *International Journal of Baudrillard Studies* (2007): n. pag. Web.

———. "Passings: Cool Memories of Susan Sontag: An American Intellectual." *International Journal of Baudrillard Studies* 2.2 (2005): n. pag. Web.

———. "Reversibility." Smith, *The Baudrillard* 181–83.

Crivelli, Paolo. *Plato's Account of Falsehood: A Study of the* Sophist. New York: Cambridge UP, 2012. Print.

Crowley, Sharon. "Response to Karlyn Kohrs Campbell, 'Agency.'" The Alliance of Rhetoric Societies. Omni-Orrington Hotel, Evanston. Sept. 2003. Response.

Crowley, Sharon, and Debra Hawhee. *Ancient Rhetorics for Contemporary Students.* Boston: Longman, 2003. Print.

Culler, Jonathan D. *Ferdinand de Saussure.* Rev. ed. Ithaca: Cornell UP, 1986.

D'Angelo, Frank J. "The Rhetoric of Intertextuality." *Rhetoric Review* 29.1 (2010): 31–47. Print.

Danto, Arthur C. "The Hyper-Intellectual." Rev. of *Selected Writings* by Jean Baudrillard, ed. Mark Poster, trans. Jacques Mourrain, and *America* by Jean Baudrillard, trans. Chris Turner, and *Jean Baudrillard: From Marxism to Postmodernism and Beyond* by Douglas Kellner. *The New Republic* 203.11–12 (1990): 44–48. PDF file.

Davis, Diane. *Inessential Solidarity: Rhetoric and Foreigner Relations.* Pittsburgh: U of Pittsburgh P, 2010. Print. Pittsburgh Series in Composition, Literacy, and Culture.

"Death." Entry 1. *The Oxford English Dictionary.* 3rd ed. 2007. Print.

Deleuze, Gilles. *The Logic of Sense.* 1969. Ed. Constantin V. Boundas. Trans. Mark Lester with Charles Stivale. New York: Columbia UP, 1990. Print.

Devitt, Amy J. *Writing Genres.* Carbondale: Southern Illinois UP, 2004. Print. Rhetorical Philosophy and Theory.

Doel, Marcus A. "Commentaries on Jean Baudrillard's 'On Disappearance.'" Clarke, Doel, Merrin, and Smith 35–37.

Duncan, Hugh Dalziel. *Communication and Social Order.* 1962. New Brunswick: Transaction, 2002. Print.

Durham, Scott. *Phantom Communities: The Simulacrum and the Limits of Postmodernism.* Stanford: Stanford UP, 1998. Print.

Duteuil, Jean-Pierre. *Nanterre 1965–66–67–68: Vers le Mouvement du 22 Mars.* Paris: Acratie, 1988. Print.

Edbauer, Jenny. "Unframing Models of Public Distribution: From Rhetorical Situations to Rhetorical Ecologies." *Rhetoric Society Quarterly* 35.4 (2005): 5–24. PDF file.

European Graduate School. "Jean Baudrillard: Biography." *egs.edu.* European Graduate School, 2015 Web. 19 Oct. 2015.

Faigley, Lester. *Fragments of Rationality: Postmodernity and the Subject of Composition.* Pittsburgh: U of Pittsburgh P, 1992. Print. Pittsburgh Series in Composition, Literacy, and Culture.

Farrell, Kathleen, and Marilyn J. Young. "The Rhetorical Situation." Kuypers 33–37.

Farrell, Thomas B. "Aristotle's Enthymeme as Tacit Reference." Gross and Walzer 93–106.

Faucher, Kane X. *Metastasis and Metastability: A Deleuzian Approach to Information.* Rotterdam: Sense, 2013. Print.

Foss, Sonja K., and Cindy L. Griffin. "A Feminist Perspective on Rhetorical Theory: Toward a Clarification of Boundaries." *Western Journal of Communication* 56 (1992): 330–49. PDF file.

Foss, Sonja K., Karen A. Foss, and Robert Trapp. "Chapter 10: Jean Baudrillard." *Contemporary Perspectives on Rhetoric.* 3rd ed. 2002. 299–338. Long Grove: Waveland, 2014, 30th anniversary ed. 303–42. Print.

Freese, John Henry, trans. Aristotle, *The Art.*

Gane, Mike. *Baudrillard: Critical and Fatal Theory.* New York: Routledge, 1991. Print.

———. *Baudrillard's Bestiary: Baudrillard and Culture.* New York: Routledge, 1991. Print.

———. "Disappearance." Smith, *The Baudrillard* 52–54.

———. "Foreword." Baudrillard, *Fragments* ix–xi.

———. "Introduction." Baudrillard, *Symbolic Exchange* viii–xiv.

———. *Jean Baudrillard: In Radical Uncertainty.* Sterling: Pluto, 2000. Print.

———. "Symbolic Exchange." Smith, *The Baudrillard* 210–13.

Gaonkar, Dilip Parameshwar. "The Idea of Rhetoric in the Rhetoric of Science." Gross and Keith 25–88.

Genosko, Gary. *Baudrillard and Signs: Signification Ablaze.* New York: Routledge, 1994. Print.

———. *McLuhan and Baudrillard: Masters of Implosion.* New York: Routledge, 1999. Print.

———. "Pataphysics." Smith, *The Baudrillard* 150–52.

———. *Undisciplined Theory.* Thousand Oaks: Sage, 1998.

Giannopoulou, Zina. Rev. of *The Unity of Plato's* Sophist: *Between the Sophist and the Philosopher*, by Noburu Notomi. *Bryn Mawr Classical Review* 11 (1999): 3. Web.

Giraudoux, Jean. *La guerre de Troie n'aura pas lieu: Piece en deux actes.* Paris: Grasset, 1935. Print.

Gogan, Brian. "Exchange in *On the Exchange:* A Baudrillardian Perspective on Isocrates's *Antidosis.*" *Rhetoric Review* 31.4 (2012): 353–70. Print.

———. "Rhetoric Re/Framed as Exchange: Baudrillard, Perlocutionary Performance, and 9/11 Ten Years Later." *Re/Framing Identifications.* Ed. Michelle Ballif. Long Grove: Waveland, 2014. 169–75. Print.

Gonzáles, José M. "The Meaning and Function of Phantasia in Aristotle's 'Rhetoric' III.1." *Transactions of the American Philological Association (1974–)* 136.1 (2006): 99–131. PDF file.

Grace, Victoria. *Baudrillard's Challenge: A Feminist Reading.* New York: Routledge, 2000. Print.

———. "Editorial: What Is Baudrillard 'Doing'?" *International Journal of Baudrillard Studies* 2.2 (2005): n. pag. Web.

Greene, Ronald Walter. "Rhetorical Materialism: The Rhetorical Subject and the General Intellect." Biesecker and Lucaites, 43–66.

Grimaldi, William M. A. "Studies in the Philosophy of Aristotle's Rhetoric." 1972. *Landmark Essays on Aristotelian Rhetoric.* Ed. Richard Leo Enos and Lois Peters Agnew. Mahwah: Lawrence Erlbaum, 1998. 15–160. Print.

Gross, Alan G., and Ray D. Dearin. *Chaim Perelman.* Albany: State U of New York P, 2003. Print. Rhetoric in the Modern Era.

Gross, Alan G., and William M. Keith. "Introduction." Gross and Keith 1–24.

———, eds. *Rhetorical Hermeneutics: Invention and Interpretation in the Age of Science.* Albany: State U of New York P, 1997. Print.

Gross, Alan G. and Arthur E. Walzer. "Preface." Gross and Walzer ix–xi.

———, eds. *Rereading Aristotle's* Rhetoric. Carbondale: Southern Illinois UP, 2000. Print.

Hamilton, Edith. Preface. *Sophist.* By Plato. Trans. Francis Macdonald Cornford. *The Collected Dialogues of Plato Including the Letters.* Ed. Edith Hamilton and Huntington Cairns. New York: Pantheon Books, 1961. 957–58. Print.

Harman, Graham. *Tool-Being: Heidegger and the Metaphysics of Objects.* Chicago: Open Court, 2002. Print.

Harris, Roy. *Reading Saussure: A Critical Commentary on the* Cours de Linguistique Générale. La Salle: Open Court, 1987. Print.

Hauser, Gerard A. *Introduction to Rhetorical Theory.* 2nd ed. Prospect Heights: Waveland, 2002. Print.

Hawhee, Debra. "Agonism and Aretê." *Philosophy and Rhetoric* 35.3 (2002): 185–207. PDF file.

———. "Looking into Aristotle's Eyes: Toward a Theory of Rhetorical Vision." *Advances in the History of Rhetoric* 14.2 (2011): 139–65. PDF file.

Hegarty, Paul. *Jean Baudrillard: Live Theory.* New York: Continuum, 2004. Print.

Heidegger, Martin. *Plato's* Sophist. Trans. Richard Rojcewicz and André Schuwer. Bloomington: Indiana UP, 1997. Print.

"Hypothesis." Entry 1. *The Oxford English Dictionary.* 3rd ed. 2007. Print.

Jameson, Fredric. "Postmodernism, or the Cultural Logic of Late Capitalism." *New Left Review* 1.146 (1984): 53–92. PDF file.

Kärreman, Dan. "The Scripted Organization: Dramaturgy from Burke to Baudrillard." *The Language of Organization.* Ed. Robert Westwood and Stephen Linstead. Thousand Oaks: Sage, 2001. 89–111. Print.

Keith, William M. "Engineering Rhetoric." Gross and Keith 225–46.

Kellner, Douglas, ed. *Baudrillard: A Critical Reader.* Cambridge: Blackwell, 1994. Print.

———. "Commentaries on Jean Baudrillard's 'On Disappearance.'" Clarke, Doel, Merrin, and Smith 40–43.

———. "Jean Baudrillard (1929–2007): A Critical Overview." Bishop 17–27.

———. *Jean Baudrillard: From Marxism to Postmodernism and Beyond.* Stanford: Stanford UP, 1989. Print.

———. "Some Reflections On Baudrillard's 'On Disappearance.'" Bishop 154–58.

Kennedy, George A., trans. Aristotle, *On Rhetoric.*

Kennerly, Michele. "Getting Carried Away: How Rhetorical Transport Gets Judgment Going." *Rhetoric Society Quarterly* 40.3 (2010): 269–91. Print.

Klossowski, Pierre. *Nietzsche and the Vicious Circle.* 1969. Trans. Daniel W. Smith. Chicago: U of Chicago P, 1997. Print.

Kraus, Chris. "Tribute to Baudrillard." *semiotext(e).com.* Semiotext(e), n.d. Web. 14 Nov. 2015.

Kuypers, Jim A., ed. *Rhetorical Criticism: Perspectives in Action.* New York: Lexington, 2009. Print.

Kuypers, Jim A., and Andrew King. "What Is Rhetoric?" Kuypers 1–12.

Lane, Richard J. *Jean Baudrillard.* New York: Routledge, 2000. Print.

Lanham, Richard A. *A Handlist of Rhetorical Terms: A Guide for Students of English Literature.* Berkeley: U of California P, 1991. Print.

Lauer, Janice M. *Invention in Rhetoric and Composition.* West Lafayette: Parlor, 2004. Print.

Lotringer, Sylvère. "Introduction: Domination and Servitude." Baudrillard, *The Agony* 7–29.

———. "Introduction: Exterminating Angel." Baudrillard, *Forget Foucault* 7–25.

Lotringer, Sylvère, Chris Kraus, and Hedi El Kholti. "Introduction: Requiem for the Masses." Baudrillard, *In the Shadow* 7–32.

Lycos, K. "Aristotle and Plato on 'Appearing.'" *Mind* 73.292 (1964): 496–514. PDF file.

Lyotard, Jean-François. *Libidinal Economy.* 1974. Trans. Iain Hamilton Grant. Bloomington: Indiana UP, 1993. Print.

Mailloux, Steven. *Disciplinary Identities: Rhetorical Paths of English, Speech, and Communication.* New York: Modern Language Association of America, 2006. Print.

Marback, Richard. "Here and Now: Remediating National Tragedy and the Purposes for Teaching Writing." *Trauma and the Teaching of Writing.* Ed. Shane Borrowman. Albany: State U of New York P, 2005. 53–68. Print.

Marcus, James. "In Short; Nonfiction." Rev of *America* by Jean Baudrillard, trans. Chris Turner. *New York Times.* New York Times, 12 Feb. 1989. Web. 26 Feb. 2012.

McComiskey, Bruce. *Gorgias and the New Sophistic Rhetoric.* Carbondale: Southern Illinois UP, 2002. Print. Rhetorical Philosophy and Theory.

McFarlane, David. "Theory as Symbolic Exchange." *International Journal of Baudrillard Studies* 13.2 (2016): n. pag. Web.

McGee, Michael Calvin. "A Materialist's Conception of Rhetoric." Biesecker and Lucaites 17–42.

McKenna, Stephen J. *Adam Smith: The Rhetoric of Propriety.* Albany: State U of New York P, 2006. Print. Rhetoric in the Modern Era.

McKerrow, Raymie E. "Critical Rhetoric: Theory and Praxis." *Communication Monographs* 56.2 (1989): 91–111.

McQueen, Sean. *Deleuze and Baudrillard: From Cyberpunk to Biopunk.* Edinburgh: Edinburgh UP, 2016. Print.

Merrin, William. *Baudrillard and the Media: A Critical Introduction.* Malden: Polity, 2005.

"Metaphor." Etymology. *The Oxford English Dictionary.* 3rd ed. 2007. Print.

Michelini, Ann N. Rev. of *The Unity of Plato's* Sophist: *Between the Sophist and the Philosopher*, by Noburu Notomi. *Classical World* 96.1 (2002): 95–96. PDF file.

Mikkonen, Kai. "Theories of Metamorphosis: From Metatrope to Textual Revision." *Style* 30.2 (1996): 309–40. PDF file.

Miller, Arthur B., and John D. Bee. "Enthymemes: Body and Soul." *Philosophy and Rhetoric* 5.4 (1972): 201–14. PDF file.

Miller, Carolyn R. "Should We Name the Tools? Concealing and Revealing the Art of Rhetoric." *The Public Work of Rhetoric: Citizen Scholars and Civic Engagement.*

Ed. John M. Ackerman and David J. Coogan. Columbia: U of South Carolina P, 2010. 19–38. Print.

———. "Writing in a Culture of Simulation: Ethos Online." *Towards a Rhetoric of Everyday Life: New Directions in Research on Writing, Text, and Discourse.* Ed. Martin Nystrand and John Duffy. Madison: U of Wisconsin P, 2003. 58–83. Print.

Modrak, Deborah K. W. *Aristotle's Theory of Language and Meaning.* New York: Cambridge UP, 2001. Print.

Morson, Gary Saul. "The Aphorism: Fragments from the Breakdown of Reason." *New Literary History* 34.3 (2003): 409–29. PDF file.

———. *The Long and Short of It: From Aphorism to Novel.* Stanford: Stanford UP, 2012. Print.

Muckelbauer, John. *The Future of Invention: Rhetoric, Postmodernism, and the Problem of Change.* Albany: State U of New York P, 2008. Print.

Neal, Gordon C. "Editor's Introduction." Bluck 9–29.

Nehamas, Alexander. *Nietzsche: Life as Literature.* Cambridge: Harvard UP, 1985.

Newman, Sara. "Aristotle's Notion of 'Bringing-Before-the-Eyes': Its Contributions to Aristotelian and Contemporary Conceptualizations of Metaphor, Style, and Audience." *Rhetorica* 20.1 (2002): 1–23. PDF file.

Norris, Christopher. *Uncritical Theory: Postmodernism, Intellectuals and the Gulf War.* London: Lawrence and Wishart, 1992. Print.

Notomi, Noburu. *The Unity of Plato's* Sophist: *Between the Sophist and the Philosopher.* New York: Cambridge UP, 1999. Print.

O'Gorman, Ned. "Aristotle's *Phantasia* in the *Rhetoric: Lexis*, Appearance, and the Epideictic Function of Discourse." *Philosophy and Rhetoric* 38.1 (2005): 16–40. PDF file.

Palmer, John A. *Plato's Reception of Parmenides.* New York: Oxford UP, 1999. Print.

Patton, Paul. "Introduction." Baudrillard, *The Gulf War* 1–21.

Pawlett, William. "Illusion." Smith, *The Baudrillard* 99–101.

———. *Jean Baudrillard: Against Banality.* New York: Routledge, 2007. Print.

———. "Simulacra + Simulacrum." Smith, *The Baudrillard* 196–99.

———. "Virtual." Smith, *The Baudrillard* 237–39.

Plato. *Sophist.* Trans. David Ambuel. *Image and Paradigm in Plato's* Sophist. Las Vegas: Parmenides, 2007. 179–247. Print.

———. *Sophist.* Trans. Francis Macdonald Cornford. *The Collected Dialogues of Plato Including the Letters.* Ed. Edith Hamilton and Huntington Cairns. New York: Pantheon Books, 1961. 958–1017. Print.

———. *Sophist.* Trans. Nicholas P. White. *Plato: Complete Works.* Ed. John M. Cooper. Indianapolis: Hackett, 1997. 235–93. Print.

Poole, Steven. "Jean Baudrillard: Philosopher and Sociologist Who Blurred the Boundaries between Reality and Simulation." *The Guardian.* The Guardian, 7 Mar. 2007. Web. 10 Oct. 2015.

Popper, Karl R. *The Logic of Scientific Discovery.* 1934. London: Hutchinson, 1968. Print.

Poulakos, John. *Sophistical Rhetoric in Classical Greece.* Columbia: U of South Carolina P, 1995. Print. Studies in Rhetoric/Communication.

"Precession." Entry 2. *The Oxford English Dictionary.* 3rd ed. 2007. Print.

Prosser, Jay. "Metaphors Kill: 'Against Interpretation' and the Illness Books.'" *The Scandal of Susan Sontag.* Ed. Barbara Ching and Jennifer A. Wagner-Lawlor. New York: Columbia UP, 2009. 188–202. PDF file.

Quandahl, Ellen. "What Is Plato? Inference and Allusion in Plato's *Sophist.*" *Rhetoric Review* 7.2 (1989): 338–48. PDF file.

Quintilian. *Institutes of Oratory; Or, Education of an Orator.* Vol. 2. Trans. John Selby Watson. New York: George Bell & Sons, 1902. Print.

Raksin, Alex. Rev. of *America* by Jean Baudrillard, trans. Chris Turner. *Los Angeles Times.* Los Angeles Times, 15 Jan. 1989. Web. 5 Nov. 2014.

Ratcliffe, Krista. *Rhetorical Listening: Identification, Gender, Whiteness.* Carbondale: Southern Illinois UP, 2005. Print. Studies in Rhetorics and Feminisms.

———. "The Twentieth and Twenty-First Centuries." *The Present State of Scholarship in the History of Rhetoric: A Twenty-First Century Guide.* Ed. Lynee Lewis Gaillet. Columbia: U of Missouri P, 2010. 185–236. Print.

Reames, Robin. "Changing Plato's *Mimēsis:* The Rhetorical Theory of Imitation in Plato's *Republic.*" 17th Biennial Rhetoric Society of America Conference. Hilton Downtown, Atlanta. 29 May 2016. Reading.

Richards, I. A. *The Philosophy of Rhetoric.* New York: Oxford UP, 1936. Print.

Rickert, Thomas. *Ambient Rhetoric: The Attunements of Rhetorical Being.* Pittsburgh: U of Pittsburgh P, 2013. Print. Pittsburgh Series in Composition, Literacy, and Culture.

Riley, Alexander Tristan. *Godless Intellectuals? The Intellectual Pursuit of the Sacred Reinvented.* New York: Berghahn, 2010. Print.

Ritivoi, Andreea Deciu. *Paul Ricoeur: Tradition and Innovation in Rhetorical Theory.* Albany: State U of New York P, 2006. Print. Rhetoric in the Modern Era.

Ritzer, George. "Introduction." Baudrillard, *The Consumer* 1–24.

Roberts, W. Rhys, trans. Aristotle, *Rhetoric.*

Rojek, Chris. "Baudrillard and Politics." Rojek and Turner 107–23.

Rojek, Chris, and Bryan S. Turner, eds. *Forget Baudrillard?* New York: Routledge, 1993. Print.

Rosen, Stanley. *Plato's* Sophist*: The Drama of Original and Image.* New Haven: Yale UP, 1983. Print.

Rowe, John Carlos. "Editorial Note." Baudrillard, *The Vital* n. pag.

Rueckert, William H. *Kenneth Burke and the Drama of Human Relations.* Minneapolis: U of Minnesota P, 1963. Print.

Schiappa, Edward. *Protagoras and Logos: A Study in Greek Philosophy and Rhetoric.* Columbia: U of South Carolina P, 2003. Print. Studies in Rhetoric/Communication.

———. "Second Thoughts on the Critique of Big Rhetoric." *Philosophy and Rhetoric* 34.3 (2001): 260–74. PDF file.

Schiappa, Edward, Alan G. Gross, Raymie McKerrow, and Robert L. Scott. "Rhetorical Studies as Reduction or Redescription? A Response to Cherwitz and Hikins." *Quarterly Journal of Speech* 88.1 (2002): 112–20. PDF file.

Schuster, Marc. "Ambivalence." Smith, *The Baudrillard* 8–10.

Scruton, Roger. *An Intelligent Person's Guide to Modern Culture.* South Bend: St. Augustine's, 2000. Print.

Senese, Guy B. *Simulation, Spectacle, and the Ironies of Education Reform.* Westport: Bergin and Garvey. 1995. Print.

Silverman, Allan. "Plato on 'Phantasia.'" *Classical Antiquity* 10.1 (1991): 123–47. PDF file.

Skloot, Rebecca. "About *The Immortal Life of Henrietta Lacks.*" *rebeccaskloot.com*, Rebecca Skloot, 2010. Web. 19 Oct. 2016.

———. "Community Reads / FYE." *rebeccaskloot.com,* Rebecca Skloot, 2016. Web. 19 Oct. 2016.

———. *The Immortal Life of Henrietta Lacks.* New York: Broadway, 2010. Print.

Smith, Daniel W. "Translator's Preface." Klossowski vii–xiii.

Smith, Richard G., ed. *The Baudrillard Dictionary.* Edinburgh: Edinburgh UP, 2010. Print.

———. "Gulf War." Smith, *The Baudrillard* 92–94.

———. "Introduction: The Words of Jean Baudrillard." Smith, *The Baudrillard* 1–4.

———. "May 1968." Smith, *The Baudrillard* 120–21.

Sontag, Susan. "Against Interpretation." *Against Interpretation and Other Essays.* 1967. New York: Farrar Straus Giroux, 1988. 3–14. Print.

———. "Artaud: An Essay." *Antonin Artaud, Selected Writings.* Ed. Susan Sontag. Berkeley: U of California P, 1988. xvii–lix. Print.

———. *Where the Stress Falls: Essays.* New York: Farrar, Straus, and Giroux, 2001. Print.

Sprague, Rosamond Kent. Rev. of *The Unity of Plato's* Sophist: *Between the Sophist and the Philosopher*, by Noburu Notomi. *Journal of the History of Philosophy* 38.4 (2000): 585–86. PDF file.

Starobinski, Jean. *Words upon Words: The Anagrams of Ferdinand de Saussure.* 1971. Trans. Olivia Emmet. New Haven: Yale UP, 1979. Print.

Swed, Mark. "Accidents to Happen, Perchance." *Los Angeles Times.* Los Angeles Times, 7 Nov. 1996. Web. 10 Oct. 2015.

———. "Hundreds, by Design, Weigh Role of Chance." *Los Angeles Times.* Los Angeles Times, 11 Nov. 1996. Web. 10 Oct. 2015.

Teh, David. "Baudrillard, Pataphysician." *International Journal of Baudrillard Studies* 3.1 (2006): n. pag. Web.

———. "Radical Alterity." Smith, *The Baudrillard* 176–78.

Thompson, Zoe. *Urban Constellations: Spaces of Cultural Regeneration in Post-Industrial Britain.* Burlington: Ashgate, 2015. Print.

Trifonova, Temenuga. *The Image in French Philosophy.* New York: Rodopi, 2007. Print.

Turner, Bryan S. "Cruising America." Rojek and Turner 146–61.

Vatz, Richard E. "The Myth of the Rhetorical Situation." *Philosophy and Rhetoric* 6.3 (1973): 154–61. PDF file.

Vitanza, Victor J. "From Heuristic to Aleatory Procedures; or, Toward 'Writing the Accident.'" *Inventing a Discipline: Rhetoric and Scholarship in Honor of Richard E. Young.* Urbana: National Council of Teachers of English, 2000. 185–206. Print.

Vivian, Bradford. *Being Made Strange: Rhetoric beyond Representation.* Albany: State U of New York P, 2004. Print.

Walker, A. D. M. Rev. of *The Unity of Plato's* Sophist: *Between the Sophist and the Philosopher*, by Noburu Notomi. *International Philosophical Quarterly* 40.4 (2000): 520–21. PDF file.

Walker, Jeffrey. *Rhetoric and Poetics in Antiquity.* New York: Oxford UP, 2000. Print.

Walzer, Arthur E. *George Campbell: Rhetoric in the Age of Enlightenment.* Albany: State U of New York P, 2003. Print. Rhetoric in the Modern Era.
Webb, Ruth. *Ekphrasis, Imagination and Persuasion in Ancient Rhetorical Theory and Practice.* Burlington: Ashgate, 2009. Print.
Weibel, Peter. "Kairos and Contingency in Photography: Jean Baudrillard's Photographs." Baudrillard, *Photographies* 206–15.
Wernick, Andrew. "Fatal." Smith, *The Baudrillard* 70–72.
Wess, Robert. *Kenneth Burke: Rhetoric, Subjectivity, Postmodernism.* New York: Cambridge UP, 1996. Print.
White, Nicholas P., trans. Plato, *Sophist* 235–93.
Wolin, Ross. *The Rhetorical Imagination of Kenneth Burke.* Columbia: U of South Carolina P, 2001. Print. Studies in Rhetoric/Communication.
Woo, Elaine. "Jean Baudrillard, 77: Kept a Sharp Eye on Blurry Reality." *Los Angeles Times.* Los Angeles Times, 11 Mar. 2007. Web. 5 Aug. 2015.
Woodward, Ashley. "Postmodernism/Postmodernity." Smith, *The Baudrillard* 168–70.
Wunderli, Peter. "Saussure's Anagrams." *The Cambridge Companion to Saussure.* Ed. Carol Sanders. New York: Cambridge UP, 2004. 174–85. Print.

Index

Brian Gogan is an associate professor at Western Michigan University, where he teaches courses in rhetorical theory, professional writing, and composition. His scholarship on Jean Baudrillard and rhetoric has appeared in journals such as *Rhetoric Review* and the *International Journal of Baudrillard Studies*, as well in the collections *Re/Framing Identifications* and *Who Speaks for Writing: Stewardship in Writing Studies in the 21st Century.*

Books in the Rhetoric in the Modern Era Series

Thomas De Quincey: British Rhetoric's Romantic Turn
Lois Peters Agnew

Jean Baudrillard: The Rhetoric of Symbolic Exchange
Brian Gogan

Chaim Perelman
Alan G. Gross and Ray D. Dearin

Adam Smith: The Rhetoric of Propriety
Stephen J. McKenna

Paul Ricoeur: Tradition and Innovation in Rhetorical Theory
Andreea Deciu Ritivoi

George Campbell: Rhetoric in the Age of Enlightenment
Arthur E. Walzer